Lecture Notes in Computer Science

Lecture Notes in Computer Science

Edited by G. Goos and J. Hartmanis

31

Samuel H. Fuller

Analysis of Drum and Disk Storage Units

Springer-Verlag
Berlin · Heidelberg · New York 1975

Author
Dr. Samuel H. Fuller
Depts. of Computer Science
and Electrical Engineering
Carnegie-Mellon University
Pittsburgh, Pennsylvania 15213
USA

Library of Congress Cataloging in Publication Data

Fuller, Samuel, 1946-
   Analysis of drum and disk storage units.

   (Lecture notes in computer science ; 31)
   Bibliography: p.
   Includes index.
   1.   Magnetic memory (Calculating-machines)--
Mathematical models.   2.   Computer storage devices--
Mathematical models.   I.   Title.   II.   Series.
TK7895.M3F84   001.6'442   75-25523

AMS Subject Classifications (1970): 60 K 25, 60 K 30, 68-00,
CR Subject Classifications (1974): 2.44, 4.40, 4.6, 5.30, 6.35

ISBN 3-540-07186-5 Springer-Verlag Berlin · Heidelberg · New York
ISBN 0-387-07186-5 Springer-Verlag New York · Heidelberg · Berlin

PREFACE

Many computer systems are operating significantly below the potential of their central processors because of inadequate support from the auxiliary storage units. Most storage units, e.g. drums and disks, store the information on rotating surfaces, and the delays associated with retrieving information from these devices are substantial; access times on the order of ten to one hundred milliseconds are not uncommon, while many central processors are capable of executing well over a million operations per second. Unless unusual care is taken in the organization and scheduling of these rotating storage units, they will become the dominant bottleneck in the computer system.

A number of problems concerning the scheduling, organization, and configuration of auxiliary storage units are analyzed in this monograph. Stochastic, combinatorial, or simulation techniques are applied, depending on the assumptions and complexity of the particular problem. For the relatively simple scheduling disciplines of first-in-first-out (FIFO) and shortest-latency-time-first (SLTF), stochastic models are used. The starting addresses of I/O requests to a file (nonpaging) drum are modeled as random variables that are uniformly distributed about the circumference of the drum; the lengths of I/O requests are modeled as random variables that are exponentially distributed. This model of I/O requests is based upon measurements from an operational computer system. The arrival times of I/O requests are first modeled as a Poisson process and then generalized to the case of a computer system with a finite degree of multiprogramming. Well-known results in queueing theory are sufficient for some models, but in other cases original approaches are required. In particular, a new model of the SLTF file drum is developed, is compared with previous models of the SLTF file drum as well as a simulation model, and is found to be a more accurate model than previously available. Furthermore, it is easily integrated into queueing network models used to analyze complete computer systems. Several simple, cyclic queueing networks that include this new model of the SLTF file drum are analyzed.

Another practical problem that is discussed is an I/O channel serving several, asynchronous paging drums. The analysis leads to the Laplace-Stieltjes transform of the waiting time and a significant observation is that the expected waiting time for an I/O request can be divided into two terms: one independent of the load of I/O requests to the drum and another that monotonically increases with increasing load. Moreover, the load-varying term of the waiting time is nearly proportional to $(2 - 1/k)$ where k is the number of paging drums connected to the I/O channel.

In addition to the FIFO and SLTF scheduling disciplines, a new scheduling discipline is presented to minimize the total amount of rotational latency (and processing time) for an arbitrary set of N I/O requests and the algorithm that is developed to implement this minimal-total-processing-time (MTPT) scheduling discipline has a computational complexity on the order of $N\log N$. The MTPT scheduling algorithm was implemented, and for more than three or four records, the most time-consuming step is the initial sorting of the records, a step also present in SLTF scheduling algorithms. It is also shown that the least upper bound of the difference between the SLTF and MTPT schedules is one drum revolution and the expected difference is the average record length.

Finally, this monograph includes an empirical study of the MTPT and SLTF scheduling disciplines. It is discovered that the MTPT discipline offers substantial advantages over the SLTF discipline for the intra-cylinder scheduling in moving-head disks. For fixed-head drums, there are many situations in which the MTPT discipline is superior to the SLTF discipline, but it is necessary to use a more sophisticated MTPT scheduling algorithm than the one shown here to have a computational complexity on the order of NlogN.

The material in this monograph is organized into relatively independent chapters. This has several implications: some definitions and concepts must be introduced more than once to minimize the dependence among the chapters, but more importantly, this redundancy in preliminary material allows individuals to immediately turn to the chapters they are interested in and begin reading, without the annoyance of being required to scan through previous chapters to find definitions and notational conventions. References to figures, tables, and equations follow a two-level structure that refers to the section within a chapter and the item within a section; for instance, Fig. 4.7 and Eq. (10.2) refer to the seventh figure of section four and the second equation of section ten respectively. Such references refer only to items within the current chapter and hence ambiguities between identically labeled items in different chatpers are avoided.

This monograph is based on a Ph.D dissertation submitted to the Dept. of Electrical Engineering at Stanford University in 1972. I am deeply indebted to Edward J. McCluskey, Forest Baskett, and Harold S. Stone (members of my reading committee) for the assistance and encouragement they provided during the initial years of my career. Harold Stone also deserves thanks for encouraging me to investigate what has now become the topic of this monograph. The research reported in Chapter 2 was done in collaboration with Forest Baskett. This research has also benefited from discussions with Norman R. Nielsen, Thomas H. Bredt, Robert Fabry, Thomas Price, and Neil Wilhelm.

I gratefully acknowledge the financial support provided by fellowships from the National Science Foundation and the Fannie and John Hertz Foundation.

I am indebted to the Computation Center of the Stanford Linear Accelerator Center, and in particular its director, Charles R. Dickens, for the support and insight gained through the use and measurement of its computer facility This work has been partially supported by the Joint Services Electronics Program under Contract N-00014-67-A-0112-0044.Also, I want to thank my wife Carol and my children, Amy, Deborah,and Matthew for their patience and unde standing during the many hours this work has kept me from them.

Pittsburgh, Pennsylvania   Samuel H. Fulle
April 1975

TABLE OF CONTENTS

Chapter 1

INTRODUCTION

This chapter discusses the impact of auxiliary storage units on the global performance of computer systems, and the direction of auxiliary storage technology in the foreseeable future. While several different problems concerning rotating storage devices are analyzed in this dissertation, a few assumptions are used consistently and this chapter discusses the relation of these assumptions to practical storage systems.

A synopsis of the chapters of this dissertation is included to guide readers interested in specific topics to the appropriate chapters.

1. Auxiliary Storage Units and the Performance of Computer Systems

An examination of most computer systems will show that they have central processors capable of executing an instruction per microsecond, or better, while the other processors in the computer systems, i.e. the secondary and mass storage units, have basic operation times on the order of tens of milliseconds. Hence, it is not too surprising that many computer systems are I/O (input/output) bound; the central processor is idle the majority of the time, not because there is no work to be done, but because all the active tasks in the systems are waiting for service at the I/O devices. For example, after several years of performance monitoring and continual tuning, the IBM 360/91 computer system at the Stanford Linear Accelerator Center has achieved an average central processor utilization of approximately 0.6[*], and the IBM 360/67 on the Stanford University campus has an average central processor utilization of 0.65[**]. Both systems suffered considerably lower central processor utilization before programs of performance evaluation and optimization were initiated.

---

[*] The mean utilization is reported in the monthly newsletters of the computation center. Other factors affecting the central processor's utilization include a main store that is 2 million bytes and on-line storage consisting of 2 fixed-head drums and 29 moving-head disks.

[**] This was estimated by sampling the 'WAIT TIME AVERAGE' statistic displayed at the campus computation center. In addition to the central processor, the computer system includes one million bytes of main storage, three fixed-head drums, and 24 moving-head disks.

In order to reduce this bottleneck at the I/O devices, the performance of the I/O devices can be improved in basically two ways: a faster technology can be used to implement the auxiliary storage units, or new organizations and scheduling strategies can be developed that will optimize the performance of the I/O devices, independent of the technology used. This dissertation focuses on the latter approach; measurement, models, techniques of analysis, and scheduling disciplines are presented and their implications with respect to the organization and performance of the storage units are discussed.

Currently, the dominant form of auxiliary storage in computer systems are drums and disks, mechanically rotating devices. Figure 1.1 is a simplified illustration of a fixed-head drum, one common form of a rotating storage unit. In order to retrieve, or store, a block of information on the surface of a drum or disk, the appropriate read-write head is selected, and then the request waits until the leading edge of the record comes under the read-write head. The information is then transmitted as the record passes under the read-write head. The rotational property of drums and disks is both what makes them so attractive economically and what causes so much trouble when we try to optimize their performance. Sharing a single read-write transducer over a large amount of data (on the order of 10^4 to 10^7 bits) enables drums and disks to realize a substantial economic advantage over random access technologies.

Before we begin the analysis of drums and disks let us consider the future application of these devices. Any suggestion to improve a drum or disk based on the work of this dissertation will take a number of years before an implementation in an operational computer system can be

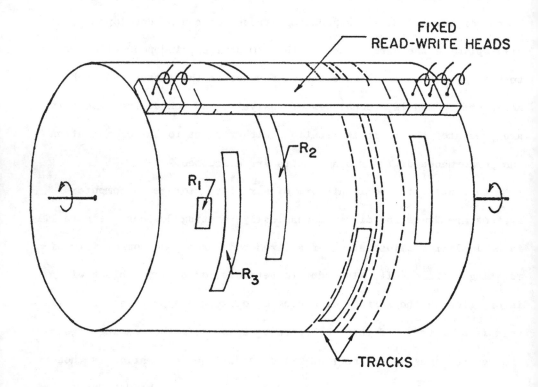

Figure 1.1. A simplified drawing of a drum storage unit.

expected, and consequently the future use of rotating storage devices
has a direct bearing on the relevance of the work discussed here.

Clearly, the widespread use of drums and disks in current computer
systems assures their continued use a considerable time into the future.
The problems, however, associated with maintaining dynamic balance and
the large centrifugal forces make the possibility of increasing the
rotational rate of drums and disks significantly beyond their current
angular velocities of about 100 revolutions/second unlikely [Matick,
1972]. For this reason, the past several years have seen a proliferation
of research into possible new technologies for auxiliary storage [Brooks,
1969; Knapp and McIntyre, 1971; Matick, 1972; McFarland and Hashguchi,
1968].

R. E. Matick [1972] has surveyed the technologies that are vying
for application as auxiliary storage devices in the future. The
proposed technologies that seem the most promising are: surface wave
acoustic delay lines, holographic storage units, magnetooptic beam-
addressed devices, magnetic bubble domain memories, and integrated
circuit memories (field-effect transistor (FET) shift registers and
charge coupled shift registers). All of the above technologies are
rotating storage memories except the holographic storage unit, but
Matick indicates that the holographic memory is also one of the most
remote contenders at the present. Of the above technologies, only the
magnetooptic beam-address device is a mechanically rotating unit;
basically it is much like a conventional drum, or disk, except that
lasers are used as the read-write transducers. The surface wave acoustic
delay lines rotate the information as surface (Rayleigh) waves on a
piezoelectric crystal, bubble memories rotate their small magnetic

domains (bubbles) around an orthoferrite wafer electrically, and the shift registers rotate their information electronically. This dissertation does not intend to discuss particular technologies for rotating storage units in any more detail than the remarks that have just been made; however, the point should be emphasized that although the exact technology of future auxiliary storage units is in substantial doubt, most proposed technologies rotate their information in order to distribute the cost of the read-write transducer among many bits of information.

Recent advances in integrated circuit, random access memories make the prospect of main storage units an order of magnitude larger than current main stores a distinct possibility. This raises the question of the relevance of embarking on a study of rotating storage units, since the current position of auxiliary storage in computer systems seems somewhat in doubt. However, the history of computer technology shows that main stores of computers increased from a few thousand words in early machines to over a million words on some current machines. Throughout this many fold increase in main storage size, computer users have found problems that have more than kept up this with increase in main storage capacity. Moreover, a recent survey reports that the amount of information in the data bases of large computation centers is on the order of 10^{12} bits [Worlton, 1971]. Even the most optimistic of integrated circuit proponents do not envision a random access, integrated circuit, main store of 10^{12} bits in the foreseeable future.

2. General Statement of Problems

Figure 1.1 illustrates the basic features of the drum-like storage units that are considered in this dissertation. The figure shows a physically rotating drum, but these comments apply to devices that rotate electronically, or acoustically, as well as mechanically.

An important assumption in all the work discussed here is that the rotating storage units revolve at a constant angular velocity. This is certainly a good assumption for mechanically and acoustically rotating devices and some implementations of electronically rotating devices. However, devices such as magnetic bubble memories and some shift registers are capable of rotating only on demand, i.e. there is no phenomenon such as inertia or electronic charge decay that requires the device to continue rotating even when the unit is idle. While most FET shift registers must be kept moving to refresh the decaying stored charge, there is usually an upper and lower bound to the rate at which the shift register can be reliably operated and some implementations will take advantage of this degree of freedom to conserve power consumption or improve performance by varying the speed of the device depending on whether the device is busy or idle.

Another assumption made throughout this dissertation is that a record, or block of information, is an indivisible unit of information; it is only possible to begin reading or writing a record at its starting address. This accurately models most drums and disks since records are written onto the surface of the drums with lengthwise error checking and correcting codes and these codes require that the reading and writing of the record begin at the front of the record and not be interrupted until the record has been completely processed.

The capacity of storage devices is not explicitly modeled here; no consideration is given to the problem of drum or disk overflow. Chapter 3, however, analyzes several drums attached to a single I/O channel, and clearly the motivation for such a configuration is to get adequate capacity.

Furthermore, no distinction is made between reading or writing records onto the storage units, and no external priorities are considered. Requests for service at the storage units are assumed to be equally important and requests are to 'process' a record at a specific starting address with a specific length. In the interests of globally optimizing the performance of computer systems, however, it may be wise to attach varying priorities to the requests sent to the storage unit, and these priorities may reflect whether the request is a read or a write operation. For instance, in a demand paging system where the rotating storage unit is used as the backing store, it may be an improvement to always process read requests before write requests since a task is sure to be blocked for every outstanding read request and, if the system is not overloaded, most write requests will just be copying old information out of main memory and no task currently executing will be blocked waiting for the completion of the write request.

In any rotating storage device there are undoubtedly a number of idiosyncrasies associated with the particular implementation constraints and the state of technology when the device was designed. It is the general principle of this work to avoid these details. This is not done because these details never affect the performance of the storage unit, some of them seriously affect performance, but to keep the models as simple as possible in order to concentrate on the fundamental properties and behavior of devices having rotational delays. After an examination of the results that are analyzed here, designers and users of specific rotating storage units should be in a better position to evaluate the performance of their particular devices and problems.

A final comment should be made concerning notation: throughout this dissertation a careful distinction is made between a scheduling discipline and a scheduling algorithm. A scheduling discipline is a strategy for sequencing jobs, or requests, through a processor and the performance of a scheduling discipline will refer to the performance of the processor while using the discipline. On the other hand, a scheduling algorithm is the statement of a procedure that orders the queued requests in a particular order and the performance of the scheduling algorithm will refer to the expense associated with executing the procedure. For example, for a processor using a random scheduling discipline, the performance of the scheduling algorithm will depend on the cost of generating random numbers and updating the list of outstanding requests while the mean waiting time of an I/O request at the processor can be predicted with the Pollaczek-Khinchine formula if the arriving requests form a Poisson process.

3. Synopsis of Dissertation

This dissertation is not a complete analysis of rotating storage units and their relation to the global performance of computer systems; too many problems are still unsolved at this time to be able to present such an analysis. This dissertation, however, does analyze a number of related questions concerning the effective use of rotating storage units and a brief outline of this dissertation is given below.

Following this introduction, Chapter 2 provides a rather broad analysis of fixed-head drum (disk) storage systems. The two major drum organizations studied are the file drum and the paging drum, and in each case both first-in-first-out (FIFO) and shortest-latency-time-first (SLTF) scheduling are considered. Some of the cases can be covered from classic results in queueing theory, e.g. the Pollaczek-Khinchine formula, while others, in particular the SLTF file drum, require original analysis. Requests to the drums are first assumed to be completely random (a Poisson arrival process) and later cyclic-queue models are used to reflect the effects of finite degrees of multiprogramming on the arrival process. The major measure of performance for the four drums studied is the expected waiting time for I/O requests at the drum, denoted $\overline{W}$, and analytic expression for $\overline{W}$ as a function of the rate of arrival of I/O requests are presented. These expressions quantify the improvement SLTF scheduling provides over FIFO scheduling and the improvement a paging drum organization provides over a file drum organization. Chapter 2 shows that $\overline{W}$, for all the cases except the SLTF file drum, exhibit hyperbolic growth; specifically, the expected waiting time for I/O requests have the basic form

$$\overline{W} = a + b\frac{\xi}{1-\xi}$$

where a and b are constant coefficients and ξ is a linear function of the arrival rate. $\overline{W}$ for the SLTF file drum grows at a slightly faster rate than hyperbolic.

Chapter 3 is also an analysis of a stochastic (queueing) model of rotating storage units. This chapter addresses the interesting, and practical, problem faced with the connection of more than one SLTF

paging drum to a single I/O channel. Analytic, as well as simulation,

results are presented to quantify the performance of an I/O channel

with multiple paging drums. A significant observation of Chapter 3 is

that the expected waiting time for an I/O request to a drum can be

divided into two terms: one independent of the load of I/O requests to

the drum and another that monotonically increases with increasing load.

Moreover, the load varying term of the waiting time is nearly

proportional to $(2 - 1/k)$ where k is the number of drums connected to

the I/O channel.

Starting with Chapter 4, we look beyond the conventional scheduling

disciplines that have been applied to rotating storage units, i.e. FIFO

and SLTF, to consider other scheduling disciplines. Severe difficulties

are encountered in extending the stochastic models of Chapters 2 and 3

to more complex scheduling strategies and consequently Chapters 4 and 5

study combinatorial, rather than stochastic, problems related to drum

scheduling. In particular, Chapter 4 presents a scheduling algorithm

that minimizes the total processing time of a set of N I/O requests and

is able to do this with computational complexity on the order of NlogN,

the same complexity associated with SLTF scheduling algorithms. The

majority of this chapter is involved with the development of the

algorithm and a proof of its correctness, but an example is also

included at the end of the chapter to illustrate the operation of the

algorithm.

Chapter 5 presents relations between the SLTF scheduling discipline

and the minimal-total-processing-time (MTPT) scheduling discipline of

Chapter 4. It shows an SLTF schedule for an arbitrary set of N records never takes as much as a full drum revolution longer to process than a MTPT schedule, and the expected difference between an SLTF and MTPT schedule for a set of N requests approaches the average record length as $N \rightarrow \infty$.

Chapter 6 is a report of the empirical results of a simulation study of MTPT scheduling disciplines when random arrivals are allowed, and a description of the simulator itself is provided in Appendix A. Situations are discovered that favor the use of the MTPT scheduling discipline over the SLTF scheduling discipline, and vice versa.   Moving-head disks show significant gains in performance when MTPT scheduling is used in place of SLTF scheduling for inter-cylinder scheduling.   This chapter also discusses the computation time required to execute the MTPT algorithm of Chapter 4, and shows that the dominant phase of the algorithm is the sorting step, a step also present in the SLTF scheduling algorithm.   The particular implementation of the MTPT algorithm used is listed in Appendix B.

Chapter 8 summarizes the work of this dissertation and discusses topics that show promise for further research.

Chapter 2

AN ANALYSIS OF DRUM STORAGE UNITS

This chapter discusses the modeling and analysis of drum-like storage units. Two common forms of drum organizations and two common scheduling disciplines are considered: the file drum and the paging drum; first-in-first-out (FIFO) scheduling and shortest-latency-time-first (SLTF) scheduling.

The modeling of the I/O requests to the drum is an important aspect of this analysis. Measurements are presented to indicate that it is realistic to model requests for records, or blocks of information to a file drum, as requests that have starting addresses uniformly distributed around the circumference of the drum and transfer times that are exponentially distributed with a mean of 1/2 to 1/3 of a drum revolution. The arrival of I/O requests is first assumed to be a Poisson process and then generalized to the case of a computer system with a finite degree of multiprogramming.

An exact analysis of all the models except the SLTF file drum is presented; in this case the complexity of the drum organization has forced us to accept an approximate analysis. In order to examine the error introduced into the analysis of the SLTF file drum by our approximations, the results of the analytic models are compared to a simulation model of the SLTF file drum.

1. Introduction

Gains in the performance of computer systems are not solely related to the power of the central processor. In particular, the I/O structure of computer systems has been an increasing cause of concern because of its relatively poor performance and high cost with respect to the central processor. This article focuses attention on one major form of I/O processor, the drum-like storage unit. Examples of drum-like stores include fixed-head disks, acoustic delay lines, and large semi-conductor shift registers, as well as storage units that actually contain physically rotating drums as shown in Fig. 1.1.

The purpose of this paper is to investigate the consequences of using a device such as a drum that must operate under the constraints of rotational delays. In the models of drum storage units that follow, every attempt has been made to keep the models as simple and free from obscuring details as possible while carefully describing those aspects of the drum relating to rotational delays. No attempt is made here to relate the capacity of the drum to the performance of the computer system. We are focusing on the response and service times of the drum and their effect on the utilization of the computer system. Furthermore, no attempt is made to differentiate read requests from write requests on the drum; when a request is made to 'process' an I/O request, only a starting address and length will be given. This assumption accurately models most drums currently in operation and should provide a base from which to analyze drum scheduling algorithms that exploit the opportunity to write a record in the most convenient empty space on the drum rather than into a fixed location.

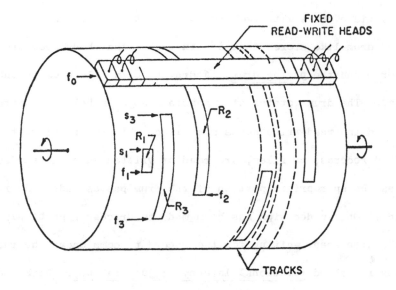

(a) A storage unit organized as a file drum.

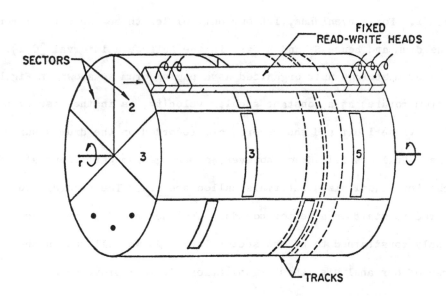

(b) A storage unit organized as a paging drum.

Figure 1.1. Two common drum organizations: the file

drum and the paging drum.

This article deals with two drum organizations that encompass the majority of drum-like stores that are in use or that have been proposed: the file drum and the paging drum. A drawing of a file drum is shown in Fig. 1.1(a). The drum rotates at a constant angular velocity, with period τ, and the read-write heads are fixed. Blocks of information, often called records, or files, are read or written onto the surface of the drum as the appropriate portion of the drum passes under the read-write heads. Once a decision has been made to process a particular record, the time spent waiting for the record to come under the read-write heads is called rotational latency or just latency. With a drum storage unit organized as a file drum we do not constrain the records to be of any particular length nor do we impose restrictions on the starting position of records. Let the random variable S_i denote the starting position of record i and the random variable R_i denote the length of record i. For convenience, let our unit of length be the circumference of the drum and hence S_i and R_i are in the half open interval $[0,1)$.

A drum storage unit organized as a paging drum is shown in Fig.1.1(b) the drum rotates at a constant angular velocity, as in the case of a file drum, with period τ and the records are recorded on the drum's surface in tracks. Unlike a file drum, however, a paging drum partitions all of its tracks into equal sized intervals called sectors. The records are required to start on a sector boundary and the record lengths are commonly constrained to be one sector long. As we will see in the course of our analysis, this organization allows improvements in performance not possible with a drum organized as a file drum.

In the analysis of both of the drum organizations just described two scheduling algorithms are considered: FIFO and SLTF. First-in-first-out (FIFO) scheduling is a simple scheduling policy that services the I/O requests in the order in which they arrive at the drum. FIFO scheduling is sometimes called first-come-first-serve (FCFS) scheduling, for obvious reasons. Shortest-latency-time-first (SLTF) is a scheduling discipline well suited for storage units with rotational latency. At all times, an SLTF policy will schedule the record that comes under the read-write heads first as the next record to be transmitted. For example, in Fig. 1.1(a), assuming the drum is not transmitting record 2, an SLTF policy will schedule record 5 as the next record to be processed. An SLTF algorithm never preempts the processing of a record once transmission of the record has begun. SLTF scheduling is often called shortest-access-time-first (SATF) scheduling. The word 'access', however, is an ambiguous term with respect to storage units (it is used both to denote the time until data transfer begins as well as the time until data transfer is complete) and to avoid possible confusion we will use the SLTF mnemonic. While SLTF is not the optimal policy to use in all situations, some remarks can be made about its near-optimality [Chapter 5], and it enjoys the important practical feature that it is straightforward to implement in the hardware of the drum controller [IBM, 1970; Burroughs, 1968]. Another drum scheduling algorithm, although not considered any further in the article, that may be of practical value is shortest-processing-time-first (SPTF), i.e. service the record whose sum of latency and transmission time is the smallest. Variants of SPTF scheduling include policies which do, or do not, allow preemptions of a request once transmission has begun. Other scheduling algorithms have been developed that are superior to SLTF under assumptions more restrictive than those considered here [Chapter 4]

Figure 1.2 applies to both paging and file drums. It defines the basic time intervals and events associated with servicing an I/O request on a drum. The four events involved in this processing of an I/O request are: (1) arrival of the I/O request at the drum, (2) decision by the scheduler that the I/O request is the next to be serviced, (3) the start of the record comes under the read-write heads and transmission begins, and finally (4) transmission of the record is completed. If the I/O request finds the drum idle upon arrival, events (1) and (2) occur at the same instant. The interval of time between events (2) and (3) is the rotational latency of the I/O request.

A drum using a SLTF scheduling algorithm may push a request back onto the queue between events (2) and (3) if a new request arrives that can begin transmission before the currently selected event. Neither SLTF nor FIFO scheduling algorithms allow a request to be preempted after event (3).

The waiting time, or response time, of an I/O request will be denoted by the random variable W and includes the time from event (1), the arrival of the request, until (4), the completion of the request. This definition of wait time was chosen, rather than from events (1) to (2) or (1) to (3), since the interval from events (1) to (4) directly measures the time a process must wait before receiving a response to an I/O request.

The utilization of the drum, call it u_d, is the long term fraction of time the drum is transmitting information. Note that only the fraction of time a drum actually transmits information is included, i.e.

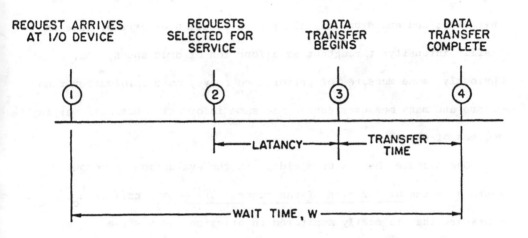

Figure 1.2.   Intervals and events associated with

servicing an I/O request.

between events (3) and (4), and intervals of rotational latency are not
included in our definition of u_d.

A wide variety of drum performance measures have been used. For
instance, some popular measures are: expected waiting time of an I/O
request as a function of queue length, or arrival rate, or traffic
intensity; cpu and drum idle times as a function of arrival rate or
traffic intensity; throughput as a function of drum speed, etc.
Obviously, some measures of performance convey more information than
others and many measures convey the same information but with varying
degrees of clarity.

One measure that is used widely in the evaluation of computer
systems is the <u>utilization of the central processor</u>, call it u_c. u_c is
a measure that is easily monitored in practice and has the advantage
that it bears a strong correlation with our intuitive concept of
"throughput".

In those cases where the utilization of the drum and central
processor cannot be used, in particular when the drum is analyzed
independently of the other processors in the computer system, the
expected waiting time of the I/O requests appears to be an appropriate
measure of performance. The expected waiting time has a more direct
interpretation than the two other common measures of processor
performance, the expected queue size or the length of the busy periods.

In this article we will present an analysis of each of the four
major drum organizations: the FIFO file drum, the FIFO paging drum, the
SLTF file drum, and the SLTF paging drum. All the organizations except
the SLTF file drum can be precisely modeled if we assume I/O requests to
the drum form a Poisson arrival process, and in these cases we will

present expressions for the expected waiting time of I/O requests at the storage units. In the case of the SLTF file drum several models are presented and compared with a simulation model of an SLTF file drum to evaluate their utility and the validity of their approximations. Finally, we remove the assumption of Poisson arrivals and explore the performance of a model of a computer system consisting of a central processor and an SLTF file drum.

2. Analysis of the FIFO Drum Scheduling Discipline

This section discusses the first-in-first-out (FIFO) scheduling discipline applied to drum storage units. Expressions are developed for the expected waiting time for I/O requests to file drums, paging drums, and a variation of the paging drum, the sectored file drum.

The FIFO file drum. First, let us consider the case of a storage unit organized as a file drum with FIFO scheduling. This is the simplest drum organization analyzed in this article, but it is worthwhile to consider explicitly each of the assumptions required to construct a tractable model even in this simple case.

The simplest arrival process to handle mathematically, and the one we will initially use to model the arrival of I/O requests to the drum is the Poisson process. This arrival process has been widely studied [cf. Cox and Smith, 1961; Feller, 1968], and the fundamental properties of a Poisson arrival process are: any two time intervals of equal length experience an arrival(s) with equal probability, and the number of arrivals during disjoint intervals are independent random events. The Poisson assumption implies that the probability of k arrivals in an arbitrary interval of time, t, is

$$\text{Pr}\{k \text{ arrivals in interval } t\} = \frac{(\lambda t)^k e^{-\lambda t}}{k!}$$

and the interarrival intervals have the exponential density function

$$\text{Pr}\{\text{interarrival time} = t\} = \lambda e^{-\lambda t}.$$

In the more specific terms of I/O requests arriving at a drum, the Poisson assumption requires that the degree of multiprogramming[*] is sufficiently large that the central processors generating requests to the drum are never idle and that the times between the generation of I/O requests can be modeled as independent, exponentially distributed random variables. In general, central processor utilization is not near unity; however, several current computer systems have been reported to enjoy this property [Sherman, Baskett, and Browne, 1971; Kimbleton and Moore, 1972]. The Poisson arrival assumption is removed in Sec. 6, and the more general case of drum performance in a computer system with arbitrary central processor utilization is studied. In this section, however, we will pursue the analysis of drum storage units with Poisson arrivals because it is our hope that the relatively straightforward results obtained will provide insight, at the most fundamental level, as to how a processor with rotational latency performs. As we progress through discussions of the various drum organizations, it will become evident that a device with rotational latency possesses several subtle, but significant, properties not encountered in more conventional processors. In the analysis that follows it is necessary to describe the starting addresses and the record lengths more completely than to

---

[*] The number of jobs, or processes, actively using the main memory resources of the computer system.

merely note they are 'random variables' as was done in the introduction.
Figure 2.1 is of considerable help in this respect; it is a histogram of
the observed service time, i.e. latency plus transmission time, for I/O
requests to the drum storage units on the IBM 360/91 computer system at
the Stanford Linear Accelerator Center where a FIFO discipline is used
to schedule the I/O requests on the drums [Fuller, Price, and Wilhelm,
1971]. The shape of this histogram suggests the following model for I/O
requests: let the starting address of a record, S_i, be a random
variable with the uniform density function

$$f_S(t) = \frac{1}{\tau}, \qquad 0 \leq t < \tau \tag{2.1}$$

$$= 0, \qquad \text{elsewhere;}$$

and let the record lengths, with mean $\overline{R}$, have the exponential density
function

$$f_R(x) = (1/\overline{R})e^{-x/\overline{R}}, \qquad x \geq 0, \tag{2.2}$$

and if we let $\mu = 1/(\tau\overline{R})$, then μ is the reciprocal of the mean transmission time and

$$f_T(t) = \mu e^{-\mu t}, \qquad t \geq 0.$$

If we assume the S_i's are independent, then it follows immediately
that the rotational latency associated with a record, denoted L_i, has
the same uniform distribution as the starting addresses, i.e. Eq. (2.1).
The service time is just the sum of the random variables L_i and τR_i, and
the density function of the service time is the convolution of $f_S(t)$ and
$f_T(t)$:

$$g(t) = \int_0^t f_T(t-\omega) \, f_R(\omega) \, d\omega$$

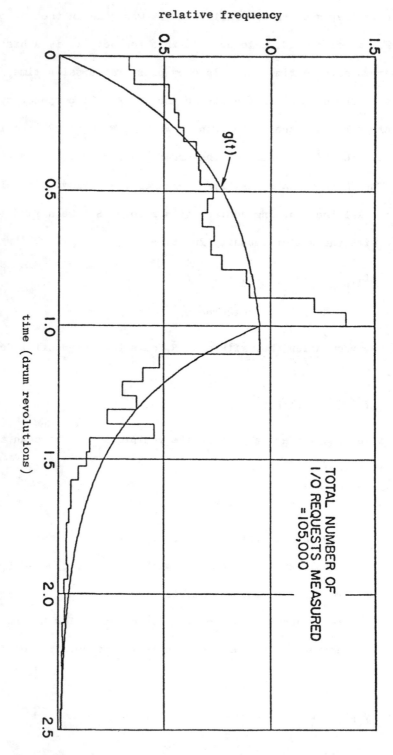

24

Figure 2.1. Histogram of latency plus transfer times for a FIFO file drum.

$$= 1 - e^{-\mu t} \qquad\qquad , \; 0 \le t < \tau \; ;$$

$$= (1 - e^{-\mu \tau}) \, e^{-\mu [t-\tau]} \qquad , \; t \ge \tau \; .$$

The relatively good fit of $g(t)$ to the histogram when $\mu = 3/\tau$ ($\bar{R} = 1/3$) indicates the appropriateness of this model of I/O requests and we will use it in our analysis of file drums.

The above assumptions concerning the arrival process and the attributes of I/O requests completely specifies our model of a file drum with a FIFO scheduling discipline. The model is in the form of the classic M/G/1 model, i.e. Poisson arrivals (M), general service time distribution (G), and one server (1), and we can use the Pollaczek-Khinchine formula [cf. Cox and Smith, 1961; Saaty, 1961] to give us the expected waiting time of an I/O request at the drum:

$$\overline{W} \; = \; (\tfrac{1}{2} + \overline{R}) \left[1 + \frac{\xi(1+c^2)}{2(1-\xi)} \right] \tau \tag{2.3}$$

where

$$\xi \; = \; \lambda (\tfrac{1}{2} + \overline{R}) \tau$$

$$c^2 \; = \; \frac{\frac{\tau^2}{12} + \sigma^2}{(\tfrac{1}{2} + \overline{R})^2 \tau^2} \qquad \text{(coefficient of variation of service time)}$$

For exponentially distributed record lengths, $\sigma = 1/\overline{R}$ in the above equations and we can achieve some simplifications. In this case, however, it is not necessary to make the exponential assumption; we need only assume the record transfer times are independent, identically distributed random variables with mean $\overline{R}\tau$ and variance σ^2.

The FIFO paging drum. The extension of the above result to a FIFO paging drum is not as straightforward as might be expected. The problem lies in accurately describing the drum when it is idle. In a FIFO file drum, the idle state is truly a Markov (memoryless) state. That is, when the drum is idle, the distance from the read-write heads to the starting address of the arriving I/O request, D_i, can be accurately modeled as a random variable with a uniform distribution, Eq. (2.1). The duration of the idle period, or any other fact about the drum's history, has no effect on the distribution of D_i.

In contrast, the idle state of a FIFO paging drum does not enjoy a similar Markovian property. The reason is readily evident: starting addresses of I/O requests always occur at sector boundaries and when a paging drum becomes idle it does so at sector boundaries. Consequently, the duration of the drum idle period has a significant effect on the latency required to service the I/O request arriving at the idle drum.

With the above comment serving as a cautionary note, let us proceed with the analysis of a FIFO paging drum. As with the file drum, assume the arrival of I/O requests form a Poisson process with parameter λ. Moreover, suppose there are k sectors on the drum and I/O requests demand service from any one of the k sectors with equal probability. In most paging drums records are required to be one sector in length and we will assume this to be true in our analysis, and consequently $\overline{R} = 1/k$.

With the above assumptions, the FIFO paging drum is an example of an abstract model developed by C. E. Skinner [1967]. The significance of Skinner's analysis is best appreciated by considering the approximations others have made in their analysis of a FIFO paging drum [Denning, 1967].

Skinner's model is depicted in Fig. 2.2. The processor services a request in time A, where A is a random variable with arbitrary distribution $F_A(t)$. After servicing a request, the processor becomes

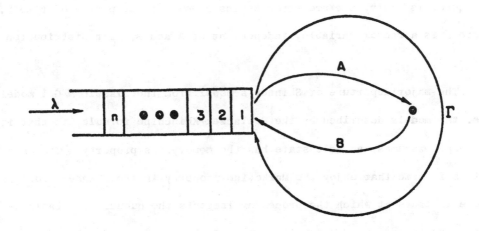

Figure 2.2.   Skinner's model of a processor

with latency.

latent for time B, where B is a random variable, possibly dependent on A, with distribution $F_B(t)$. Let Z denote the sum of A and B, and $F_Z(t)$ the distribution function of Z. After a service-latency cycle, the processor inspects the queue to see if there are any outstanding requests. If the queue is not empty, a new service period begins. If the queue is empty, the processor begins a new latency period of time Γ, where Γ is a random variable, independent of A and B, with distribution $F_\Gamma(t)$.

The major departure of Skinner's model from the classic M/G/1 model, i.e. the models described by the Pollaczek-Khinchine formula, is that it no longer assumes the idle state has the memoryless property. The only points in time that enjoy the Markovian property in the Skinner model are those instants at which the processor inspects the queue. The Laplace-Stieltjes transform of the waiting time for Skinner's model is [Skinner, 1967]:

$$\underset{\sim}{W}(s) = \frac{(1 - \lambda\overline{Z})(\underset{\sim}{\Gamma}(s) - 1)\underset{\sim}{A}(s)}{\lambda\,\overline{\Gamma}\,[1 - \frac{s}{\lambda} - \underset{\sim}{Z}(s)]}$$

Consequently, the expected waiting time of a request at the server is:

$$\overline{W} = \underset{s \to 0}{\text{limit}}\,\{-\underset{\sim}{W}'(s)\} = \frac{\overline{\Gamma^2}}{2\overline{\Gamma}} + \frac{\lambda\overline{Z^2}}{2(1-\lambda\overline{Z})} + \overline{A} \qquad (2.4)$$

where l'Hôpital's rule must be applied twice to find the limit as $s \to 0$.

The interpretation of Skinner's model as a FIFO paging drum is straightforward. From the assumptions that the starting addresses are independent random variables that are equally likely to have the value of any of the k sector boundaries and all records are one sector long it follows that

$$F_A(t) = \frac{1}{k} \sum_{0 \leq i \leq k-1} \underset{\sim}{U} \left(t - \frac{i\tau}{k} \right)$$

where $\underset{\sim}{U}(x)$ is the unit step function:

$$\underset{\sim}{U}(x) = \begin{cases} 1 \text{ for } x \geq 0 \\ 0 \text{ for } x < 0. \end{cases}$$

The first two moments of A are

$$\bar{A} = \frac{k+1}{2k} \tau,$$

$$\overline{A^2} = \frac{(k+1)(k+\frac{1}{2})}{3k^2} \tau^2.$$

Since all the records are one sector long, the paging drum is in a position to begin servicing a new request immediately after finishing the previous one; this is reflected in Skinner's model by setting B to zero. This leads to the simplifying result that $F_Z(t) = F_A(t)$.

If the queue is empty after the paging drum finishes servicing a request, it must remain latent for the time to traverse one sector before examining the queue again. Hence, for a paging drum Γ is not a random variable at all, it is always τ/k, and

$$\bar{\Gamma} = \frac{\tau}{k}$$

$$\overline{\Gamma^2} = \left(\frac{\tau}{k} \right)^2$$

Therefore, the mean waiting time for I/O requests at a FIFO paging drum is

$$\bar{W} = \left\{ \left(\frac{1}{2} + \frac{1}{k} \right) + \frac{\lambda(\frac{1}{2} + \frac{1}{2k})(1 + \frac{1}{2k})\tau}{3[1 - \lambda(\frac{1}{2} + \frac{1}{2k})\tau]} \right\} \tau \qquad (2.5)$$

The FIFO sectored file drum. Suppose the record lengths are exponentially distributed rather than the constant size required by a paging drum, but assume records are still constrained to begin at sector boundaries. This type of drum will be called a <u>sectored file drum</u>, and the IBM 2305[*] is a good example of this type of drum organization. The IBM 2305 has 128 sectors, its track capacity is roughly 3/4ths of the track capacity of an IBM 2301, and from the histogram in Fig. 2.1 it is clear most records will be considerably longer than a sector. Skinner's model is adequate to describe the behavior of a sectored file drum using the FIFO scheduling discipline. Let A be the sum of the latency plus the transmission time, as in the case of a paging drum, and we see immediately that

$$\overline{A} = (\overline{R} + \frac{1}{2} - \frac{1}{2k})\tau$$

Let B be the time required to get from the end of the record to the next sector boundary, and let R_p denote the sum of the record length and B, i.e. R_p is the record length rounded up to the nearest integer number of sectors. The probability mass function of R_p is

$$\Pr\{R_p = \frac{i\tau}{k}\} = (e^{\mu\tau/k} - 1)e^{-i\mu\tau/k}, \quad i = 1,2,\ldots$$

and

$$\overline{R}_p = \frac{\tau}{k(1-e^{-\mu\tau/k})}$$

$$\overline{R_p^{\,2}} = \frac{\tau^2(1+e^{-\mu\tau/k})}{k^2(1-e^{-\mu\tau/k})^2}$$

In order to find $\overline{Z}$ and $\overline{Z^2}$, it is more helpful to treat Z as the sum of R_p and the latency interval rather than the sum of A and B. Hence

---

[*] As will be discussed later, a more efficient way to schedule a position-sensing, sectored drum like the IBM 2305 is with a SLTF scheduling discipline.

$$\overline{z} = [\frac{k-1}{2k} + \frac{1}{k(1-e^{-\mu\tau/k})}]\tau$$

$$\overline{z^2} = \frac{\tau^2(k-1)(1-e^{-\mu\tau/k})^2[(k-\frac{1}{2})(1-e^{-\mu\tau/k})+3] + 3e^{-\mu\tau/k}[1-e^{-\mu\tau/k}]}{3k^2(1-e^{-\mu\tau/k})^3}$$

Now using Eq. (2.4) we see that the expected waiting time for I/O requests at a sectored file drum with FIFO scheduling is

$$\overline{W} = (\frac{1}{2} + \overline{R})\tau + \frac{\lambda\overline{z^2}}{2(1-\lambda\overline{z})} \tag{2.6}$$

Note that in the limit as $k \to \infty$, the above equation approaches the Pollaczek-Khinchine formula for a FIFO file drum, Eq. (2.3).

3. Analysis of the SLTF Drum Scheduling Discipline

In this section we attempt to provide the same analysis for the shortest-latency-time-first (SLTF) scheduling discipline that we provided for the FIFO scheduling discipline in the last section. We will continue to model the I/O requests as a Poisson arrival process, and both file and paging drum organizations are considered. In contrast to FIFO scheduling, it is considerably simpler to analyze an SLTF paging drum than a SLTF file drum, and in fact several articles exist that analyze an SLTF paging drum with a Poisson arrival process [Coffman, 1969; Skinner, 1967]. The difficulty of defining an exact, tractable model of a SLTF file drum leads here to the presentation of three alternate models that vary in the approximations they make as well as the complexity of their analysis and results.

The SLTF paging drum. For the analysis of an SLTF paging drum, let us use the same notation that was developed for the FIFO paging drum, as well as the same assumptions concerning the I/O requests: all requests are for records of size 1/k and a request is equally likely to be directed to any one of the k sectors. Referring back to Fig. 2.2, let the queue shown be for the I/O requests of a single sector, rather than the entire paging drum as in the case of the FIFO scheduling discipline. It follows as an obvious consequence of the Poisson assumption that the arrival process at an individual sector queue is also a Poisson process with rate λ/k. Let $A = \tau/k$, the time to transmit a record, and let $B = (k-1)\tau/k$, the time to return to the start of the sector after finishing the service of a request. Γ is the time between inspections of the sector queue after the queue is found to be empty, and hence Γ is simply the period of the drum revolution, τ. Interpreting Fig. 2.2 as a sector queue of a SLTF paging drum is a simple application of Skinner's model since neither A, B, nor Γ is a random variable. Note that

$$\overline{A} = \frac{\tau}{k}$$

$$\overline{Z} = \overline{\Gamma} = \tau$$

$$\overline{Z^2} = \overline{\Gamma^2} = \tau^2$$

Therefore, using Eq. (2.4), the expected waiting time for I/O requests at a SLTF paging drum is:

$$\overline{W} = \{(\frac{1}{2} + \frac{1}{k}) + \frac{\rho}{2(1-\rho)}\}\tau , \qquad 0 \leq \rho < 1 . \tag{3.1}$$

$$\rho = \lambda\tau/k = \lambda\overline{R}\tau$$

Define the utilization of a drum, denoted u_d, to be the equilibrium, or long term, probability that the drum is transmitting information. From basic conservation principles it follows that the utilization of a paging drum is $\lambda\tau/k$ and hence $u_d = \rho$.

Coffman [1969] derives this same result from first principles[*] and those interested in a more complete discussion of SLTF paging drums are encouraged to read Coffman's article.

The SLTF file drum. For the remainder of this section we turn our attention to the SLTF file drum. This form of drum organization is becoming more important to understand as drums that provide hardware assistance to implement SLTF scheduling gain wider acceptance.

Let us use the same model of I/O requests for the SLTF file drum that was used for the FIFO file drum; in other words, the successive arrival epochs form a Poisson process with parameter λ; starting addresses are independent random variables, uniformly distributed about the drum's circumference, Eq. (2.1); and the record lengths are exponentially distributed, Eq. (2.2).

The most difficult aspect of an SLTF file drum to model is its latency intervals. Since the initial position of the read-write heads of the drum is not related (correlated) to the starting addresses of the outstanding I/O requests, S_i, it follows that the distance from the read-write heads to S_i, denoted D_i, is uniformly distributed between zero and a full drum revolution and hence

$$\Pr\{D_i > t\} = 1 - \frac{t}{\tau} \qquad 0 \le t < \tau \text{ and } 1 \le i \le n.$$

Since the distances to the starting addresses from the read-write heads are independent,

$$\Pr\{D_1 > t \text{ and } D_2 > t \text{ and } \ldots \text{ and } D_n > t\} = [1 - \frac{t}{\tau}]^n, \ 0 \le t < \tau.$$

---

[*] Coffman's definition of $\overline{W}$ does not include the data transmission time, and hence his expression for $\overline{W}$ is smaller than Eq. (3.1) by the quantity τ/k.

The SLTF scheduling discipline requires that the first record processed is the one whose starting address is the first to encounter the read-write heads; call the time until processing begins L_n. We can now state the cumulative distribution function of L_n, as well as its density function, mean, and variance

$$F_n(t) = \Pr\{L_n < t\} = 1 - [1 - \frac{t}{\tau}]^n, \qquad 0 \le t < \tau; \qquad (3.2)$$

$$f_n(t) = F_n'(t) = \frac{n(\tau - t)^{n-1}}{\tau^n}, \qquad 0 \le t < \tau;$$

$$\bar{L}_n = \frac{\tau}{n+1};$$

$$\text{var}(L_n) = \{1 - \frac{2n}{n+1} + \frac{n}{n+2} - \frac{1}{(n+1)^2}\}\tau^2$$

Although the above distribution of L_n is relatively simple, significant simplification in the analysis will result by replacing Eq. (3.2) with the exponential distribution

$$G_n(t) = 1 - e^{-(n+1)t/\tau}, \qquad t \ge 0. \qquad (3.3)$$

Let L_n' be the random variable with distribution $G_n(t)$. $G_n(t)$ has several attractive properties as an approximation to $F_n(t)$:

$$\bar{L_n'} = \bar{L}_n = \frac{\tau}{n+1},$$

and if we let C_n' be the coefficient of variation for L_n' and C_n be the coefficient of variation for L_n we have

$$C_n = \sqrt{\frac{n}{n+2}} < 1 = C_n'$$

but

$$\lim_{n \to \infty} C_n = 1$$

Consequently, $G_n(t)$ becomes a better approximation to $F_n(t)$ as the depth of the queue at the drum increases. We cannot ignore the fact $G_n(t)$ is a rough approximation for small n, but note how quickly C_n' approaches 1:

$$C_1 = .577$$

$$C_2 = .707$$

.
.
.

$$C_{10} = .910$$

.
.
.

The above discussion makes no mention of how well the higher order moments (greater than 2) of $G_n(t)$ approximate $F_n(t)$. However, we feel somewhat justified in ignoring these higher moments since both the Pollaczek-Khinchine formula, Eq. (2.2), and the Skinner formula, Eq. (2.4), show that the expected waiting time (and queue size) is only a function of the first two moments of the service time. Unfortunately neither the Pollaczek-Khinchine or Skinner formulas directly apply here since service time, in particular latency, is queue size dependent. However, it appears likely that the first two moments of the service time are also the dominant parameters in a SLTF file drum and comparison of models based on the exponential approximation to latency shown in Sec. 4 behave very similarly to models not using the approximation.

Figure 3.1 is the model of a SLTF file drum based on the assumptions discussed above. We have a Poisson arrival process with parameter λ, a single queue, and the server is made up of two exponential servers in series. The second server, with servicing rate μ, models the transmission of records and reflects our assumption of exponentially distributed record lengths.

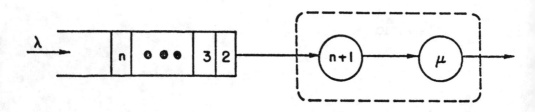

Figure 3.1.   Two-stage Markov model of the SLTF file drum.

The first of the two servers has service time distribution $G_n(t)$, and hence service rate $(n+1)/\tau$, and models the latency incurred accessing a record when there are n I/O requests demanding service. This 'latency' server is the result of our recent discussion and one further assumption: we assume that the latency is purely a function of queue depth and not related to the past performance of the drum. Although this is normally a very good approximation, it is not entirely true. In Sec. 4 we will explore why this is an approximation and show its relation to Feller's waiting-time paradox [Feller, 1970].

Since both servers in our model have exponential service times and the arrival process is Poisson, our model is a birth-and-death Markov process. Let $E_{0,n}$ be the state where n I/O requests are queued or in service and the latency server, server 0, is active; define $E_{0,0}$ as the idle state. Similarly, let $E_{1,n}$ be the state with n I/O requests and the transmission server, server 1, active. If $P_{i,j}(t)$ is the probability of being in state $E_{i,j}$ at time t, then the differential equations describing the SLTF file drum are

$$P'_{0,0}(t) = -\lambda\, P_{0,0}(t) + \mu\, P_{1,1}(t),$$

$$P'_{1,1}(t) = -(\lambda + \mu)\, P_{1,1}(t) + \frac{2}{\tau}\, P_{0,1}(t),$$

$$P'_{0,n}(t) = -(\lambda + \frac{n+1}{\tau})\, P_{0,n}(t) + \lambda\, P_{0,n-1}(t) + \mu\, P_{1,n+1}(t),$$
$$n = 1, 2, \ldots;$$

$$P'_{1,n}(t) = -(\lambda+\mu)\, P_{1,n}(t) + \lambda\, P_{1,n-1}(t) + \frac{n+1}{\tau}\, P_{0,n}(t),$$
$$n = 2, 3, \ldots$$

In this article we are primarily interested in the steady state solution, or more precisely, the solution at statistical equilibrium. Consequently let $p_{i,j} = \lim_{t \to \infty} P_{i,j}(t)$, and the above set of differential equations reduce to the following set of recurrence relations (often called balance equations):

$$\lambda p_{0,0} = \mu\, p_{1,1} , \qquad (3.4)$$

$$(\lambda+\mu)p_{1,1} = \frac{2}{\tau}\, p_{0,1} , \qquad (3.5)$$

$$(\lambda + \frac{n+1}{\tau})\, p_{0,n} = \lambda p_{0,n-1} + \mu\, p_{1,n+1} , \qquad n = 1,2,\ldots; \qquad (3.6)$$

$$(\lambda+\mu)p_{1,n} = \lambda p_{1,n-1} + \frac{n+1}{\tau}\, p_{0,n+1} , \qquad n = 2,3,\ldots \qquad (3.7)$$

The most direct solution of the above set of balance equations lies in working with their associated generating functions:

$$P_0(z) = \sum_{0 \le n < \infty} p_{0,n}\, z^n$$

$$P_1(z) = \sum_{0 < n < \infty} p_{1,n}\, z^n .$$

Equation (3.6), using Eq. (3.4) as an initial condition yields

$$z\, P_0'(z) + (1 + \lambda\tau - \lambda\tau z)\, P_0(z) = \frac{\mu\tau}{z}\, P_1(z) + p_{0,0} . \qquad (3.8)$$

Similarly, Eqs. (3.5) and (3.7) yield

$$\tau(\mu + \lambda - \lambda z)\, P_1(z) = z\, P_0'(z) + P_0(z) - p_{0,0} . \qquad (3.9)$$

$P_1(z)$ can be eliminated from the above set of simultaneous equations and we get a linear, first-order differential equation in $P_0(z)$:

$$P_0'(z) + (\frac{1}{z} - \lambda\tau + \frac{\lambda\tau\rho}{\rho z-1})\, P_0(z) = \frac{1}{z}\, p_{0,0} \qquad (3.10)$$

where $\rho = \lambda/\mu$. Using

$$\int(\frac{1}{z} - \lambda\tau + \frac{\lambda\tau\rho}{\rho z-1})dz = \ln z - \lambda\tau z + \lambda\tau\cdot\ln(\rho z-1) + C$$

as an integrating factor, we find the following explicit form for $P_0(z)$

$$P_0(z) = \frac{p_{0,0}e^{\lambda\tau z}}{z(1-\rho z)^{\lambda}}\left[\int e^{-\lambda\tau z}(1-\rho z)^{\lambda\tau}dz + C\right] \tag{3.11}$$

where C is the constant of integration. We can eliminate C by replacing

the indefinite integral by the correct definite integral. Clearly

$\lim\limits_{z \to 0} P_0(z) = p_{0,0}$, and thus C vanishes if the indefinite integral is

replaced by a definite integral with limits from 0 to z:

$$P_0(z) = \frac{e^{\lambda\tau z}p_{0,0}}{z(1-\rho z)^{\lambda}}\int_0^z e^{-\lambda\tau w}(1-\rho w)^{\lambda\tau}dw$$

A more useful generating function for the subsequent analysis than

$P_0(z)$ is

$$Q(z) = \sum_{0 \le n < \infty}(p_{0,n} + p_{1,n})z^n = P_0(z) + P_1(z) .$$

From Eqs. (3.8) and (3.9) it follows that

$$P_1(z) = \frac{\rho z}{1-\rho z} P_0(z)$$

and hence

$$Q(z) = \frac{1}{1-\rho z} P_0(z)$$

$$Q(z) = \frac{e^{\lambda\tau z}p_{0,0}}{z(1-\rho z)^{-\lambda\tau+1}}\int_0^z e^{-\lambda\tau w}(1-\rho w)^{\lambda\tau}dw \tag{3.12}$$

It is impossible to integrate, in closed form, the integral in the

above equations. However it is in the form of the well-known, and

extensively tabulated, incomplete gamma function [Abramowitz and Stegun,

1964]:

$$\gamma[\alpha,x] = \int_0^x e^{-y} y^{\alpha-1} dy$$

Restating Eq. (3.12) in terms of the incomplete gamma function gives

$$Q(z) = \frac{\mu \ e^{(\lambda z - \mu)\tau} p_{0,0}}{\lambda z} \left\{ \frac{\gamma[\lambda\tau+1, -\mu\tau] - \gamma[\lambda\tau+1, (\lambda z - \mu)\tau]}{[(\lambda z - \mu)\tau]^{\lambda\tau+1}} \right\}.$$

It is now possible to find an explicit expression for $p_{0,0}$, the equilibrium probability that the drum is idle, since it is clear that $\lim\limits_{z \to 1} Q(z) = 1$. Hence, from Eq. (3.12)

$$p_{0,0} = e^{-\lambda\tau}(1-\rho)^{\lambda\tau+1} \left\{ \int_0^1 e^{-\lambda\tau w}(1-\rho w)^{\lambda\tau} dw \right\}^{-1} \tag{3.13}$$

Equation (3.12) can be used to find the mean queue length, $\overline{L}$:

$$\overline{L} = \lim\limits_{z \to 1} Q'(z) = \lambda\tau - 1 + \frac{\rho(\lambda\tau+1) + p_{0,0}}{1-\rho}$$

Using Little's formula, $\overline{L} = \lambda\overline{W}$ [cf. Jewell, 1967], we can state the expected waiting time of I/O requests at an SLTF file drum for this two-stage Markov model:

$$\overline{W} = \frac{\mu\tau+1}{(\mu-\lambda)} + \frac{1}{\lambda} \left[\left\{ \left\{ \int_0^1 \left[\frac{e^{(1-w)}(1-\rho w)}{1-\rho} \right]^{\lambda\tau} dw \right\}^{-1} - 1 \right\} \right] \tag{3.14}$$

Figure 3.2 displays the expected waiting time, $\overline{W}$, as a function of both λ and μ for this two-stage model of the SLTF file drum.

The expression for $\overline{W}$ is not given in terms of the incomplete gamma function since numerical integration of the integral in Eq. (3.14) is routine.

In the analysis of the two-stage model of an SLTF file drum just discussed, a concerted attempt was made to closely approximate the behavior of the drum. It is interesting, even if for comparative purposes only, to briefly discuss a simplification of the two-stage model. The

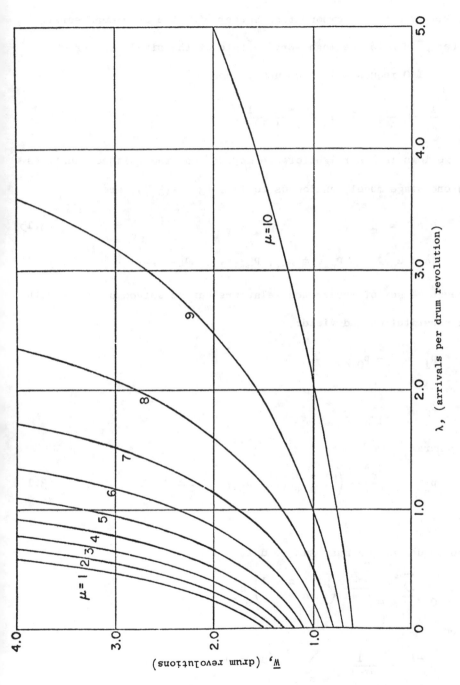

Figure 3.2. $\overline{W}$, the expected waiting time, of the two-stage Markov model of the SLTF file drum.

most obvious simplification is to replace the two series-coupled servers

in Fig. 3.1 by a single exponential server with the same mean service

rate. Let μ_n denote the mean service rate of the single server when

there are n I/O requests in the queue, then

$$\frac{1}{\mu_n} = \frac{\tau}{n+1} + \frac{1}{\mu} = \frac{\mu\tau + n + 1}{\mu(n + 1)} .$$

It follows in a straightforward manner that the balance equations

for the one-stage model, analogous to Eqs. (3.4)-(3.7), are

$$\lambda \, p_0 = \mu_1 \, p_1 , \tag{3.15}$$

$$(\lambda + \mu_n)p_n = \lambda p_{n-1} + \mu_{n+1} \, p_{n+1} , \qquad n = 1, 2, \ldots \tag{3.16}$$

The above set of recurrence relations can be solved directly with

forward substitution and yield:

$$p_1 = \frac{\lambda}{\mu_1} \, p_0 ,$$

$$p_2 = \frac{\lambda^2}{\mu_1 \mu_2} \, p_0 ,$$

and in general

$$p_n = \frac{\rho^n}{\mu\tau + 1} \left(\begin{array}{c} \mu\tau + n + 1 \\ n + 1 \end{array} \right) p_0 , \qquad n \geq 0 ; \tag{3.17}$$

where $\rho = \frac{\lambda}{\mu}$.

The sequence $\{p_n\}$ must sum to unity, i.e.

$$\sum_{0 \leq n < \infty} \frac{\rho^n}{\mu\tau+1} \left(\begin{array}{c} \mu\tau + n + 1 \\ n + 1 \end{array} \right) p_0 = 1$$

and hence

$$p_0^{-1} = \frac{1}{\mu\tau+1} \sum_{0 \leq n < \infty} \left(\begin{array}{c} \mu\tau + n + 1 \\ n + 1 \end{array} \right) \rho^n .$$

With the aid of the binomial theorem the above relation reduces to

$$p_0 = \frac{\rho(\mu T+1)(1-\rho)^{\mu T+1}}{1-(1-\rho)^{\mu T+1}} \tag{3.18}$$

Using Eqs. (3.17) and (3.18) we see that for this simple model of a SLTF file drum we are able to get explicit expressions for the probability of being in any state E_n. However, only $\overline{W}$ will be used in comparing this single-stage model to the two-stage model and $\overline{W}$ is most easily determined from the generating function for the model.

$$P(z) = \sum_{0 \le n < \infty} p_n z^n$$

$$= \sum_{0 \le n < \infty} \frac{\rho^n}{\mu T+1} \binom{\mu T+n+1}{n+1} p_0 z^n$$

Applying the binomial theorem as before, and using the expression for p_n in Eq. (3.17),

$$P(z) = \frac{(1-\rho)^{\mu T+1}[1-(1-\rho z)^{\mu T+1}]}{z(1-\rho z)^{\mu T+1}[1-(1-\rho)^{\mu T+1}]} \tag{3.19}$$

The expected waiting time for I/O requests at the single-stage model of a SLTF file drum is

$$\overline{W} = \lim_{z \to 1} P'(z) = \frac{1}{\lambda}\left(\frac{\rho(\mu T+1)}{(1-\rho)(1-(1-\rho)^{\mu T+1})} - 1\right). \tag{3.20}$$

For our third model of the SLTF file drum we turn to an article by Abate and Dubner [1969]. Although the majority of their paper is concerned with a particular variant of the SLTF scheduling discipline implemented by Burroughs [1968], their approach can be applied to the SLTF file drum discussed here.[*]

---

[*] Abate and Dubner do in fact briefly discuss the model of a SLTF file drum presented here, and Eq. (3.22) is their Eq. (14), with appropriate changes in notation.

Abate and Dubner's analysis, when applied to a file drum with pure SLTF scheduling, is surprisingly simple. They divide the waiting time into three, independent terms:

$$W = D + R + \tau(K - 1) . \tag{3.21}$$

D is the distance from the read-write heads to the start of the I/O request at the instant of the request's arrival. Consistent with our previous discussions, D is a random variable uniformly distributed from zero to a full drum revolution; hence $\overline{D} = 1/2$. R is the length of the record that must be read or written to the drum; Abate and Dubner make no assumptions concerning the distribution of R; they only use the mean of the record length, $\overline{R}$. With the same conservation argument following Eq. (3.1), Abate and Dubner also note the drum utilization is just λ/μ, or ρ, and that on the average, the drum is free to begin servicing a record at its starting address with probability $(1 - \rho)$, which is the equilibrium probability the drum is not busy transmitting a record. Furthermore, they assume successive attempts to read a record can be modeled as independent, Bernoulli trials with probability of success $(1 - \rho)$. The random variable K in Eq. (3.21) is the number of trials required until the record is serviced, and hence K is geometrically distributed with probability mass function:

$$\Pr\{K = k\} = (1 - \rho)\rho^{k-1} , \qquad k = 1, 2, \ldots$$

and mean

$$\overline{K} = \frac{1}{1 - \rho} .$$

Therefore, the expected waiting time for I/O requests at Abate and Dubner's model of an SLTF file drum is:

$$\overline{W} = \{\tfrac{1}{2} + \overline{R} + \frac{\rho}{1 - \rho}\}\tau \ . \tag{3.22}$$

This concludes the development of models for the SLTF file drum. Unlike the FIFO file drum, the FIFO paging drum, and the SLTF paging drum, we do not have a model that is exact; in each of the three models of the SLTF file drum, assumptions are made that do not exactly reflect the actual behavior of a SLTF file drum.

4. Verification of SLTF file drum models

We have presented three different models of the SLTF file drum: the one-stage Markov model; the 2-stage Markov model, and Abate and Dubner's model. In order to resolve the relative merits of these models we will compare each of them to the results of a simulation model of the SLTF file drum. The simulation uses all of our original assumptions, i.e. (1) Poisson arrival process, (2) exponential distribution of record lengths and (3) starting addressing uniformly distributed around the surface of the drum.

The precision of the summary statistics of the simulation model is described in detail in [Appendix A]. All the points on the graphs in this article represent the result of simulation experiments that are run until 100,000 I/O requests have been serviced; this number of simulated events proved sufficient for the purposes of this article. The sample means of the I/O waiting times, for example, are random variables with standard deviations less than .002 for $\rho = .1$ and slightly more than .1 for $\rho = .75$.

A plot of the results from the models of the SLTF file drum are shown in Fig. 4.1 for an expected record size of 1/3 of the drum's

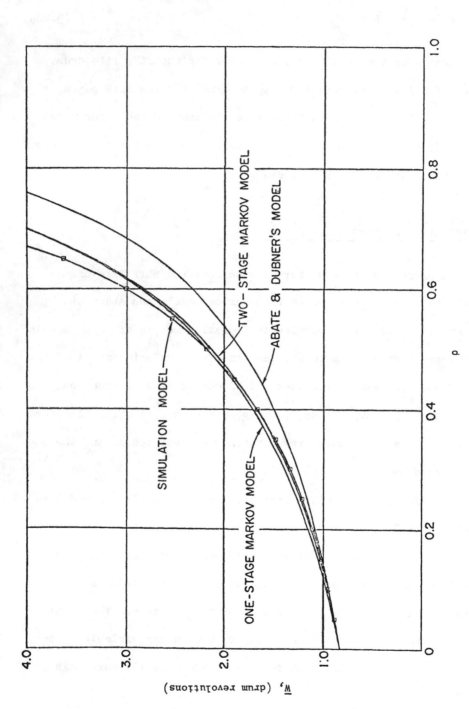

Figure 4.1. The expected waiting time of the four models of the SLTF file drum for $\overline{R} = 1/3$.

circumference. Specifically, $\overline{W}$, the mean waiting time for I/O requests

at the SLTF file drum are shown as a function of drum utilization, ρ.

Figure 4.2 is a similar plot except the expected records size is 1/8 of

the drum's circumference. We use 1/3 because this is close to the

measured value of record sizes discussed in Sec. 2 and 1/8 because Abate

and Dubner thought their model should be a good approximation for

$\overline{R} < 1/4$. For $\overline{R} = 1/3$ and $\rho < .45$ the results are encouraging: the two-

stage model tracks the simulated waiting time very closely, but is a

slight overestimate; the one-stage model follows the simulation fairly

closely but is more of an overestimate than the two-stage model; and

Abate and Dubner's model is an underestimate, but they warned their

model might not apply very accurately for $\overline{R} > 1/4$. When we estimated

the latency intervals by the exponential distribution with mean of

$\tau/(n+1)$, we slightly overestimated the coefficient of variation. It has

been shown in other queueing models that the mean waiting time is

positively related to the mean service time as well as the coefficient

of variation of the service time. Therefore, it is not surprising that

the two-stage model is an overestimate of the results found by simulation.

Lumping the latency and transmission servers into one server in the one-

stage model further over-approximates the coefficient of variation of

service time, even though the mean is still exact, and hence the one-

stage model is a larger overestimate of the waiting time than the two-

stage model.

Examination of Fig. 4.2 for small ρ, i.e. $\overline{R} = 1/8$ and $\rho < .45$,

shows several significant features of the SLTF file drum models. Most

striking is the degradation of the one and two-stage models. The reason,

however, is quite simple; since the record lengths are not uniformly

48

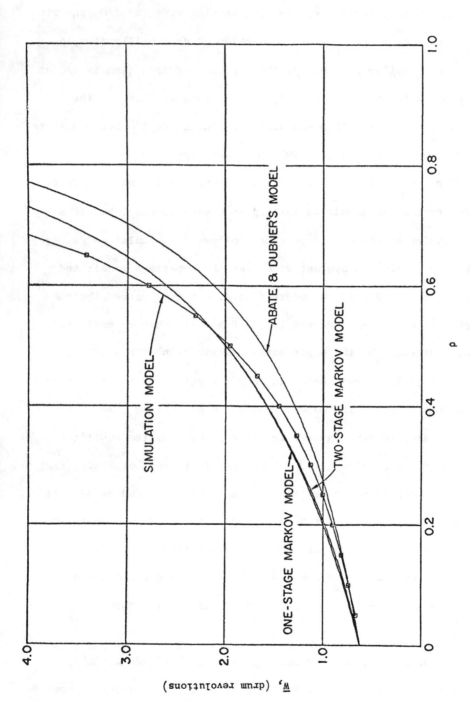

Figure 4.2. The expected waiting time of the four models of the SLTF file drum for $\bar{R} = 1/8$.

distributed over some integer number of drum revolutions, the finishing

address of an I/O request is not independent of its starting address.

In particular, as the expected record length goes to zero, the average

wait time for an I/O request approaches $\tau/2$, regardless of the arrival

rate of I/O requests.

Figure 4.2 illustrates an interesting phenomenon with respect to

the Abate and Dubner model: no change, to within the accuracy of the

simulation model, is detectable between the difference in the simulation

model and Abate and Dubner's model for $\bar{R} = 1/3$ and $\bar{R} = 1/8$. Counter to

original intuition [Abate and Dubner, 1969], no improvement in the Abate

and Dubner model is detected as $\bar{R}$ becomes smaller. If instead of

comparing the curves for $\bar{R} = 1/3$ and $\bar{R} = 1/8$ at points of equal ρ, as is

suggested by Figs. 4.1 and 4.2, we compare them at points of equal λ,

then as $\bar{R}$ is reduced, we do see a significant improvement in the Abate

and Dubner model.

The most outstanding feature of Figs. 4.1 and 4.2 is when ρ becomes

large, i.e. $\rho > 0.45$: the one and two-stage models, as well as Abate

and Dubner's model, are underestimates of the expected waiting time

found by the simulation model, and the underestimates become increasingly

pronounced as $\rho \to 1$. The following illustration gives an intuitive

explanation for this phenomena. Suppose we have n outstanding I/O

requests. From the arguments that lead to Eq. (3.3) we know the expected

distance from the read-write heads to the first starting address is

$1/(n+1)$. However, the reasoning can be applied to distances opposite to

the drum's rotation and again the distance from the read-write heads to

the closest starting address behind the read-write heads is $1/(n+1)$.

Hence the expected size of the interval between the starting addresses,

punctuated by the read-write heads, is $2/(n+1)$. If we consider the n
I/O requests by themselves, however, since the starting addresses are
independent random variables, from symmetry it follows that the expected
distance between adjacent starting addresses is $1/n$. Therefore we see
that when we randomly position the read-write head on the drum, we are
most likely to fall into a larger than average interval between
starting addresses. In other words, those starting addresses that end
large intervals are most likely to be chosen first by an SLTF schedule
and as the SLTF schedule processes I/O requests, the remaining starting
addresses exhibit an increasing degree of clustering, or correlation. A
more complete discussion of this phenomenon, and related topics, are
discussed by Feller [1970] under the general heading of waiting-time
paradoxes.

Let us consider in more detail why the two-stage model underestimates the wait time. Let $S_{(1)}$, $S_{(2)}$, and $S_{(3)}$ denote the starting
addresses in order of increasing distance from the read-write head,
denoted H, and let $F_{(1)}$ be the finishing address of the record beginning
with $S_{(1)}$. Let $F_{(1)}$ be a random variable uniformly distributed around
the circumference of the drum, and for this example suppose it is
independent of $S_{(1)}$. Suppose initially there are n I/O requests, the
$S_{(i)}$'s, H, and $F_{(1)}$'s make up n+2 random variables, and they can form the
following three basic configurations with respect to H:

$$H \; F_{(1)} \; S_{(1)} \; S_{(2)} \; \cdots \; S_{(n)} \tag{4.1a}$$

$$H \; S_{(1)} \; \cdots \; S_{(n)} \; F_{(1)} \tag{4.1b}$$

$$H \; S_{(1)} \; \cdots \; S_{(j)} \; F_{(1)} \; S_{(j+1)} \; \cdots \; S_{(n)} \; ; \quad 1 < j < n-1 \tag{4.1c}$$

We know that the density function of the distance between any two adjacent random variables is $(n+2)(1-x)^{n+1}$, $0 \leq x < 1$, and has a mean of $1/(n+2)$. Moreover, an obvious extension of the above expression leads to the following distribution functions for the difference between any two random variables separated by k-1 other points on the drum [Feller, 1970]:

$$(n+2)\binom{n+1}{k-1} x^{k-1}(1-x)^{n-k} , \qquad 0 \leq x < 1 .$$

with mean $k/(n+2)$.

Referring to the n+2 situations in (4.1) we can see that

$$\Pr(L_n = t) = (n+1)(1-t)^n , \qquad 0 \leq t < \tau$$

and

$$\bar{L}_n = \tau/n+1$$

and this is precisely what we found $\bar{L}_n$ to be by a much simpler argument in Sec. 3. However, now consider $\bar{L}_{n-1}$ in the same example. In (4.1a) and (4.1b) the latency is the distance from $F_{(1)}$ to $S_{(2)}$ and in the n-1 cases of (4.1c) the latency is the distance from $F_{(1)}$ to $S_{(j+1)}$. Hence

$$\bar{L}_{n-1} = \frac{1}{n+1} \cdot \frac{2}{n+2} + \frac{1}{n+1} \cdot \frac{3}{n+2} + \frac{n-1}{n+1} \cdot \frac{1}{n+2}$$

$$= \frac{n+4}{(n+2)(n+1)} > \frac{1}{n} .$$

The above inequality illustrates that latency is dependent on the past history of the drum; and that unlike the SLTF and FIFO paging drums, as well as the FIFO file drum, the SLTF file drum does not experience a Markov epoch upon completion of an I/O request. The only instances in which the drum's future performance truly uncouples from the past behavior is when the drum is idle. This fact makes the precise analysis of a SLTF file drum, even with the simple arrival process described here, very difficult.

In concluding this section we might pause to consider the relative errors introduced by the approximations used to make a tractable model of the SLTF file drum. In the best analytic model, the two-stage Markov model, we made three assumptions, all with regard to latency, that are not entirely correct: (1) we approximated Eq. (3.2) by the exponential distribution Eq. (3.3), (2) we assumed the position of the read-write heads at the end of a record transmission is independent of its position at the start of transmission, and (3) we assumed that latency is a function only of the current queue length and not influenced by previous queue sizes. The first two approximations are dominant for $\rho < .4$ but the error introduced by these approximations is slight for large $\overline{R}$, and as $\overline{R}$ becomes small, the second assumption causes large overestimations of numbers. However, for larger ρ, the third approximation, related to Feller's waiting time paradox, dominates and the error it introduces becomes severe as $\rho \rightarrow 1$. Consequently, attempts to make a significant practical improvement over the two-stage model should not dwell on removing the exponential approximation to the latency interval, but rather on the second and third approximations.

5. An Empirical Model of the SLTF File Drum

In this section we develop a simple, empirical expression for the expected waiting time of the SLTF file drum. Such an empirical expression has a limited utility, but in conjunction with the other models available for the SLTF file drum it can be a useful tool.

The expressions for the expected waiting time for the FIFO file drum, the FIFO paging drum, the SLTF paging drum, and Abate and Dubner's model of the SLTF file drum all have the basic hyperbolic form:

$$\overline{W} = \{\tfrac{1}{2} + \overline{R} + b(\tfrac{\rho}{1-\rho})\}\tau \qquad (5.1)$$

and consequently this form is a likely candidate for a model of the SLTF

file drum. All that must be empirically determined is the coefficient b,

and whether or not an expression of the form of Eq. (5.1) is adequate to

describe the SLTF file drum. Figure 5.1 is a plot of

$$[\overline{W} - (\tfrac{1}{2} + \overline{R})](1 - \rho) \qquad (5.2)$$

for all four models of the SLTF file drum for $\overline{R} = 1/3$. Curves that are

of the form of Eq. (5.1) will appear as straight lines in Fig. 5.1.

Note Abate and Dubner's model appears as a straight line with a slope of

one, and both of the Markov models approach finite, nonzero value as

$\rho \to 1$, indicating they are also fundamentally hyperbolic in form. The

simulation points, however, do not appear to approach a finite value as

$\rho \to 1$, and hence Eq. (5.1) does not capture all the significant behavior

of the SLTF file drum. In order to model the part of the SLTF waiting

time that is growing faster than $\rho/(1-\rho)$, we will add another term to

Eq. (5.1) to get:

$$\overline{W} = \{\tfrac{1}{2} + \overline{R} + b\tfrac{\rho}{1-\rho} + c(\tfrac{\rho}{1-\rho})^2\}\tau \ . \qquad (5.3)$$

From Fig. 5.1 we see that for small ρ, the simulation curve appears to

have a slope of about one, and hence if Eq. (5.2) is an adequate model

of the SLTF file drum, the expression

$$[\overline{W} - (\tfrac{1}{2} + \overline{R}) - \tfrac{\rho}{1-\rho}]\tfrac{(1-\rho)^2}{\rho}\tau \qquad (5.4)$$

should appear as a straight line when plotted as a function of ρ.

Figure 5.2 shows Eq. (5.4) as a function of ρ. Clearly the simulation

results are not growing as fast as Eq. (5.3) suggests and it over-

estimates the rate of growth of $\overline{W}$ as $\rho \to 1$.

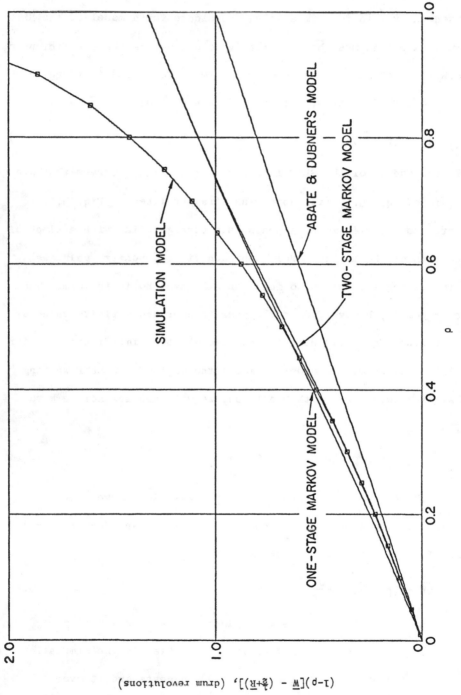

Figure 5.1. The expected waiting time of the SLTF file drum models transformed to test hyperbolic dependence on $(1-\rho)$.

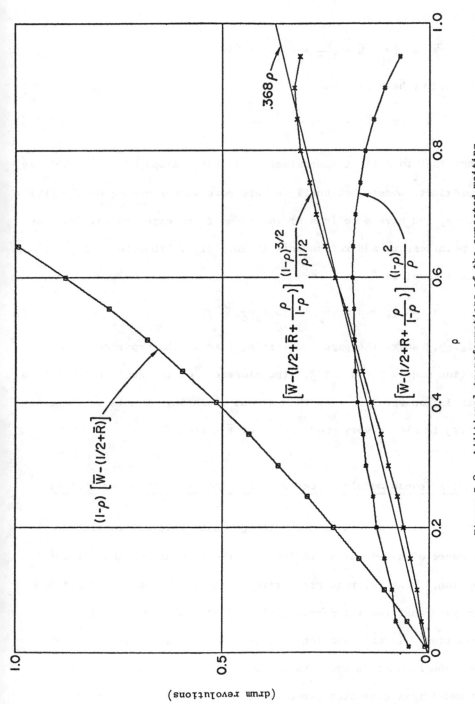

Figure 5.2. Additional transformations of the expected waiting time for the simulation model.

Another expression for $\overline{W}$ that may lead to an adequate empirical model is

$$\overline{W} = \{\tfrac{1}{2} + \overline{R} + \tfrac{\rho}{1-\rho} + c(\tfrac{\rho}{1-\rho})^{3/2}\}\tau \ . \tag{5.5}$$

In Fig. 5.2 we have plotted

$$[\overline{W} - (\tfrac{1}{2} + \overline{R}) - \tfrac{\rho}{1-\rho}] \frac{(1-\rho)^{3/2}}{\rho^{1/2}} \tag{5.6}$$

and show that to a first approximation it has a slope of .368. This is an approximate model, but until we have more understanding of the SLTF file drum, and have some idea of the form of the expected waiting time, it is pointless to add refinements to Eq. (5.5). Therefore, our empirical model is

$$\overline{W} = \{\tfrac{1}{2} + \overline{R} + \tfrac{\rho}{1-\rho} + .368(\tfrac{\rho}{1-\rho})^{3/2}\}\tau \tag{5.7}$$

and Fig. 5.3 shows the expected waiting time of the empirical and simulation models for $\overline{R} = 1/3$. The closeness of the empirical model to the simulation results makes them almost indistinguishable in the figure. Eq. (5.7) is also a very good model for $\overline{R} = 1/8$.

6. Cyclic queue models of central processor-drum computer systems

The previous models of drum storage units have all considered the performance of a drum as an isolated system by means of the Poisson assumption. That is, requests arrive at the drum from some undefined source such that the interarrival times follow an exponential distribution. In this section we extend the previous models by removing the Poisson assumption and consider a simple case of the type of environment that generates requests to be processed by the drum. Cyclic queue models with a FIFO file drum can be treated by Gaver's [1967]

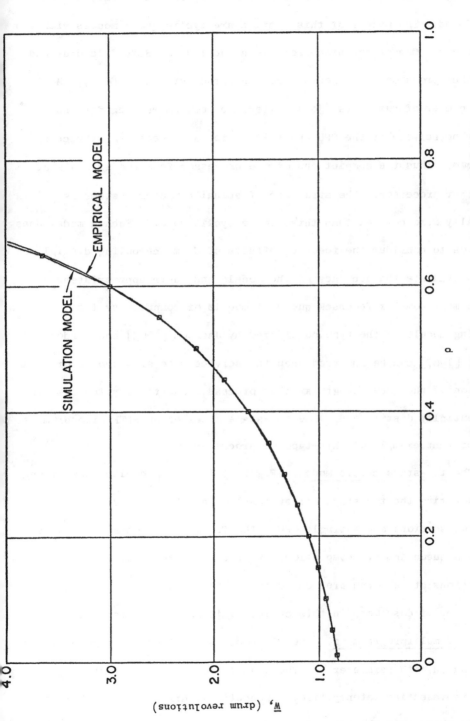

Figure 5.3. The expected waiting time of the empirical and simulation
models of the SLTF file drum for $\mu = 3$.

analysis, and for a SLTF and FIFO paging drum, an exact analysis has not been found. The models of this section are cyclic queue models with two processors. One of the processors is a model of an SLTF file drum and the other processor represents a central processing unit (CPU). A fixed number of customers (jobs) alternate between waiting for and receiving service at the CPU and waiting for and receiving service at the drum. Thus the completions of one processor form the arrivals at the other processor. The structure of actual computer systems is typically more complex than this simple cyclic model. Such a model does allow us to consider the feedback effects of drum scheduling disciplines and to evaluate the accuracy of the models and their appropriateness for use in more complex feedback queueing models of computer systems. Closed queueing models of the type considered by Jackson [1963] and Gordon and Newell [1967] can be analyzed when the service rate of a processor is a function of the queue length at that processor and the service time is exponentially distributed. The one-stage model of an SLTF file drum is an important example of this type of processor.

The two-stage cyclic model. Figure 6.1 shows a cyclic queue model incorporating the two-stage Markov model of an SLTF file drum of the previous sections and a single CPU. The CPU server processes requests from its queue and its completions are routed to the drum queue. Completions at the drum are routed to the CPU queue. There are a fixed number, m, of customers in this cycle. This number, m, is called the degree of multiprogramming. The CPU processing times are exponentially distributed with parameter λ. The drum is composed of two stages, the first representing latency time, exponentially distributed with rate $(n+1)/\tau$ where n is the size of the drum queue and τ is the period of

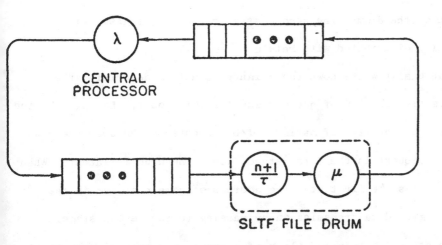

Figure 6.1.   Cyclic queue model of CPU-drum system

with two-stage Markov model of SLTF file drum.

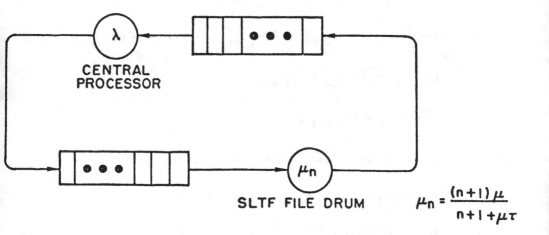

$$\mu_n = \frac{(n+1)\mu}{n+1+\mu\tau}$$

Figure 6.2.   Cyclic queue model of CPU-drum system

with one-stage Markov model of SLTF file drum.

revolution of the drum. The second stage represents transmission time, exponentially distributed with rate μ.

We can easily write down the balance equations describing the equilibrium distribution of queue sizes for this model. Let $p_{0,n}$ be the steady state probability of having n I/O requests in the drum queue and having some request in the first stage, i.e., the drum is latent. When the drum reaches the first starting address of some customer in the queue, it begins data transmission by passing to the second stage. Denote the steady state probability of transmission with n requests at the drum by $p_{1,n}$. For convenience let $p_{0,0}$ denote an idle drum and let $p_{1,0}$ be identically zero. The balance equations are then:

$$\lambda p_{0,0} = \mu p_{1,1}$$

$$(\lambda+\mu)p_{1,n} = \frac{(n+1)}{\tau} p_{0,n} + \lambda p_{1,n-1} , \qquad 1 \leq n < m$$

$$(\lambda+\frac{n+1}{\tau})p_{0,n} = \mu p_{1,n+1} + \lambda p_{0,n-1} , \qquad 1 \leq n < m \qquad (6.1)$$

$$\mu p_{1,m} = \frac{(m+1)}{\tau}p_{0,m} + \lambda p_{1,m-1}$$

$$(\frac{m+1}{\tau})p_{0,m} = \lambda p_{0,m-1} .$$

These equations can be transformed to the following form

$$p_{1,n} = \rho_0(p_{0,n-1} + p_{1,n-1}) , \qquad 1 \leq n \leq m$$

$$p_{0,n} = \rho_n(p_{0,n-1} + p_{1,n}) , \qquad 1 \leq n < m \qquad (6.2)$$

$$p_{0,m} = \rho_m \, p_{0,m-1}$$

where $\rho_0 = \lambda/u$ and $\rho_n = \lambda\tau/(n+1)$. Remembering that $p_{1,0} = 0$, we have 2m+1 equations in 2m+2 variables. We get the final (nonhomogeneous) equation by recalling that all the variables must sum to unity in order to represent a discrete probability distribution. Now note that if a value for $p_{0,0}$ were known, the values of all the other variables could be computed directly from Eqs. (6.2). Note also that $p_{0,0}$ is a factor of all the other variables; that is, if $p_{0,0}$ were incorrect by a factor of α, all the other values computed from Eqs. (6.2) would be incorrect by a factor of α. Thus to find the correct value for $p_{0,0}$ assume some arbitrary, nonzero value for $p_{0,0}$, say one, and use Eqs. (6.2) to compute the sum of all the variables. The reciprocal of the resulting sum is the factor by which the initial value of $p_{0,0}$ was incorrect. Thus if we assumed an initial value of one, the correct value would be the reciprocal of the sum. Now we can either correct the computed values of the other variables or recompute them using the correct value of $p_{0,0}$.

The expected waiting time at the two-stage drum, $\overline{W}$, (the queueing time plus the service time) will be

$$\overline{W} = \lambda^{-1} \sum_{n=0}^{m} n(p_{0,n} + p_{1,n}) \ .$$

The utilization of the CPU will be

$$u_c = 1 - (p_{0,m} + p_{1,m}) \ .$$

The one-stage cyclic model. Figure 6.2 shows a cyclic queue model using the one-stage Markov model of an SLTF file drum. There is one exponential server for the drum, the service rate of which is queue size dependent. Let μ_n be the service rate when n customers are in the drum queue. Since we want the mean service time to be $\tau/(n+1) + 1/\mu$, where $1/\mu$ is the mean transmission time, we see that

$$\mu_n = \frac{(n+1)\mu}{n+1+\mu\tau} \ .$$

The balance equations for this model are

$$\lambda p_0 = \mu_1\, p_1$$

$$(\lambda + \mu_n) p_n = \lambda p_{n-1} + \mu_{n+1}\, p_{n+1}, \qquad 1 \le n < m$$

$$\mu_m\, p_m = \lambda p_{m-1}.$$

These are equations for a simple queue with arrival and service rates dependent on queue size [cf. Cox and Smith, p. 43] so the solution is

$$p_n = \left(\prod_{i=1}^{n} \rho_i \right) p_0, \qquad 1 \le n \le m$$

$$p_0 = \left\{ \sum_{i=0}^{m} \prod_{j=0}^{i} \rho_j \right\}^{-1}$$

where $\rho_n = \lambda / \mu_n$.

Comparison of the models. Figure 6.3 shows the expected waiting time, $\overline{W}$, for a drum service request versus the ratio of drum transmission time and computing time, λ/μ, when the expected record size is one-third of a drum revolution for three models and four different degrees of multiprogramming, $m = 2, 4, 8, 16$. The model results depicted by the square plotting symbol are from a modification of the simulation model discussed in the earlier sections. The drum server captures the true latency of an SLTF drum. A CPU server and a fixed number of customers have been substituted for the Poisson source. The model results depicted by the smooth curves are from the two-stage model. The one-stage model results are indicated by the curves with the ● plotting symbol. Both of the analytic models are very close to the simulation model except for large degrees of multiprogramming $(m > 8)$, but the two-stage model gives slightly better results than the one-stage model.

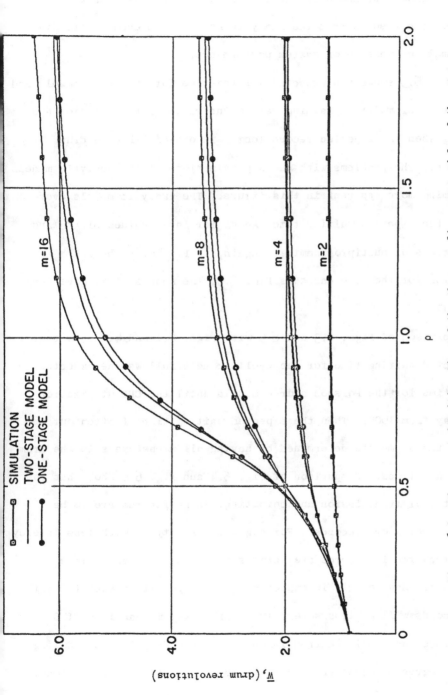

Figure 6.3. The expected waiting time of the three cyclic queue models of the CPU-drum system for $\overline{R} = 1/3$.

Figure 6.4 shows the CPU utilization for all of the cases shown in Fig. 6.3. The results from the analytic models seem even better for this normalized measure of system performance.

Figure 6.5 shows the expected waiting time for the three models and four degrees of multiprogramming versus the ratio of transmission and computing when the expected record length is one-eighth of a drum revolution. The problems with the approximations of the analytic models are becoming more apparent in this figure. The analytic models over-estimate the expected waiting time except for large values of λ/μ and large degrees of multiprogramming. Again, in Fig. 6.6, the CPU utilization for the same cases as Fig. 6.5, the models still give very good results.

Comparison of Figs. 6.3 and 6.5 with Figs. 4.1 and 4.2 show that the expected waiting time for the cyclic models follows the expected waiting time for the Poisson source models until the CPU utilization falls away from 100%. Then the expected waiting times flatten out and approach the asymptote determined by having all m customers in the drum queue at all times. Comparison of Fig. 6.4 and Fig. 6.6 show that for a given ratio of transmission and computing, large records are to be preferred over short records. For a given quantity of work less latency will be incurred if records are large since fewer records will be transmitted. However, it is expected that the penalty associated with short records will be less severe in an SLTF system than in a FIFO system since the total incurred latency is reduced by SLTF scheduling.

The degree of agreement among the curves for the different models encourages us to use the analytic models of SLTF file drums in more complex models of computer systems at least until a more exact treatment

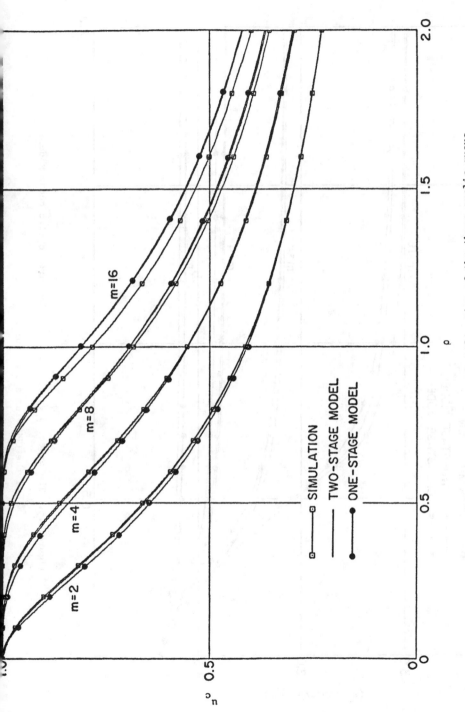

Figure 6.4. Central processor utilization of the three cyclic queue
models of the CPU-drum system for $\overline{R} = 1/3$.

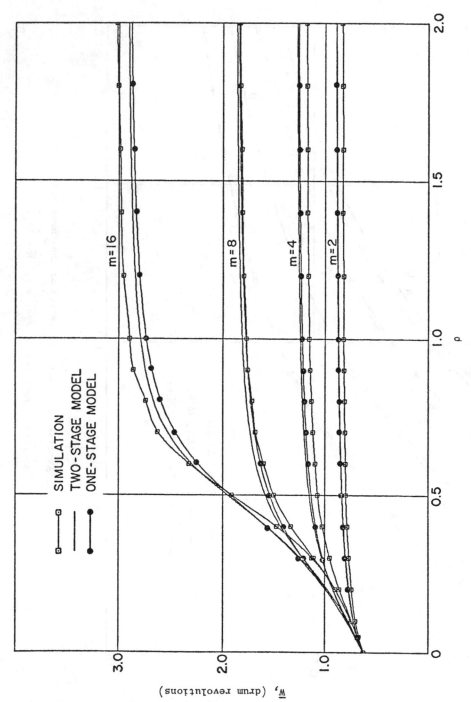

Figure 6.5. The expected waiting time of the three cyclic queue models of the CPU-drum system for $\bar{R} = 1/8$.

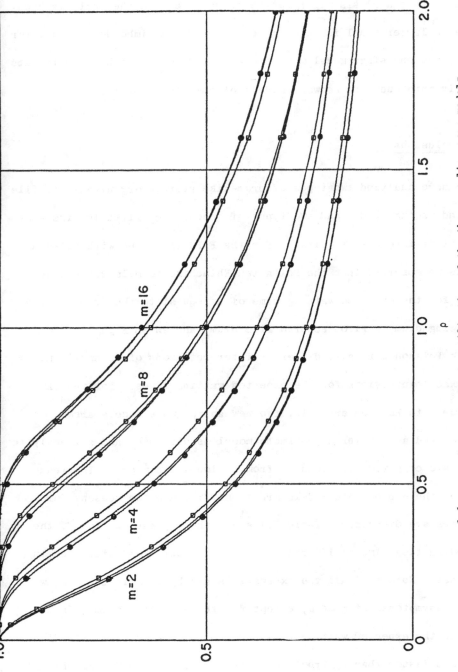

Figure 6.6. The central processor utilization of the three cyclic queue models of the CPU-drum system for $\overline{R} = 1/8$.

of SLTF scheduling can be developed. Even if an exact analysis were
available, that analysis might not be compatible with the analysis used
to treat a larger model in which an exact model was imbedded. Thus, for
example, the one-stage model may be useful for some time because it fits
naturally into queueing network models of computer systems.

7. Conclusions

We have analyzed two types of drum-like storage organizations, file
drums and paging drums, and two types of scheduling, first-in-first-out
and shortest-latency-time-first. For the FIFO file drum with Poisson
arrivals we observed that the Pollaczek-Khinchine formula gives exact
results for the expected waiting time of a request to the drum. For a
FIFO paging drum, a FIFO sectored file drum, and an SLTF paging drum,
all with Poisson arrivals, different interpretations of Skinner's model
yield exact expressions for the expected waiting times. For the SLTF
file drum with Poisson arrivals, two new approximate models are
developed and an earlier approximate model is discussed and all analytic
results are compared with results from a simulation model. The weak
points of the approximate models are identified and the reasons for
the errors are discussed. Table 7.1 shows the expressions for $\overline{W}$, the
expected waiting time of I/O requests for the four drums discussed in
this paper. Note that all the expressions are hyperbolic in form, with
vertical asymptotes at ξ and ρ, except for the SLTF file drum. In Sec. 5
we showed the expected waiting time for I/O requests at the SLTF file
drum grows faster than hyperbolically as $\rho \to 1$. Figure 7.1 graphically
illustrates the relative performance of the different drum organizations
and scheduling disciplines. (The two-stage Markov model is used for the

Table 7.1. Expressions for the Expected Waiting Times of I/O Requests at a drum with Poisson arrivals.

scheduling discipline	drum organization	$\overline{W}$
FIFO	file	$\left(\frac{1}{2} + \overline{R}\right)\left[1 + \frac{\xi(1+C^2)}{2(1-\xi)}\right]\tau$
FIFO	paging	$\left\{\left(\frac{1}{2} + \frac{1}{k}\right) + \dfrac{\xi'(1 + \frac{1}{2k})}{3(1-\xi)}\right\}\tau$
SLTF	file	two-stage Markov model $$\frac{\mu\tau+1}{(\mu-\lambda)} + \frac{1}{\lambda}\left[\left\{\int_0^1\left[e^{(1-w)}(1-\rho w)\right]^{\lambda\tau}dw\right\}^{-1} - 1\right]$$ empirical model $$\left\{\frac{1}{2} + \overline{R} + \frac{\rho}{1-\rho} + .368\left(\frac{\rho}{1-\rho}\right)^{3/2}\right\}\tau$$
SLTF	paging	$\left\{\frac{1}{2} + \overline{R} + \dfrac{\rho}{2(1-\rho)}\right\}\tau$

$$\rho = \lambda\overline{R}\tau; \quad \xi = \lambda\left(\frac{1}{2} + \overline{R}\right)\tau = \frac{\lambda\tau}{2} + \rho; \quad \xi' = \lambda\left(\frac{1}{2} + \frac{1}{2k}\right)\tau;$$

$$C = \left\{\frac{(\tau^2/12 + \sigma^2)^{\frac{1}{2}}}{\frac{1}{2} + \overline{R}}\right\}\tau.$$

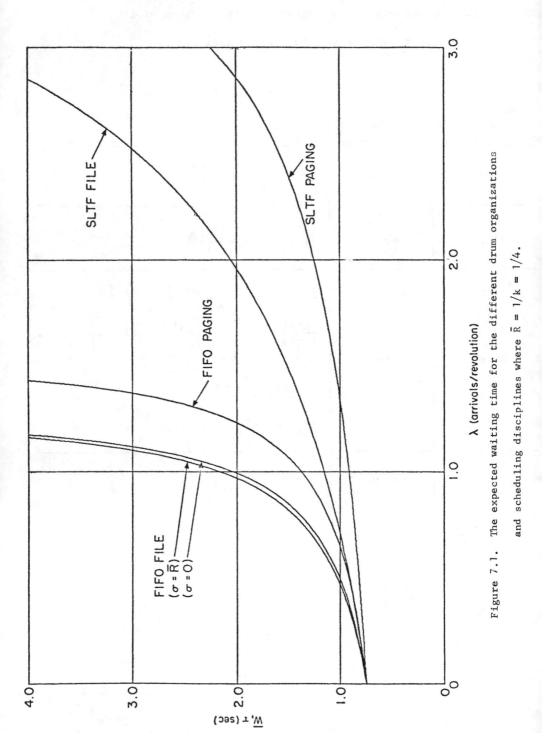

Figure 7.1. The expected waiting time for the different drum organizations and scheduling disciplines where $\bar{R} = 1/k = 1/4$.

SLTF file drum).

The one-stage and two-stage Markov models are incorporated into a cyclic queueing model and these results are compared with simulation results. The comparisons indicate the suitability of these models of SLTF file drums for use in more complex queueing network models of computer systems. A reasonably accurate model of an SLTF paging drum that could be easily incorporated into larger queueing network models would be a valuable addition to this work.

Chapter 3

PERFORMANCE OF AN I/O CHANNEL WITH MULTIPLE PAGING DRUMS

For rotating storage units, a paging drum organization is known to offer substantially better response time to I/O requests than is a more conventional (file) organization [Abate and Dubner, 1969; Chapter 2]. When several, asynchronous paging drums are attached to a single I/O channel, however, much of the gain in response time due to the paging organization is lost; this article investigates the reasons for this loss in performance.

A model of an I/O channel with multiple paging drums is presented and we embed into the model a Markov chain that closely approximates the behavior of the I/O channel. The analysis then leads to the moment generating function of sector queue size and the Laplace-Stieltjes transform of the waiting time. A significant observation is that the expected waiting time for an I/O request to a drum can be divided into two terms: one independent of the load of I/O requests to the drum and another that monotonically increases with increasing load. Moreover, the load varying term of the waiting time is nearly proportional to $(2 - 1/k)$ where k is the number of drums connected to the I/O channel. The validity of the Markov chain approximation is examined in several cases by a comparison of the analytic results to the actual performance of an I/O channel with several paging drums.

1. Introduction

The performance of computer systems has become increasingly dependent on secondary storage in the past years as the relative performance gap has widened between central processors on the one hand, and secondary storage on the other. This article focuses attention on the performance of one major form of secondary storage, the drum-like storage unit. Examples of drum-like stores include fixed-head disks, semiconductor storage units built from large shift registers, magnetic bubble shift registers, and delay lines, as well as storage units that actually contain physically rotating drums as shown in Fig. 1.1. The purpose of this article is to investigate exactly how the performance of several drums attached to the same I/O channel, as shown in Fig. 1.2, compares to the simpler case of a single drum per I/O channel.

An attractive organization for a drum storage unit is as a shortest-latency-time-first (SLTF), paging drum, often just called a paging drum; Fig. 1.1 is an illustration of a paging drum. The drum rotates at a constant angular velocity and information is read or written onto the surface of the drum as the surface passes under the fixed read-write heads. That fraction of the drum's surface that passes under a particular read-write head is called a track, and a block of information, or a record, is recorded serially onto a track. In a paging drum, the angular co-ordinate of the drum is partitioned into a number of equal size intervals called sectors. Furthermore, we impose the restriction that records be stored at the intersection of a track and a sector. In other words, we require that records start at sector boundaries and all records are the same size, the length of a sector. The scheduling policy used by a paging drum is , as we already mentioned, shortest-latency-time-first.

74

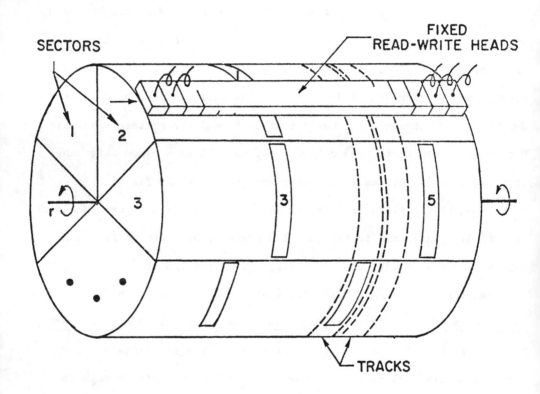

Figure 1.1. A drum storage unit organized as a paging drum.

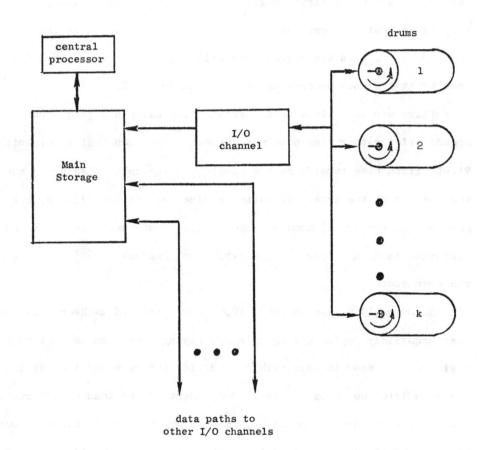

data paths to
other I/O channels

Figure 1.2. Data paths between drums, I/O channel, and main storage.

This simply means that when a new sector arrives at the read-write heads, if there is an outstanding I/O request on the sector it will begin service immediately. If more than one I/O request requires service at a particular sector, a first-in-first-out (FIFO) policy is used. In Fig. 1.1, if requests to read records 2, 3, and 5 in sector 3 arrived in the order 3, 5, 2, then the paging drum will begin servicing record 3 as soon as it finishes processing record 1 in sector 2.

There are several important reasons for using a paging drum organization rather than some more general, less constrained organization. First, fixed size records considerably ease the task of managing space on the surface of the drum. If variable size records are allowed, the same problems of (external) memory fragmentation that have received so much attention in main storage [cf. Knuth, 1968; Randell, 1969] also occur in the drum store.

Skinner [1967] and Coffman [1969] have analyzed mathematical models that accurately depict a single, SLTF, paging drum. An inspection of their results show it is possible to divide the response time of I/O requests into two terms: a term independent of the load of I/O requests placed upon the drum, denoted W_{LI}, and a term that monotonically increases with increasing load, denoted W_{LV}. The general form of the expected I/O waiting time, $\overline{W}$, a single paging drum is

$$\overline{W} = W_{LI} + W_{LV} , \tag{1.1}$$

the specific composition of W_{LI} and W_{LV} is discussed in detail later in this article. For an SLTF file (nonpaging) drum it has been shown that the expected I/O waiting time is [Chapter 2]

$$\overline{W} > W_{LI} + 2W_{LV} , \tag{1.2}$$

where W_{LI} and W_{LV} are the same expressions shown in Eq. (1.1). A comparison of the above two equations gives an indication of the substantial gains in performance offered by a paging drum over a file drum. However, economic and hardware constraints often require that more than one drum must be attached to a single I/O channel, as shown in Fig. 1.2. When an I/O channel must manage several drums, much of the gain in response time achieved by using a paging drum organization is lost. The reason for this loss is that each drum on the I/O channel is driven by a separate, asynchronous motor. The records on one drum that are carefully stored in non-overlapping sector positions now overlap by some arbitrary, and slowly varying, amount with all the other records on the remaining drums attached to the I/O channel.

In the analysis that follows we will see that the expected I/O waiting time of an I/O channel with k paging drums is approximately

$$\overline{W} = W_{LI} + (2 - \frac{1}{k})W_{LV} .$$

Note that the load varying term increases by $\frac{1}{2}$ with the addition of a second drum to the I/O channel and doubles in the limit as $k \to \infty$.

Should an individual decide, after seeing how much is lost with several drums on a single channel, that he would like to regain the lost performance there are several possible solutions. The most obvious one is to replace all the drums on the I/O channel by a single drum large enough to hold all the information once contained on the several smaller drums. This solution unfortunately runs counter to efforts to maintain modularity and reliability in the I/O structure of the computer system. A more attractive solution would be to provide sufficient hardware in the drum controllers so that all the paging drums on the same I/O channel can remain in synchronization and hence reply to I/O requests with the responsiveness of a single drum.

In the next section, Sec. 2, we develop a mathematical model of an I/O channel supporting several drums and discuss the assumptions involved in the development of the model. An analysis of the model follows in Sec. 3 and an alternate approach to the analysis is presented in Appendix D. While an understanding of the techniques used in the appendix are not necessary to derive any of the results of this article, attempts to extend the results to other practical situations may require either, or both, of these alternate methods. Section 4 compares the results of our analysis with simulation results to verify the validity of our model. Section 5 presents an example in which the parameters of the model are chosen to characterize some actual computer systems.

2. Description of Mathematical Model

In this section a model of an I/O system is described that has several drums communicating with the main store of the computer system via a single I/O channel as illustrated in Fig. 1.2. It is assumed that the remaining I/O structure will not have a significant effect on the performance of the drums and can be ignored in the analysis that follows. This is a reasonable assumption in most computer systems and only in those systems where other heavily used devices, such as movable head disks, are on the same I/O channel will this assumption have to be reconsidered.

Figure 2.1 illustrates the conceptual model of a paging drum that is used in this article. Let r be the number of records, or sectors, per track on the paging drum and let k be the number of drums attached to the I/O channel. Associated with each of the r sectors is a queue

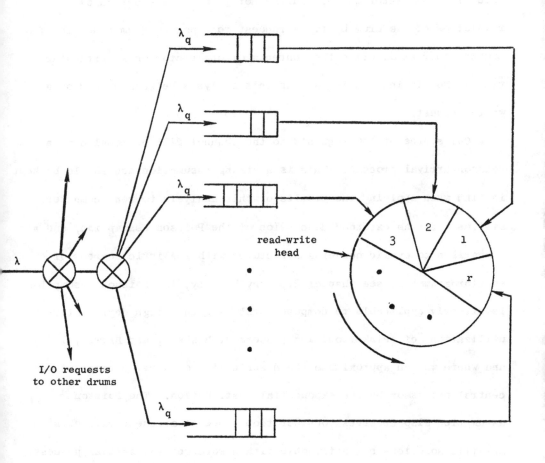

Figure 2.1.   Queue Structure for Paging Drum.

for requests for that sector. First-in-first-out (FIFO) scheduling is
used within a sector queue. Furthermore, denote the period of
revolution of the drum by τ. A request to a paging drum consists of a
command to read or write the contents of one sector on a particular
track. No distinction is made in this analysis between a read or a
write request.

Our source of I/O requests to the channel will be modeled as a
Poisson arrival process. This is a strong assumption and should be kept
in mind when applying the results of this analysis to real computer
systems. For an extended discussion of the Poisson assumption, and a
comparison to cyclic queueing structures with realistic degrees of
multiprogramming, see Chapter 2. Very briefly, the Poisson assumption
is directly applicable to computer systems with a high degree of CPU
utilization [cf. Pinkerton, 1968; Sherman, Baskett, and Browne, 1971]
and where we can approximate the distribution of service times at the
central processor by the exponential distribution. The Poisson
assumption also deserves consideration since it frequently results in
analytic solutions not attainable with a more general arrival process.
Hence, the results provide insight into the dynamics of the queueing
structure that is otherwise unattainable.

We assume that it is equally likely an arriving request will go to
any one of the drums, and equally likely the request enqueues on any one
of the r sector queues. While the above two assumptions are not crucial
in the analysis that follows, they considerably reduce the algebra;
should it be necessary to model an uneven distribution of requests, the
following analysis can be generalized in a straightforward manner to
reflect this effect.

Let λ be the mean arrival rate of the Poisson process. Then

$$\Pr\{n \text{ arrivals in interval } \tau\} = \frac{(\lambda\tau)^n}{n!} e^{-\lambda\tau} . \qquad (2.1)$$

Assuming each I/O request goes to any of the k*r sector queues with equal probability, it follows directly from the fundamental properties of a Poisson process that the arrival process at an individual sector queue is also Poisson with an arrival rate of $\frac{\lambda}{kr}$ requests per second.

3. Analysis of the Mathematical Model

This section is concerned with the analysis of the model of an I/O channel with several drums that has been described in the previous sections.

We can start our analysis with a few direct observations based on the long-run behavior of the model. We are assuming the mean arrival rate of requests to the I/O channel is λ and from the definition of a paging drum each request will need the I/O channel for $\frac{\tau}{r}$ seconds to transfer the record between the drum and main storage. Therefore, if we denote the mean utilization of the I/O channel as u_{IO}, by a direct application of the Law of Large Numbers [cf. Feller, 1968] to the long-run behavior of our model we see

$$u_{IO} = \frac{\lambda\tau}{r} \qquad (3.1)$$

and furthermore, the equilibrium (long-run) probability that a particular drum is transmitting information is $\frac{u_{IO}}{k}$, from similar arguments.

Figure 3.1 is a representation of the sequence in time in which sectors of three typical drums come under their respective read-write heads; note that the sector boundaries are out of phase. Suppose we are interested in the probability that the I/O channel will be free to

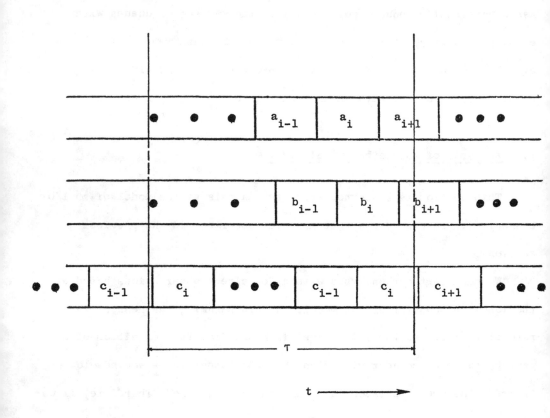

Figure 3.1. Timing diagram to show interference among

drums on same I/O channel.

service a request at the beginning of a sector, for example sector c_i on the bottom drum in Fig. 3.1. At time t, some instant arbitrarily close to the beginning of sector c_i, the equilibrium probability of the I/O channel being busy is u_{IO} and the probability the channel is busy processing a request on sector c_{i-1} of the bottom drum is just u_{IO}/k. Assuming the drum can commence servicing a request on sector c_i, after having just completed servicing a request on c_{i-1}, we see the equilibrium probability of the I/O channel being free to service sector c_i is

$$\Pr\{\text{channel free}\} = 1 - u_{IO} + \frac{u_{IO}}{k}$$

$$= 1 - \frac{(k-1)}{k} u_{IO} \qquad (3.2)$$

In this analysis Eq. (3.2) is used to describe the probability of finding the I/O channel free at the beginning of a sector, independent of the number of I/O requests in that sector. Strictly speaking, however, this is not true. Referring back to Fig. 3.1, we see sector c_i recurs every τ seconds in the diagram. Both the state of c_i's queue and the status of the I/O channel at time t are potentially affected by the state of c_i's queue the last time it passed under the read-write heads. However, it is a reasonable approximation to assume the sector's queue length and the probability the sector finds the channel free are independent. This assumption is critically re-examined in Sec. 4 when we compare the results of this analysis with several simulations. This independence assumption is very similar to an assumption Abate and Dubner [1969] make in their analysis of a file (nonpaged) drum.

The behavior of an arbitrary sector queue can now be described by embedding a Markov chain into our model. Let the states of the Markov chain be $\{E_i\}$ where $i = 1,2,\ldots$ and E_i is the state in which the sector queue has i requests awaiting service. Furthermore, let an epoch of the Markov chain be defined each time the read-write heads of the drum encounter the beginning of the sector. For example, if we consider sector c_i of Fig. 3.1, the epochs of time in which the Markov chain for sector c_i is defined is t, $t+\tau$, $t + 2\tau$, $\ldots$ as well as $t - \tau$, $t - 2\tau$, $\ldots$. Let g_i denote the equilibrium probability of being in state E_i. Now in statistical equilibrium we know

$$g_j = \sum_{0 \leq i < \infty} p_{ij}\, g_i, \qquad j = 0,1,2,\ldots \tag{3.3}$$

where the $p_{i,j}$'s are the single-step transition probabilities of our Markov chain. From direct consideration of the Poisson arrival process and our model of the I/O channel and drums we can determine the transition probabilities. Let $\underset{\sim}{F}$ denote the probability that the I/O channel is free i.e. Eq. (3.2) and let

$$\lambda_q = \frac{\lambda}{kr}$$

and

$$\alpha_n(t) = \frac{(\lambda_q t)^n}{n!}\, e^{-\lambda_q t}.$$

Then,

$$p_{o,j} = \alpha_j(\tau), \qquad j = 0,1,2,\ldots \tag{3.4}$$

$$p_{i,j} = \underset{\sim}{F}\alpha_{j-i+1}(\tau) + (1-\underset{\sim}{F})\alpha_{j-i}, \qquad j = 1,2,\ldots \tag{3.5}$$

Using Eqs. (3.3)-(3.5), the set of recurrence relations can now be written that define the behavior of the Markov chain.

$$g_o = \underset{\sim}{F}(\alpha_o(\tau)g_1) + \alpha_o g_o \tag{3.6}$$

$$g_1 = \underset{\sim}{F}(\alpha_o(\tau)g_2 + \alpha_1(\tau)g_1 + \alpha_1(\tau)g_o)$$

$$\qquad + (1-\underset{\sim}{F})(\alpha_o(\tau)g_1 + \alpha_1(\tau)g_o) \tag{3.7}$$

and in general

$$g_n = \underset{\sim}{F}(\alpha_n(\tau)_n g_o + \sum_{0 \leq i \leq n} \alpha_i(\tau)_i g_{n-i+1})$$

$$+ (1-\underset{\sim}{F}) \sum_{0 \leq i \leq n} \alpha_i(\tau) g_{n-i} ; \qquad n = 0,1,2,\ldots \qquad (3.8)$$

if we let $G(z)$ be the moment generating function of the sequence $\{g_n\}$,

i.e.

$$G(z) = \sum_{0 \leq n < \infty} g_n z^n$$

then Eq. (3.8) can be used to find the following expression for $G(z)$,

$$G(z) = \underset{\sim}{F}[\frac{1}{z} A(z,\tau)(G(z) - g_o) + g_o A(z,\tau)]$$

$$+ (1 - \underset{\sim}{F}) A(z,\tau) G(z)$$

where

$$A(z,t) = \sum_{0 \leq n < \infty} \alpha_n(t) z^n$$

$$= e^{-\lambda q t(1-z)} .$$

Rearranging the above relation to find an explicit form for $G(z)$ we get

$$G(z) = \frac{g_o \underset{\sim}{F}(1 - z) A(z)}{z - A(z)[\underset{\sim}{F} + z(1 - \underset{\sim}{F})]} \qquad (3.9)$$

Now consider those epochs immediately after the drum has completed serving of an I/O request from the sector being examined. These epochs can be used to define the embedding of another Markov chain. Let this new Markov chain have states $\{E_i{}'\}$ and associated equilibrium probabilities $\{q_i\}$. Relating q_n to the $\{g_n\}$ requests we see

$$q_n = \sum_{1 \le i \le n+1} \frac{g_i}{1-g_o} \alpha_{n-i+1} \left(\frac{\tau}{r}\right), \qquad n = 1,2,\ldots$$

where α_{n-i+1} (τ/r) is just the probability n-i+1 new requests arrive at the sector queue while the I/O channel and drum are servicing the just completed I/O request, and the term $g_i/(1-g_o)$ is an expression for the conditional probability that the sector queue is in state E_i when the read-write heads encounter the beginning of the sector, given the drum will service a request in the sector queue, i.e. the sector queue is not empty and the I/O channel is free. If we let Q(z) be the moment generating function of $\{q_n\}$ it follows from the above equation for q_n that

$$Q(z) = \frac{A(z,\frac{\tau}{r})}{z(1-g_o)} \left(G(z) - g_o\right) . \tag{3.10}$$

Now eliminating G(z) from Eqs. (3.7) and (3.8) we find

$$Q(z) = \frac{g_o A(z,\frac{\tau}{r}) [1 - A(z,\tau)]}{(1-g_o)\{\underset{\sim}{F} A(z,\tau)(1-z) - z[1 - A(z,\tau)]\}} \tag{3.11}$$

The importance of Q(z) can be seen from Fig. 3.2, an example of how the queue size for an arbitrary sector queue might vary with time. The shaded regions represent those intervals when the read-write heads of the drum are over the sector. Those points on the time axis labeled ① mark epochs of the first Markov chain and those labeled ② mark epochs of the second Markov chain. Note that the queue size always changes by a single unit, i.e. I/O requests arrive and depart individually. For every departure leaving behind a queue size of n, there exists a corresponding arrival that enters to find a queue size of n. Therefore, Eq. (3.11) is the moment generating function for the queue size that arriving requests see, as well as a generating function for queue size

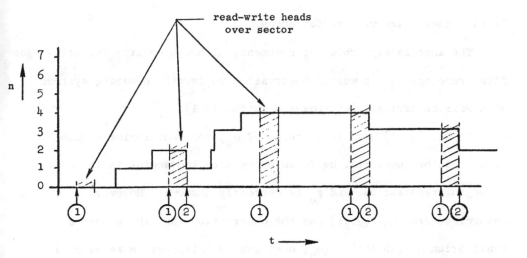

Figure 3.2.   Size of the sector queue as a function of time.

after departures. Furthermore, since we are assuming the arrival process is Poisson, the arrival of an I/O request is completely independent of other arrivals, as well as the state the sector queue, and consequently the distribution of queue sizes an arriving request sees is in fact just the equilibrium distribution of queue sizes. Therefore Eq. (3.11) is the moment generating function of the equilibrium queue size of a sector queue.

The immediately preceding argument, although counter intuitive upon first reading, is a powerful observation concerning queueing systems with Poisson arrivals [cf. Cox and Smith, 1961].

In Eq. (3.11) $Q(z)$ is in terms of g_o, the equilibrium probability that a sector queue will be found empty when the sector is in position to begin transmission, and g_o is currently unknown. However, g_o can be determined from Eq. (3.11) and the observation that the sequence of equilibrium probabilities $\{q_n\}$ must sum to unity, or in terms of its generating function $Q(z)$,

$$\lim_{z \to 1} Q(z) = 1 .$$

Taking the limit as z approaches 1 in Eq. (3.9) requires the application of l'Hospital's rule, but is otherwise straightforward.

$$\lim_{z \to 1} Q(z) = \frac{g_o}{1-g_o} \left(\frac{\lambda_q \tau}{1-k\lambda_q \tau} \right)$$

The above relation and Eqs. (3.6) and (3.7), the defining recurrence relations, yield

$$g_o = \frac{1 - k\lambda_q \tau}{1 - (k-1)\lambda_q \tau}$$

and

$$q_o = \frac{g_o}{\lambda q\tau} e^{-\lambda q\tau/r} (e^{\lambda q\tau} - 1)$$

$Q(z)$ can now be stated in terms of the explicit parameters of our drum model

$$Q(z) = \frac{(1 - k\lambda_q\tau) A(z,\frac{\tau}{r}) [1 - A(z,\tau)]}{\lambda_q\tau\{z - A(z,\tau)[1 + (z-1)(k-1)\lambda_q\tau]\}} \qquad (3.12)$$

We are now in a position to use the moment generating function $Q(z)$ to find the expected queue size, denoted by $\overline{Q}$.

$$\overline{Q} = \lim_{z\to 1} Q'(z)$$

$$= \{(\tfrac{1}{2} + \tfrac{1}{r}) + \frac{k\lambda_q\tau(2 - \tfrac{1}{k})}{2(1 - k\lambda_q\tau)} \} \lambda_q\tau \qquad (3.13)$$

Little's formula [Little, 1961 ; Jewell, 1967], $\overline{Q} = \lambda\overline{W}$, can be used to find the expected waiting time for an I/O request at the drum, denoted $\overline{W}$.

$$\overline{W} = \{(\tfrac{1}{2} + \tfrac{1}{r}) + \frac{u_{IO}(2 - \tfrac{1}{k})}{2(1 - u_{IO})} \}\tau \qquad (3.14)$$

Recall that in the introduction the statement was made that the mean expected waiting time for I/O requests consists of two terms: W_{LI}, an expression independent of the arrival rate of I/O requests, and W_{LV}, an expression that monotonically increases with increasing load. From Eq. (3.14) we can immediately see

$$W_{LI} = (\tfrac{1}{2} + \tfrac{1}{r})\tau$$

and

$$W_{LV} = \{\frac{u_{IO}(2 - \tfrac{1}{k})}{2(1 - u_{IO})} \}\tau \ .$$

The above expression for W_{LV} not only indicates that it is monotonically increasing over u_{IO}'s entire range, the unit interval from 0 to 1, but that it is increasing hyperbolically, becoming unbounded as $u_{IO} \to 1$.

There are two special cases of Eq. (3.14) that have been studied before; (1) $k = 1$ and (2) $k \to \infty$. For $k = 1$ we just have a single drum on the I/O channel and Eq. (3.14) reduces to the same formula found by Skinner [1967] and Coffman [1969]

$$\overline{W} = \{(\tfrac{1}{2} + \tfrac{1}{r}) + \frac{u_{IO}}{2(1-u_{IO})}\}\tau \ .$$

As $k \to \infty$ we approach the situation where the starting addresses of I/O requests are uniformly distributed around the drum circumference. This case was studied by Abate and Dubner [1969] using a more direct approach than developed here, and interestingly Eq. (3.14) reduces to a special case of Abate and Dubner's formula as $k \to \infty$

$$\overline{W} = \{(\tfrac{1}{2} + \tfrac{1}{r}) + \frac{u_{IO}}{1-u_{IO}}\}\tau \ .$$

It is sometimes of interest to know more than just the expected value of the waiting time for an I/O request. The following argument can be used to get the Laplace-Stieltjes transform of the waiting time, call it $\underset{\sim}{W}(s)$

$$\underset{\sim}{W}(s) = \int_0^\infty e^{-st} \, dW(t)$$

$$= \int_0^\infty e^{-\lambda_q t} e^{(\lambda_q - s)t} \, dW(t)$$

$$= \int_0^\infty e^{-\lambda_q t} \sum_{0 \le k < \infty} \frac{[(\lambda_q s)t]^k}{k!} \, dW(t)$$

$$= \sum_{0 \leq k < \infty} (1 - \frac{s}{\lambda_q})^k \int_0^\infty e^{-\lambda_q t} \frac{(\lambda_q t)^k}{k!} \, dW(t)$$

The integral in the last line is just the probability of an I/O request

leaving behind k remaining requests, i.e. q_k. Hence

$$\underset{\sim}{W}(s) = \sum_{0 \leq k < \infty} p_k (1 - \frac{s}{\lambda_q})^k$$

and finally

$$\underset{\sim}{W}(s) = Q(1 - \frac{s}{\lambda_q}) \, .$$

$$\underset{\sim}{W}(s) = \frac{(1 - k\lambda_q \tau) \, e^{\tau s / r} \, (1 - e^{-\tau s})}{\lambda_q \tau \{1 - \frac{s}{\lambda_q} - e^{-\tau s} [1 - s(k-1)\tau]\}} \tag{3.15}$$

As with the moment generating functions, the Laplace-Stieltjes

transform can be used to find the moments of the waiting time.

$$\overline{W} = \lim_{s \to 0} \{-\underset{\sim}{W}'(s)\}$$

$$\text{var}(W) = \overline{W^2} - (\overline{W})^2 = \lim_{s \to 0} \{\underset{\sim}{W}''(s)\} - \overline{W^2}$$

$\overline{W}$ is shown in Eq. (3.14) and var(W)* is

$$\text{var}(W) = \{\frac{1}{12} + \frac{(1 - \frac{2}{3k})u_{IO}}{1 - u_{IO}} + [\frac{(2 - \frac{1}{k})u_{IO}}{2(1 - u_{IO})}]^2\}\tau^2 \tag{3.16}$$

---

* The calculation of var(W), while conceptually straightforward, is in

reality quite laborious. Taking the second derivative of Eq. (3.15)

is not difficult, but carrying through the application of l'Hospital's

rule four times in order to get a nonvanishing numerator and

denominator is tedious. This appears to be an ideal situation in

which to use a symbolic manipulation language such as REDUCE [Hearn,

4.   Verification and Discussion of Results

In this section we examine the results of the analysis in the
previous section, and discuss how well the results conform to reality.

As a basis for comparison, we use a simple Monte Carlo simulation
model.   The simulation model is just the model of a set of drums on a
single I/O channel described in Sec. 2.   In other words, the simulation
assumes there are k drums on the I/O channel, r sectors per track, all
the drums are out of synchronization but have the same period of
revolution τ, and I/O requests form a Poisson arrival process with a
request going with equal probability to any one of the sector queues.
Note the simulation model does not require any assumptions as to when
the channel is free.   In the results of the simulation models that
follow, the results for $u_{IO} < .75$ are within $\pm$ .01 τ of the equilibrium
values.   This precision is in part due to the simplicity of the model
and in part due to running each simulation until 100,000 I/O requests
had been completed.   For a more complete discussion of the simulator,
and its accuracy, see Appendix A.

1967].   However, several attempts to find Eq. (3.16) with a naive
program written in REDUCE only resulted in long computations
aborted by memory overflow messages.   It would be of value if
someone with more knowledge of symbolic manipulation than the author
were to write a working program to find the central moments of a
distribution, given its generating function or Laplace-Stieltjes
transform.   This would verify, or correct, the 11 pages of algebra
leading up to Eq. (3.16) as well as provide a useful tool for
manipulating queueing models.

Figs. 4.1 through 4.3 compare the expected waiting time for an I/O

request as given by Eq. (3.14) with the simulated value. The figures

show the cases for $r = 4,8$ and $k = 1,2,4,\infty$. As expected, for a single

drum on the I/O channel, i.e. $k = 1$, and $r = 4$ or $r = 8$ the simulation

precisely tracks the theoretical values, and these curves give a graphic

illustration of the precision of the simulation. In all the figures, $\overline{W}$

and $\overline{Q}$ are plotted as a function of u_{IO}, the utilization of the I/O

channel. This facilitates comparisons between the plots since $u_{IO} = \frac{\lambda\tau}{r}$

and hence for all r, τ, and k, u_{IO} takes on values in the unit interval

$[0,1)$. The abscissa of all these plots can be thought of as λ, the mean

arrival rate, normalized by the factor τ/r. In many discussions of

queueing systems the fraction (mean interarrival rate)/(mean service

rate), called traffic intensity, is used. However, in the discussion of

devices with rotational latency this term can be misleading since

confusion easily arises as to whether or not latency is included in the

service time. If, however, we define the drum service time to be the

actual transmission time, i.e. τ/r, then u_{IO} is in fact also an

expression for the traffic intensity.

As the number of drums on the I/O channel increases, Figs. 4.1 to

4.3 show that the analytic expression for expected wait time increasingly

underestimates the real expected wait time. However, if we direct our

attention to those regions of the figures where current computer systems

operate: $u_{IO} < .5$ and $k = 2$, 3 or 4, we see that our analytic

expression does a very reasonable job of estimating the expected waiting

time. In particular, for the case of two drums attached to a single I/O

channel, a common situation in practice, our analytic expression closely

approximates $\overline{W}$ as u_{IO} varies from 0 to .5.

94

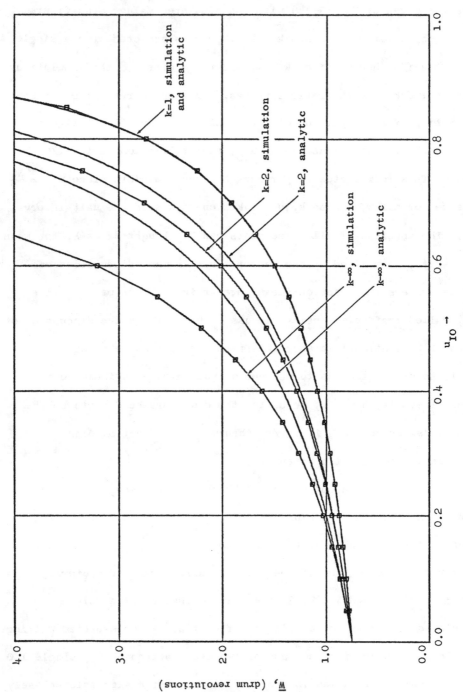

Figure 4.1. The expected waiting time for paging drums with 4 sectors/track.

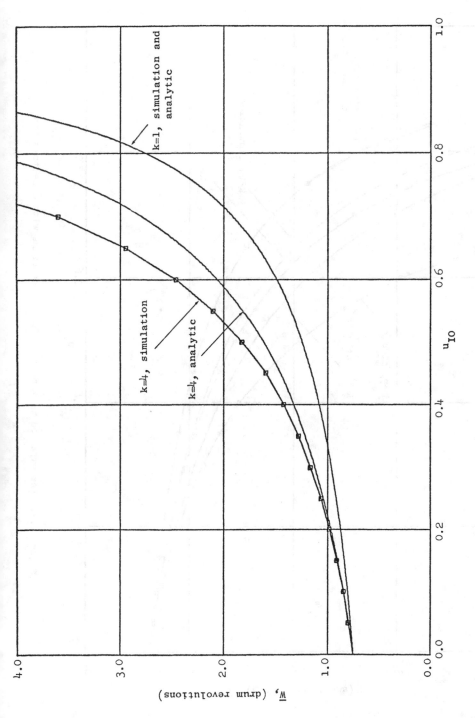

Figure 4.2. Expected waiting time for paging drums with 4 sectors/track.

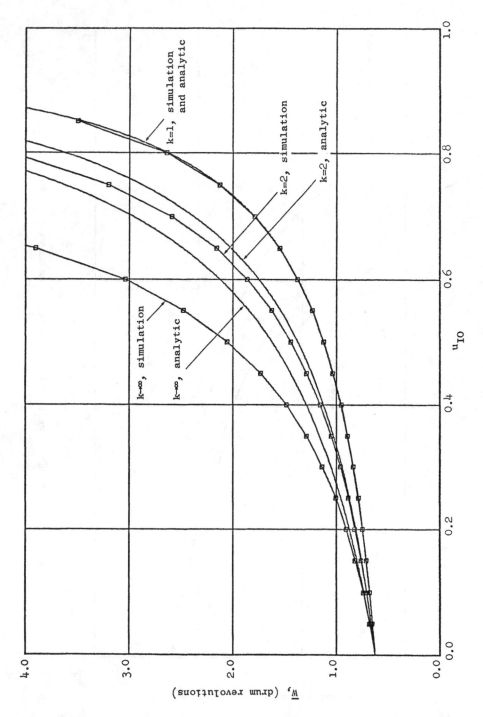

Figure 4.3. The expected waiting time for paging drums with 8 sectors/track.

The reason the analytic expression for expected waiting time is an underestimate of the simulation can be traced back to an assumption made in Sec. 3. Referring back to Fig. 3.1, recall that we assume the probability of finding the I/O channel free at time t is independent of the size of the queue for sector c_i.

The importance then, of this analysis is that by making the above approximation, a simple expression for the expected waiting time and expected queue size of the drum can be derived and yields a good approximation to the actual results when we operate in regions of practical interest.

Our analysis in the last section yields several other results in addition to the expected waiting time for an I/O request. Figure 4.4 is a plot of the number of outstanding I/O requests on all the drums attached to the I/O channel as a function of load; Eq. (3.13) provides the analytic results seen in Fig. 4.4.

Fig. 4.5 is a plot of the standard deviation of the waiting time, $\sqrt{var(W)}$, for k = 1 and k = 4; recall var(W) is given in Eq. (3.16). The expected waiting time for k = 1 is also plotted on the same graph in order to show the relative magnitudes of the mean and standard deviation.

Fig. 4.5 serves to illustrate what should be clear from Eqs. (3.14) and (3.16): the standard deviation of the waiting time, and queue size, grows at a rate similar to that of the mean waiting time as more drums are added to the I/O channel.

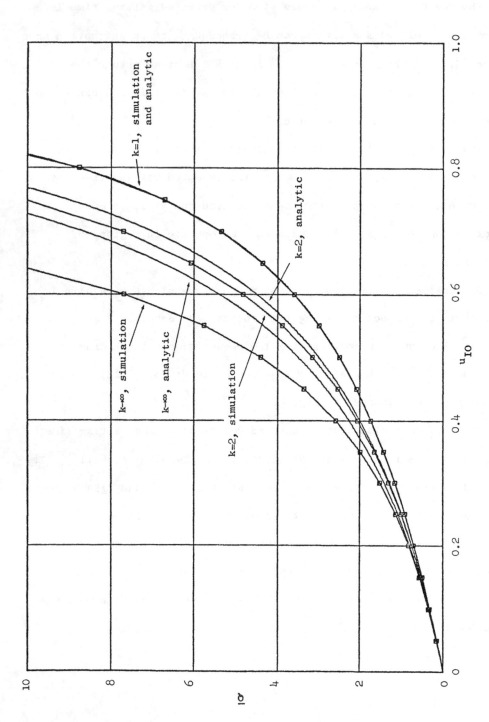

Figure 4.4.   The expected queue size for paging drums with 4 sectors/track.

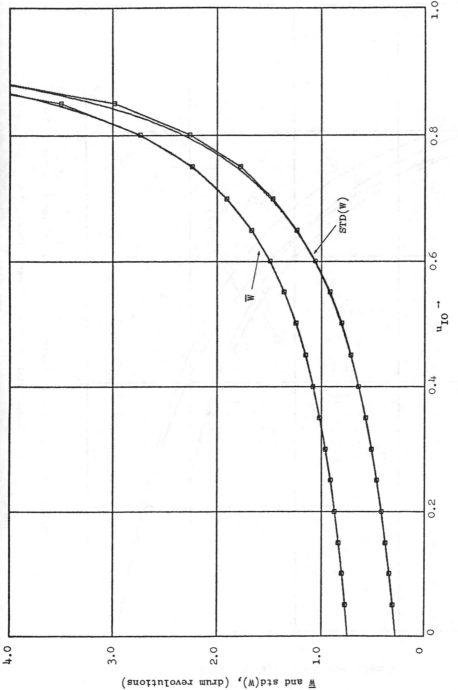

Figure 4.5(a). Mean and standard deviation of waiting time for an I/O channel with one 4 page/track drum.

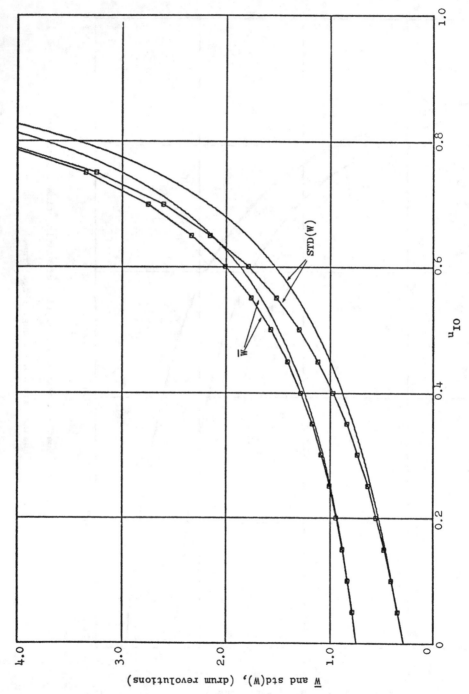

Figure 4.5(b). Mean and standard deviation of waiting time for an I/O

channel with two 4 page/track drums.

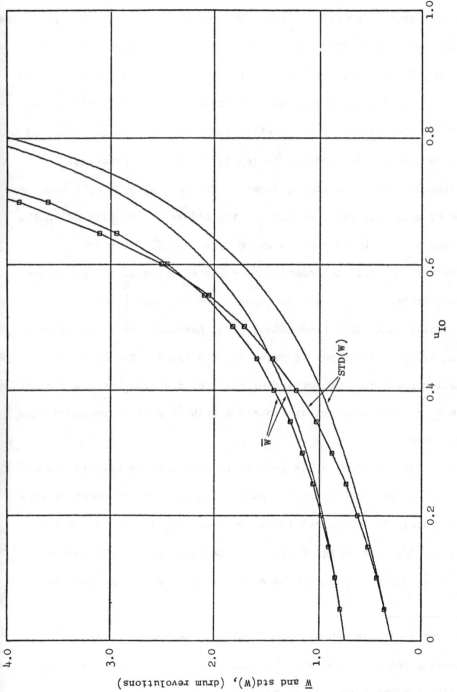

Figure 4.5(c). Mean and standard deviation of waiting time for I/O channel with four 4 page/track drums.

5.   An Example: the IBM 360/67

In this section we will consider an interesting practical application
of our analysis. The IBM 360/67 is the only central processor in the
IBM system 360 series with a paged, virtual memory capability. The IBM
2301 drum is the highest performance rotating storage unit offered for
use with the 360 series. Consequently, there exists a large number of
computation centers that include an IBM 360/67 central processor and
several IBM 2301 drums as paging drums.* However, using a 2301 drum
with the 67 processor poses an interesting dilemma. The size of an IBM
360/67 page is 4096 bytes and the capacity of a 2301 track is
unfortunately too small to accommodate 5 pages, but allocating 4 pages
to a track wastes over 10% of the capacity of the drum [IBM, 1965]. A
possible solution to this predicament, that has been chosen by several
operating systems, is to put $4\frac{1}{2}$ pages on each track. The $4\frac{1}{2}$ page/track
organization makes good use of the capacity of the drum but now a single
drum takes on the appearance of two drums with respect to response time
to page requests.

The analysis of Sec. 3 can be used to quantify the performance we
can expect from an IBM 2301 drum organized in each of two possible ways.
First, to model the 4 page per track organization, let $k = 1$ and $r = 4$.
However, the $1/r$ term in Eq. (3.14) must be replaced by $9/2$, corresponding to a page occupying 2/9ths of a track. The $4\frac{1}{2}$ page per track

---

* It is difficult, though not impossible, to implement an SLTF
   scheduling policy on an IBM 2301 since they do not have rotational
   position sending hardware and software techniques must be used to
   keep track of the angular position of the drum.

organization can be modeled if we let $k = 2$ and $r = 4.5$. A comparison of these two alternative drum organizations is shown in Fig. 5.1. The 4 page/track organization shows a small but distinct improvement in response time over the $4\frac{1}{2}$ page-track organization for all but extremely heavy loads; the mean waiting time can be reduced by over two milliseconds for arrival rates between two and three page requests per drum revolution. Hence we are faced with a trade-off between drum capacity and response time.

A possible solution to the above dilemma may lie in a new device, the IBM 2305 drum. With a loss of less than 10% of the drum's capacity it seems possible to organize it as a 3 page-track paging drum where $\tau = 10$ msec. [IBM, 1971]. Figure 5.2 compares the proposed[*] IBM 2305 paging drum with the two alternate organizations for the IBM 2301 drum.

6. Conclusions and Comments

This paper can best be summarized by Eq. (3.14) and (3.16), the moment generating function of the sector queue size and the Laplace-Stieltjes transform of the waiting time for an I/O request:

$$Q(z) = \frac{(1 - k\lambda_q\tau)\, e^{-\lambda_q\tau(1-z)/r}(1 - e^{-\lambda_q\tau(1-z)})}{\lambda_q\tau\{z - e^{-\lambda_q\tau(1-z)}[1 + (z-1)(k-1)\lambda_q\tau]\}}$$

---

[*] This is only a proposal since IBM 2305 drums are presently not compatible with IBM 360 processors.

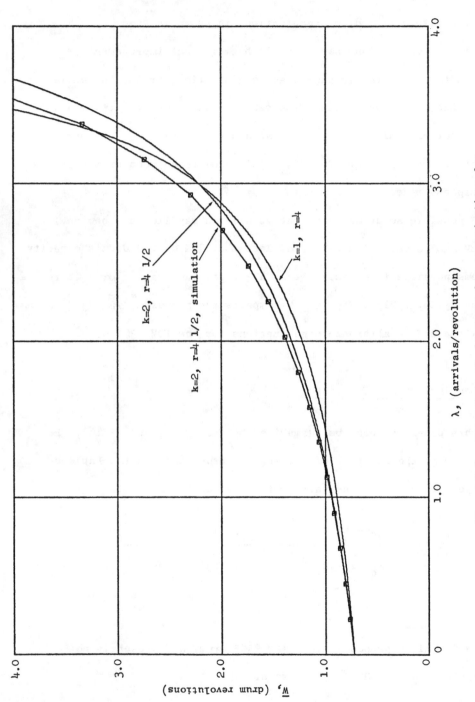

Figure 5.1. Comparison of alternate drum organizations for
IBM S360/67 computer systems.

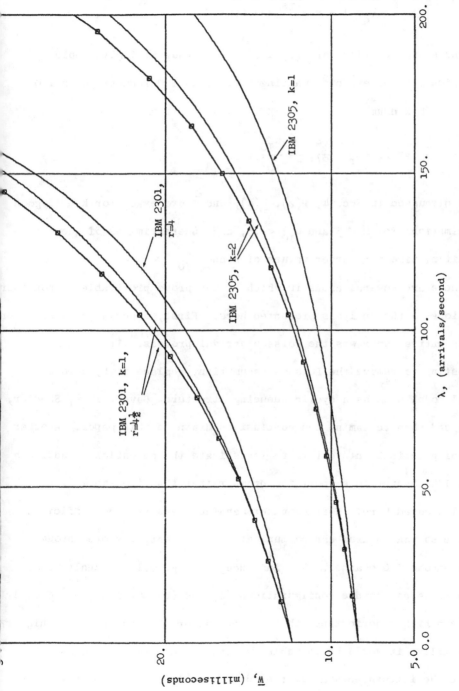

Figure 5.2. Comparison of IBM 2301 and 2305 drums organized as paging drums.

$$\underset{\sim}{W}(s) = \frac{(1 - k\lambda_q \tau) \; e^{-\tau s/r} \; (1 - e^{-\tau s})}{\lambda_q \tau \{1 - s \; e^{-\tau s}[1 - s(k-1)\tau]\}} = Q(1 - \frac{s}{\lambda_q})$$

The above relation for $\underset{\sim}{W}(s)$ leads to the surprisingly simple expression for the expected waiting time of an I/O request to an I/O channel with k drums

$$\overline{W} = \{\tfrac{1}{2} + \frac{1}{r} + \frac{(2 - \frac{1}{k})u_{IO}}{2(1 - u_{IO})}\}\tau$$

As was discussed in Sec. 4, $P(z)$, $\underset{\sim}{W}(s)$, and $\overline{W}$ are exact for $k = 1$, good approximations for $k < 5$ and $u_{IO} < .5$, and underestimates of queue size and waiting time for larger values of k and u_{IO}.

There are several areas in which it may prove profitable to consider extensions to the analysis presented here. First, a pervading assumption in this entire paper was the Poisson arrival process. It would be interesting to remove the Poisson assumption, replace it by a more general model such as a cyclic queueing structure [Gaver, 1967; Shedler, 1970], and then reexamine the conclusions drawn in this paper. Another topic of practical interest is to investigate the potential of adding a second I/O channel to support the drums rather than the single I/O channel assumed here. Most computer manufacturers provide sufficient hardware so that a drum can communicate to the central store through more than one I/O channel. For instance, in Fig. 6.1 the analysis of this article can handle configurations (a) and (b) but not (c). Clearly (c) has a higher performance than either (a) or (b), but how much higher?

Finally, it would be valuable to find an analysis that does not require the independence assumption discussed in Sec. 2 and that would then give exact results.

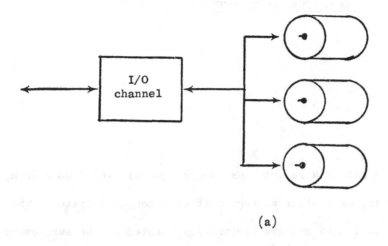

(a)

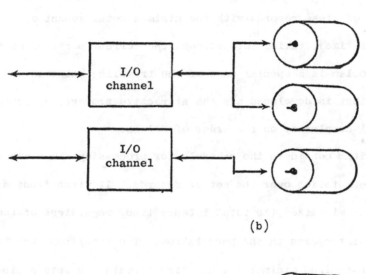

(b)

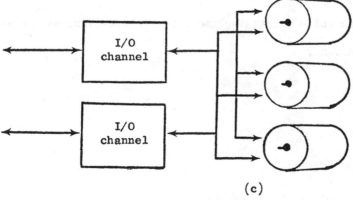

(c)

Figure 6.1. Possible I/O channel-drum configurations.

Chapter 4

AN OPTIMAL DRUM SCHEDULING ALGORITHM

Suppose a set of N records must be read or written from a drum,
fixed-head disk, or similar storage unit of a computer system. The
records vary in length and are arbitrarily located on the surface of the
drum. The problem considered here is to find an algorithm that schedules
the processing of these records with the minimal total amount of rotationa
latency (access time), taking into account the current position of the
drum. This problem is a special case of the traveling salesman problem.
The algorithm that is developed has the attractive property of exhibiting
a computational complexity on the order of N*logN.

The algorithm considers the schedule for processing the records as a
single cycle permutation over the set of records. It first finds a
permutation that minimizes the total latency time, regardless of the
number of disjoint cycles in the permutation. The algorithm then transforms the unconstrained minimal latency time permutation into a single
cycle permutation while increasing the total latency time of the schedule
by the minimal amount.

1. Introduction

Consider the problem of processing information on a drum, fixed-head disk, or similar storage unit of a computer system. Data is stored on the surface of the rotating drum, as shown in Fig. 1.1, in blocks called records. Reading and writing of the records is accomplished with the use of fixed read-write heads. Consequently, any given piece of information can be processed only when it is positioned directly under a read-write head, which occurs once each revolution in a single head per track drum[1]. There usually exist many independent tracks for records on the surface of the drum. Hence, as illustrated in Fig. 1.1, it will often be the case that records occupy overlapping regions on the circumference of the drum. If the order of processing the records is carelessly chosen, considerable time can be wasted waiting for the drum to rotate from the end of one record to the beginning of the next record to be processed. This delay is referred to as rotational latency, or just simply latency.

Suppose the drum receives requests to process N records. An algorithm will be presented which constructs the sequence that will process these N records in the minimal amount of time. The algorithm has a computational complexity on the order of N*logN. This is considerably better than the exponential growth rate experienced by the other known algorithm for optimally scheduling a drum [Gill, 1960].

------

1. An M head-per-track drum, in the context of this article, is equivalent to a single head-per-track drum revolving at M times the speed of the single head per track drum.

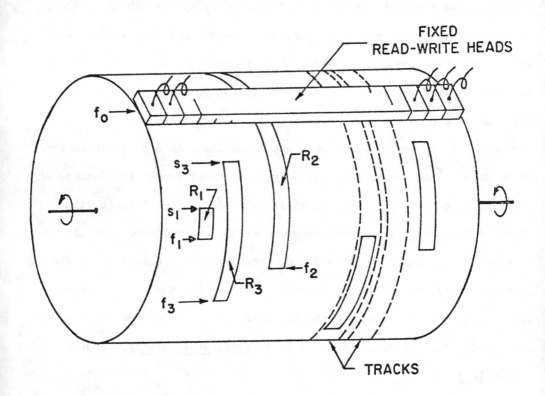

Figure 1.1.   A drum storage unit.

Conventional integer programming or branch and bound techniques can be used to construct an optimal schedule but again the computation experiences exponential growth [cf. Hillier and Lieberman, 1967].

The drum scheduling problem discussed in this article can be stated precisely as follows. A set of N records, denoted by R_i, $1 \le i \le N$, must be read or written onto the drum's surface. The angular position of the drum will be described by the single variable x. Associated with each R_i is a starting position, $x = s_i$, where the processing of the record must start and a final position, $x = f_i$, where the drum is left when the processing of the record is complete. When the record processing begins the drum is in position $x = p$.

Let $t_{i,j}$ be defined as the rotational latency incurred in accessing R_j after having just finished R_i. Assume the drum rotates at a constant angular velocity such that a complete revolution of the drum takes one unit of time. Similarly, let the perimeter of the drum be our unit of length, i.e. s_i and f_i will be in the real interval $0 \le X < 1$. Now we have the following simple expressions for $t_{i,j}$.

$$t_{i,j} = s_j - f_i \qquad \text{if } s_j \ge f_i \qquad\qquad (1.1)$$

$$t_{i,j} = 1 + (s_j - f_i) \qquad \text{if } s_j < f_i \qquad\qquad (1.2)$$

In order to represent the sequence of records accesses as a permutation a _pseudo record_ is introduced and given the index of 0. Conceptually, the pseudo record, R_0, starts where the last record to be accessed ends, and ends at the initial position of the read-write heads. The location of the end points of R_0 can be restated formally with the relations

$$f_0 = p \qquad\qquad (1.3)$$

$$\text{and} \quad t_{i,0} = 0, \qquad 0 \le i \le N. \qquad\qquad (1.4)$$

R_0 effectively changes the problem from one of finding a sequence of the N original records to one of finding a cycle, or permutation, of N+1 records.

Now that the problem can be formulated in terms of a permutation ϕ on the set of N+1 records, the objective function can be stated as

$$\text{minimize:} \quad T(\phi) = \sum_{i=0}^{N} t_{i,\phi(i)} \tag{1.5}$$

subject to the constraint that ϕ be a permutation with a single cycle. In the above equation, $\phi(i)$ is the successor of i on ϕ. The desired sequence can be found from the permutation ϕ; the first record processed will be $\phi(0)$, the second record will be $\phi(\phi(0))$, etc.

Modeling the drum in this manner has some obvious, but important, implications not yet discussed. First, for simplicity, Fig. 1.1 is drawn as a single drum, but the analysis of this article is directly applicable to the scheduling of several, identical drums communicating with the central store via a single I/O channel. The only restriction we must impose is that for the time period required to service the set of I/O requests, all the drums on the I/O channel revolve at the same angular velocity. Second, applications exist where it is important to differentiate between read and write operations, and scheduling algorithms have been proposed that exploit this difference [cf. Greenberg, 1971]. In this article, however, we choose to make no distinction between the reading or writing of a record in order to concentrate on understanding the nature of algorithms that truly minimize our objective function, Eq. (1.5).

To clarify these definitions consider the following simple example. Suppose there are three records that must be read from the drum, R_1, R_2, and R_3, and the position of these records on the surface of the drum is as shown in Fig. 1.2. The read-write heads are initially in position $x = p = 0.1$. We can represent the motion of the drum by letting p increase in value at a constant rate. Since $x = 0.0$ and $x = 1.0$ are in reality the same point on the drum's surface, when $p = 1.0$ we reset p to 0.0 and then continue to let p increase in value.

First, suppose we access the three records of Fig. 1.2 with the shortest-latency-time-first (SLTF) scheduling discipline. SLTF simply means that whenever the drum is free to read or write another record, it begins accessing the first record, among those records remaining to be processed, to come under the read-write heads. Therefore, the order of processing for the SLTF schedule will be R_1, R_3, R_2. This sequence is described by the permutation ϕ^1 where

$$\phi^1 = (0,1,3,2) \ . \tag{1.6}$$

The total latency time can now be calculated.

$$
\begin{aligned}
T(\phi^1) &= \sum_{i=0}^{3} t_{i,\phi^1(i)} \\
&= t_{0,1} + t_{1,3} + t_{2,0} + t_{3,2} \\
&= 0.1 + 0.1 + 0.0 + 0.9 \\
&= 1.1 \text{ drum revolutions}
\end{aligned}
\tag{1.7}
$$

A reexamination of the problem will show that the SLTF schedule does not minimize the total latency time. There exist two other schedules for this problem which do minimize the total latency time: R_1, R_2, R_3 and R_2, R_1, R_3. These two sequences can be described by the permutations

$$\phi^2 = (0,1,2,3) \tag{1.8}$$

$$\phi^3 = (0,2,1,3) \tag{1.9}$$

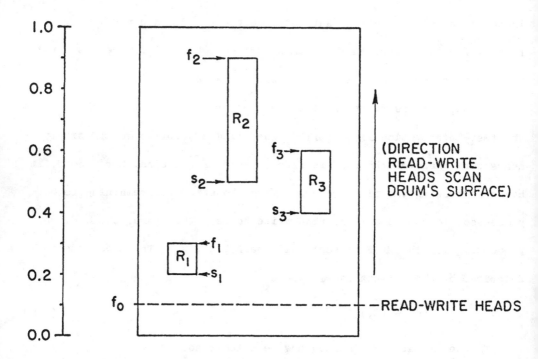

Figure 1.2. Location on the drum's surface of the three records and
the initial position of the read-write heads.

respectively.   Now calculating the total latency time for ϕ^2 and ϕ^3 we

see

$$T(\phi^2) = t_{0,1} + t_{1,2} + t_{2,3} + t_{3,0}$$
$$= 0.1 + 0.2 + 0.5 + 0.0$$
$$= 0.8 \text{ drum revolutions} \tag{1.10}$$

$$T(\phi^3) = t_{0,2} + t_{1,3} + t_{2,1} + t_{3,0}$$
$$= 0.4 + 0.1 + 0.3 + 0.0$$
$$= 0.8 \text{ drum revolutions} \tag{1.11}$$

Even for this simple example, the optimal schedules are significantly

better than SLTF.

The approach that is taken in this article to find an optimal drum

schedule is to relax the constraint that ϕ contain a single cycle and

find the permutation ψ that minimizes the objective function, Eq. (1.5).

Then a procedure is developed that transforms ψ into the single cycle

permutation ϕ^0 while increasing the cost of the permutation by as little

as possible.   This general approach was suggested by Gilmore and Gomory

[1964] in a paper in which they solved a special case of the traveling

salesman problem that has some similarities to the problem considered

here.

This section has defined the basic elements of the problem; Sec. 2

introduces some necessary notation and describes the method we will use

to transform one permutation (schedule) into another permutation

(schedule).   Sections 3 through 7 develop the optimal drum scheduling

algorithm and prove its correctness.   Section 8 contains a complete

statement of the algorithm, and then Sec. 9 gives an example to help

illustrate the algorithm's essential features.

2.   Ordered Bipartite Graphs, Matchings, and Interchanges

In the next few sections we will use the following notions from graph theory, and in particular matching theory, in order to construct the permutation ψ that will minimize the objective function over all possible permutations of the N+1 records.

A bipartite graph is commonly defined as a graph, the nodes of which can be divided into two disjoint subsets such that no node in a subset is directly connected to another node in the same subset by any edge [cf. Liu, 1968]. Figure 2.1 is an example of a bipartite graph. An ordered bipartite graph is defined in this paper to be any bipartite graph that has a value assigned to every node and has an arc (directed edge) defined from every f_i, a node in the left subset, to every s_i, a node in the right subset. The cost of an arc from f_i to s_j is $t_{i,j}$, as defined by Eq. (1.1) and (1.2). It is important to notice at this point that any subset of the nodes of an ordered bipartite graph can also define an ordered bipartite graph. Figure 2.2(a) is an ordered bipartite graph and Fig. 2.2(b), which contains a subset of the nodes of Fig.2.2(a), is also an ordered bipartite graph.

Unfortunately, the cost of an arc from any f_i to s_0, the beginning of the pseudo record, is a special case and must be defined separately by Eq. (1.4), i.e. $t_{i,0} = 0.0$. In order to make s_0 look as much like the other s_i's as possible, whenever we discuss an arc from any f_i to s_0 we will show s_0 directly opposite f_i to suggest $s_0 = f_i$ and hence $t_{i,0} = 0.0$ For example, see Fig. 2.3.

A matching in an ordered bipartite graph is any set of arcs of the graph such that no two arcs are incident with the same node, either an s_i or f_i node. Figure 2.3 is a matching on an ordered bipartite graph.

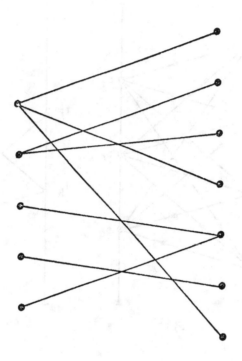

Figure 2.1.   A bipartite graph.

118

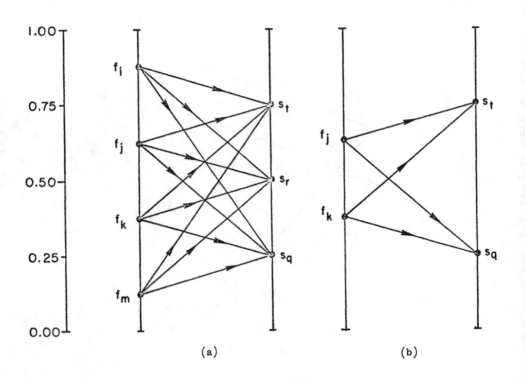

Figure 2.2. Ordered bipartite graphs.

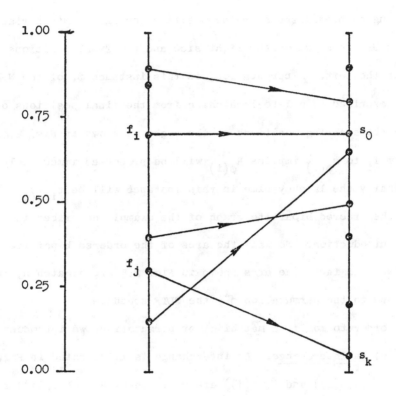

Figure 2.3.   A matching on an ordered bipartite graph.

For convenience denote the cost of a matching, in this instance E with arcs $\{e_1, \ldots, e_N\}$, as

$$C(E) = \sum_{i=1}^{N} e_i \ . \tag{2.1}$$

Figure 2.4 is an ordered bipartite graph representation of the drum scheduling problem. The starting positions on the drum's surface of all N+1 records are shown on the right side and the final positions are shown on the left. A permutation, in this instance ϕ, of the N+1 records can be described by a 1-to-1 matching from the final positions on the left to the starting positions on the right as shown in Fig. 2.4. The arc from f_i to $s_{\phi(i)}$ implies $R_{\phi(i)}$ will be processed immediately after R_i. Clearly the latency time in this instance will be $t_{i,\phi(i)}$. Figure 2.5 is the ordered bipartite graph of the example described in Fig. 1.2 of the introduction. Not all the arcs of the ordered bipartite graph are shown. In fact, the arcs shown in Fig. 2.5 are a matching and correspond to the permutation ϕ^1, the SLTF schedule.

In order to modify a matching, or permutation, we introduce the concept of an __interchange__. An interchange is illustrated in Fig. 2.6 where arcs $(i,\phi(i))$ and $(j,\phi(j))$ are replaced by arcs $(i,\phi(j))$ and $(j,\phi(i))$. This interchange can be represented as the permutation $X_{i,j}$ where

$$X_{i,j}(i) = j \tag{2.2}$$

$$X_{i,j}(j) = i \tag{2.3}$$

$$X_{i,j}(k) = k, \quad \text{if } k \neq i,j. \tag{2.4}$$

Applying an interchange to ϕ yields a new permutation $\phi\dagger$ given by

$$\phi\dagger = \phi * X_{i,j}. \tag{2.5}$$

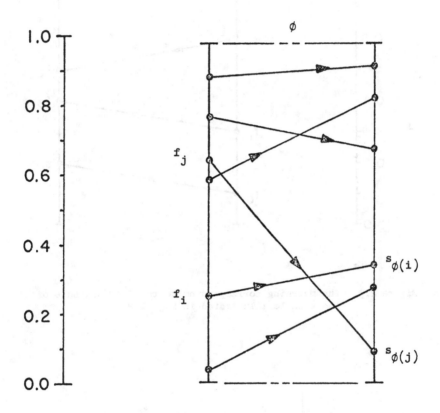

Figure 2.4.   Graphic representation of the drum scheduling problem.

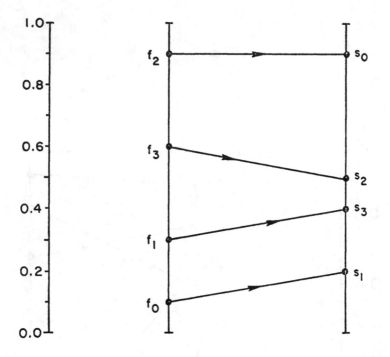

Figure 2.5. The matching corresponding to the SLTF schedule of the example illustrated in Fig. 1.2.

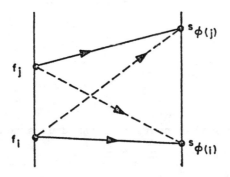

Figure 2.6. The interchange $X_{i,j}$.

In other words, first apply $X_{i,j}$ and then ϕ to get $\phi\dagger$. Hence

$$\phi\dagger(i) = \phi(j) \qquad\qquad (2.6)$$

$$\phi\dagger(j) = \phi(i) \qquad\qquad (2.7)$$

$$\phi\dagger(k) = \phi(k), \quad \text{if } k \neq i,j. \qquad\qquad (2.8)$$

The following equation defines the cost associated with an interchange. It accurately describes the increase in time required to process the N records as a result of applying $X_{i,j}$ to ϕ.

$$\Delta T(X_{i,j}, \phi) = T(\phi * X_{i,j}) - T(\phi). \qquad\qquad (2.9)$$

This equation can be directly applied to determine the cost of an interchange. However, interchanges can be partitioned into several distinguishable cases, and this structure can be used to our advantage in the following discussion. These cases, as tabulated in Fig. 2.7 add an intuitive understanding that cannot be gained directly from Eq. (2.9).

3. Minimal Cost Matchings on Ordered Bipartite Graphs

As mentioned in the introduction, we first relax the constraint that the permutation must contain a single cycle and consider only the objective function, Eq. (1.5). This section is concerned with the task of finding the matching from $\{f_0, \ldots, f_N\}$ onto $\{s_1, \ldots, s_N\}$ such that the sum of the costs of the arcs in the matching is as small as possible, i.e. a minimal cost matching. This matching problem is now in the form of the conventional assignment problem and a minimal cost matching can be found with algorithms developed for the general assignment problem [Kuhn, 1955]. However, by exploiting the particular manner in which arc costs are defined for an ordered bipartite graph, we can use a much more efficient algorithm to find the minimal cost matching.

Class	Type	Conditions[1]	$\Delta T(X_{i,j},Q)$	Examples
Zero Cost	1	$s_{Q(i)} \in [i,j]$ [2] and $s_{Q(j)} \in [i,j]$ or $s_{Q(i)} \notin [i,j]$ and $s_{Q(j)} \notin [i,j]$	0	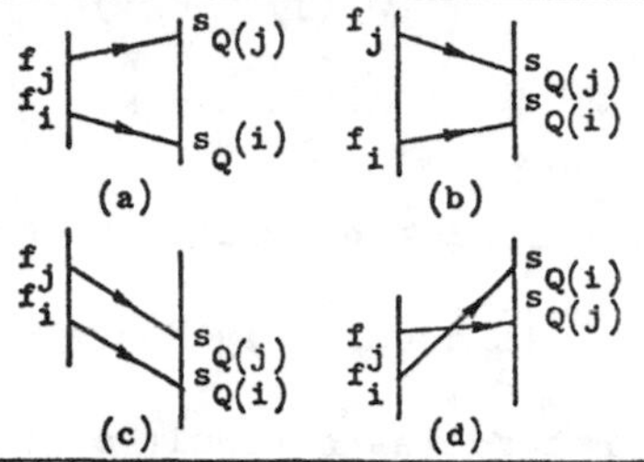 (a) (b) (c) (d)
Positive Cost	2	$s_{Q(i)} \in [i,j]$ and $s_{Q(j)} \notin [i,j]$	1	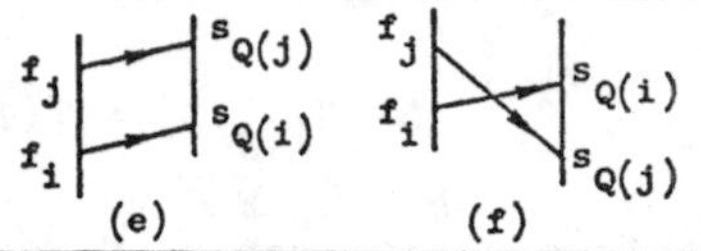 (e) (f)
	2a	$Q(i) = 0$ and $s_{Q(j)} \notin [i,j]$	$f_j - f_i$	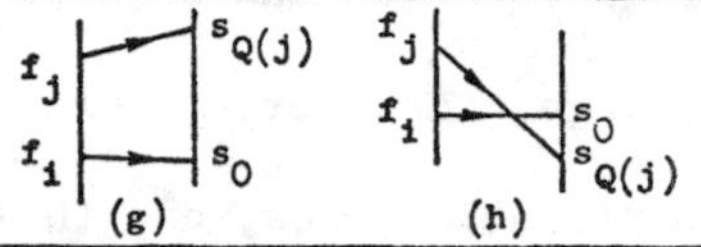 (g) (h)
	2b	$s_{Q(i)} \in [i,j]$ and $Q(j) = 0$	$1 - f_j + f_i$	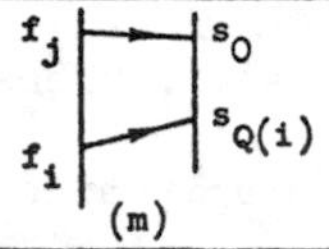 (m)
Negative Cost	3	$s_{Q(i)} \notin [i,j]$ and $s_{Q(j)} \in [i,j]$	-1	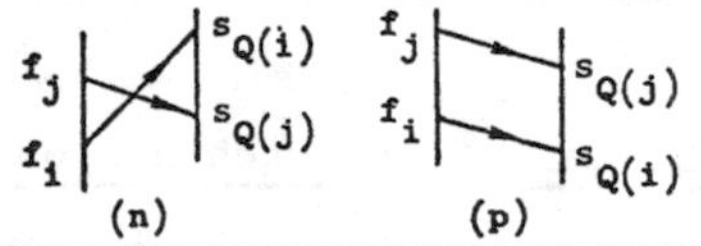 (n) (p)
	3a	$s_{Q(i)} \notin [i,j]$ and $Q(j) = 0$	$-(f_j - f_i)$	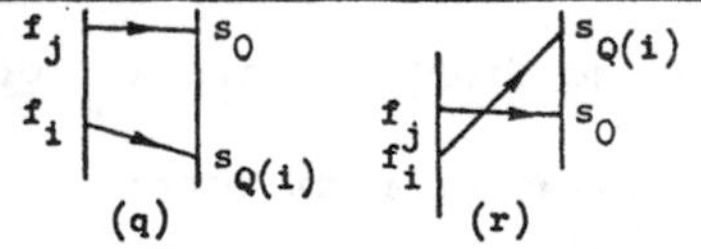 (q) (r)
	3b	$Q(i) = 0$ and $s_{Q(j)} \in [i,j]$	$-(1 - f_j + f_i)$	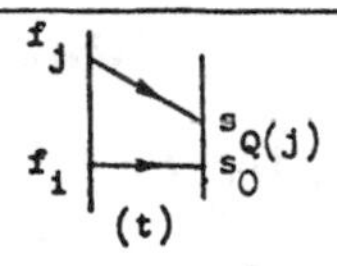 (t)

1. i and j are defined such that $f_i \le f_j$.
2. $y \in (i,j)$ implies $f_i \le y < f_j$.

Figure 2.7. Cost of Interchanges (in drum revolutions).

Before discussing the matching algorithm itself we develop an important property of ordered bipartite graphs. A matching is called a complete matching on the ordered bipartite graph G if there exists no remaining arcs in G which can be added to the matching. In other words, all arcs in G but not in the complete matching of G share at least one node with an arc in the complete matching. Since ordered bipartite graphs have the property that an arc is defined from every s_i to every f_i, all complete matchings will have the same number of arcs (cardinality) which we call the rank of G. Clearly

$$\text{rank of } G = \min(|S|, |F|) \tag{3.1}$$

where $|S|$ denotes the size of the set of s_i's and $|F|$ denotes the size of the set of f_i's. We assume in the remaining discussion that matchings mean complete matchings unless otherwise stated.

Consider the matching of an ordered bipartite graph G that is lexicographically the smallest; call this matching A. This means that for any other matching, say B, on G there exists the following relation. Let

$$A = \{a_1, \ldots, a_n\} \tag{3.2}$$

$$B = \{b_1, \ldots, b_n\} \tag{3.3}$$

Where in both of the above matchings the set of arcs are arranged in order of increasing cost. Then from the fact A is lexicographically less than B we see

$$a_i < b_i \tag{3.4}$$

where i is the smallest index such that $a_i \neq b_i$.

Referring to the example of Fig. 1.2 again, we see that A, the lexicographically least matching, is

$$A = \{t_{3,0}, t_{0,1}, t_{1,3}, t_{2,2}\}$$
$$= \{0.0, 0.1, 0.1, 0.6\} \tag{3.5}$$

and $C(A) = 0.8$ drum revolutions. $\tag{3.6}$

Now consider the matching corresponding to the SLTF schedule and call it B

$$B = \{t_{2,0}, t_{0,1}, t_{1,3}, t_{3,2}\}$$
$$= \{0.0, 0.1, 0.1, 0.9\} \tag{3.7}$$

and $C(B) = 1.1$ drum revolutions. $\tag{3.8}$

Let the matching A be called <u>sum-optimal</u>[1] if for any other matching B on G

$$\sum_{i=1}^{k} a_i \leq \sum_{i=1}^{k} b_i, \qquad 1 \leq k \leq N. \tag{3.9}$$

From the definition of the sum-optimal matching it is easy to see that if a matching is sum-optimal, it is the lexicographically smallest as well as the minimal cost matching on G. A lexicographically least matching of an arbitrary bipartite graph is not necessarily sum-optimal. However, the following theorem shows that for every ordered bipartite graph there exists one or more sum-optimal matchings.

Theorem 1. If G is an ordered bipartite graph then there exists a sum-optimal matching on G.

Proof. By induction on the rank of G.

Basis step. Suppose G is an ordered bipartite graph of rank 1. In other words, either its set of s nodes or set of f nodes is limited to

------

1. The word 'sum-optimal' has been chosen to suggest a similarity to the concept of 'optimal' as defined by Gale in connection with matroid theory [Gale, 1968].

one element. In this trivial case every matching on G consists of a single arc and clearly the minimal cost arc constitutes the sum-optimal matching for G.

Induction step. Assume there exist sum-optimal matchings for all ordered bipartite graphs of rank 1 through k. It will now be shown that an ordered bipartite graph of rank k+1 also has a sum-optimal matching.

Consider the matching of an ordered bipartite graph G of rank k+1 that is lexicographically the smallest. Call this matching A and let its set of arcs be as denoted in Eq. (3.2).

Recall the cardinality of all matchings on G are equal to the rank of G. This implies any matching on G must saturate either all initial or final nodes of G. Hence for any two matchings on G, every arc of one matching must share at least one terminal node with an arc in the other matching. Therefore when comparing A with some other matching, say B, we only need consider the cases where (i) a_1 is an element of B, (ii) a_1 shares one terminal node with an arc in B, and (iii) a_1 shares both terminal nodes with arcs in B. As with A, let the arcs of B be arranged in order of increasing cost and denoted as in Eq. (3.3). These three cases are discussed below and in each instance we will show that the cost of A does not exceed the cost of B.

Case I. Let B be any matching other than A such that a_1 is an element of B. Since the arcs of B are arranged in increasing order of their cost, the name of a_1 in B must be b_1 or else b_1 is an arc with the same cost as a_1, in which case the arcs of B can be rearranged, still in increasing order, such that a_1 is called b_1 in the new arrangement of B.

Delete the initial and terminal nodes of a_1 from G and call this subgraph G'. Note that G' is an ordered bipartite graph of rank k and the set of arcs $A-\{a_1\}$ and $B-\{b_1\}$ are matchings on G'.

From the induction hypothesis we know G' must have a sum-optimal matching. Except for the matching $A-\{a_1\}$, every other matching on G' is related to a unique B in G such that the arcs of the matching on G' are just the arcs of the related B matching minus b_1. $A-\{a_1\}$ must be lexicographically smaller than any $B-\{b_1\}$ since

$$a_1 = b_1 \tag{3.10}$$

which implies $i > 1$ in Eq. (3.4). Therefore $A-\{a_1\}$ must be the sum-optimal matching in G' and we have

$$\sum_{i=2}^{k+1} a_1 \leq \sum_{i=2}^{k+1} b_i \tag{3.11}$$

for any B.

From Eqs. (3.10) and (3.11) it directly follows

$$C(A) \leq C(B) . \tag{3.12}$$

Case II. Let B be any matching other than A such that a_1 is not an element of B but a_1 shares exactly one node, initial or final, with the arcs of B; see Fig. 3.1. Let this neighboring element of B be called b'. We can construct a new matching B_1 such that B_1 is identical to B except b' is replaced by a_1. Clearly

$$a_1 \leq b' \tag{3.13}$$

and hence $C(B_1) \leq C(B) .$ \hfill (3.14)

Now since a_1 is an element of B_1, from case I we can conclude

$$C(A) \leq C(B_1) \leq C(B). \tag{3.15}$$

Case III. Let B be any matching other than A such that a_1 is not an element of B but a_1 shares both terminal nodes with the members of B as shown in Fig. 3.2. Let these neighboring elements of B be called b' and b''. We can define a new matching, call it B_2, such that

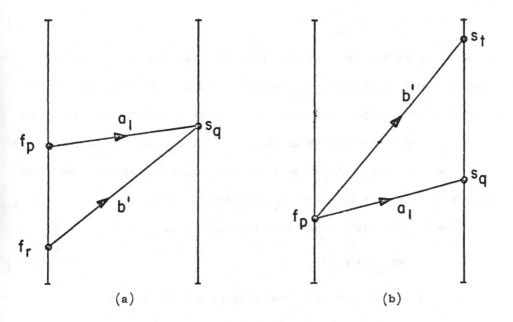

Figure 3.1. Case II -- a_1 adjacent to one element of B matching.

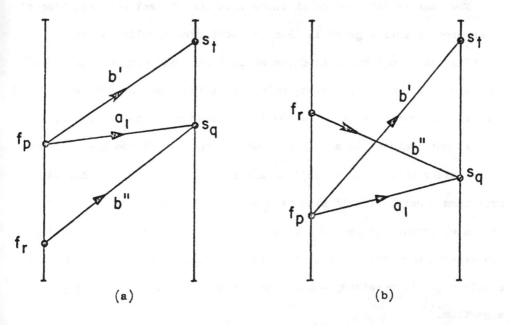

Figure 3.2. Case III -- a_1 adjacent to two elements of B matching.

$$B_2 = B*X_{p,r} \; . \tag{3.16}$$

Since a_1 is the shortest arc in G, the interchange $X_{p,r}$ must be either a ⁺vpe 1 (zero cost) or type 3 (negative cost) interchange. It cannot be a type 2 (positive cost) interchange since this would require f_r and s_t to be inside the interval from f_p to s_q, the terminal nodes of a_1. However, if there did exist a node in this interval the node would create an arc of less cost than a_1, a contradiction.

Since $X_{p,r}$ involves a non-positive cost we see

$$C(B_2) \leq C(B) \; . \tag{3.17}$$

Now a_1 is an element of B_2 and from case I it follows

$$C(A) \leq C(B_2) \leq C(B) \; . \tag{3.18}$$

Hence it has been shown that the cost of A, the lexicographically smallest matching on G, is less than any other matching on G. Therefore G, an ordered bipartite graph of rank k+1, has a sum-optimal matching.

Now that it has been established that the minimal cost matching of an ordered bipartite graph is also the lexicographically smallest matching, an algorithm to find the minimal cost matching can be stated very simply as follows. First, select a minimal cost arc of the ordered bipartite graph; then pick the smallest (least cost) arc remaining in G that is not incident to a node already having an assigned arc. In other words, after this step, as well as after the first step, the selected arcs form a matching. If after the second step the matching is not complete, repeat the second step until we do have a complete matching on the ordered bipartite graph. This type of algorithm which chooses the smallest (best) remaining arc at each stage is described as a greedy algorithm.

The procedure presented below constructs the minimal cost matching of an ordered bipartite graph in at most two scans of the nodes of G. The procedure in its entirety will first be presented and then we will show it is equivalent to a greedy algorithm over the arcs of G.

The Minimal Matching Procedure for Ordered Bipartite Graphs

1. Based on the unique value associated with each node, sort f_0, f_i, and s_i $(1 \leq i \leq N)$ into one circular list. If $f_i = s_j$ for any i and j then f_i must precede s_j.

2. Set the list pointer to an arbitrary element in the list.

3. Scan in the direction of nodes with increasing value for the next (first) f_i in the list.

4. Place this f_i on a pushdown stack and remove it from the circular list.

5. Move the pointer to the next element and if it is an f_i go to Step 4, else continue on to Step 6. In the latter case, the element must be an s_i.

6. Pop the top f_i from the stack, delete the current s_i in the circular list, and let these two elements define a match.

7. If the circular list is empty stop, else if the stack is empty go to Step 3, otherwise go to Step 5.

Theorem 2. The minimal matching procedure for ordered bipartite graphs is equivalent to a greedy algorithm.

Proof. If the minimal matching procedure exhibits the greedy attribute when applied to G, an ordered bipartite graph, it must at some point in its execution select the minimal cost arc of G. The minimal cost arc of G is illustrated in Fig. 3.3. Certainly there cannot be any

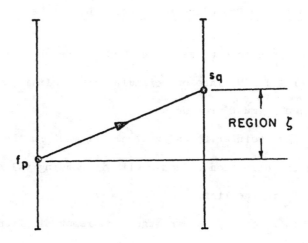

Figure 3.3.   The minimal cost arc.

f_i's or s_i's in the interval ζ else one of these internal vertices will define a lower cost arc with f_p or s_q. The arc (f_p, s_q) must be an element of the matching since immediately after f_p is placed on the pushdown stack in Step 4 of the minimal matching procedure s_q is recognized in Step 4 and they are then paired off in Step 6.

The remainder of this proof is by induction on the rank of G.

Basis step. Suppose the rank of G is 1. Obviously the matching selected by a greedy algorithm is just the shortest arc in G, and we have just shown the minimal matching procedure does select the shortest arc.

Induction step. Let the rank of G be k+1. Note that the minimal cost arc is selected independent of the other arcs in G. The pushdown stack is identical before and after both nodes of a_1 were recognized. The circular list is the same except the terminal nodes of a_1 have been removed. In fact, we can obtain the same matching that the minimal matching procedure constructs by first deleting the nodes of a_1 from the circular list, since we know they will be paired off. The list now represents the subgraph of G we have previously called G' in Theorem 1. Recall G' is an ordered bipartite graph of rank k. Now simply let the minimal matching procedure work on G', and then add a_1 to the resulting matching. Since

$$a_1 \leq e \tag{3.19}$$

where e is any other arc of G and by the induction hypothesis we know that the minimal matching procedure is equivalent to a greedy algorithm on G', it follows that the minimal matching algorithm is equivalent to a greedy algorithm when applied to G.

4. A Minimal Cost Permutation

Now that a minimal cost matching has been constructed from the N+1 f_i's onto the N s_i's, it is a simple matter to extend this matching to a minimal cost permutation. Since N+1 f_i's are matched with N s_i's, there must exist one remaining unmatched f_i on the pushdown stack at the completion of the minimal matching procedure. Let this one remaining f_i be identified as f_δ and pair it off with s_0. Hence s_0 behaves as if $s_0 = f_\delta$. The minimal cost permutation is now completely defined on the N+1 records.

Theorem 3. Let ψ be the permutation constructed from the minimal matching procedure. Then the total latency time for ψ satisfies

$$T(\psi) = \min\{T(\phi)\} \tag{4.1}$$

where the minimum is taken over all possible permutations ϕ of the N+1 records.

Proof. Let A be the matching constructed by the minimal matching procedure. It follows immediately that

$$T(\psi) = \sum_{i=0}^{N} t_{i,\psi(i)}$$

$$= \sum_{j=0}^{N} t_{\psi^{-1}(j),j}$$

$$= \sum_{j=1}^{N} t_{\psi^{-1}(j),j} = C(A) \tag{4.2}$$

since $t_{\delta,0} = 0$ from the definition of the pseudo record. Clearly there exists a similar relation between any other permutations ϕ and a matching B. Hence by Theorems 1 and 2 we know

$$T(\psi) = C(A) \le C(B) = T(\phi) . \tag{4.3}$$

Although ψ has just been shown to be a minimal cost permutation, it is not necessarily unique. There may exist many zero cost (type 1) interchanges in ψ which could be used to transform ψ into another permutation of the same cost.

Now let all the f_i's and s_i's be redefined relative to f_δ to simplify the subsequent analysis. The new values for the f_i's and s_i's will in no way alter their relative positions on the drum; we merely shift our point of reference on the drum to f_δ. We can represent this redefinition of all f_i's and s_i's ($0 \leq i \leq N$) as

$$z := z - f_\delta \qquad \text{if } z \geq f_\delta \qquad\qquad (4.4)$$

$$z := 1 + (z - f_\delta) \qquad \text{if } z < f_\delta \qquad\qquad (4.5)$$

where z is either an f_i or s_i.[2]

All references to the values of any f_i or s_i in the remainder of this paper will refer to their new values as defined in the preceding two equations. The result of this reassignment can be seen in the following lemma and this property of ψ will prove very useful in the remainder of this article.

Lemma 1. Let ψ be the permutation constructed from the minimal matching procedure. Then

$$f_i \leq s_{\psi(i)} \qquad \text{for } 0 \leq i \leq N. \qquad\qquad (4.6)$$

Proof. The case for $f_i = f_\delta$ is trivial since $f_\delta = s_0 = 0$.

For $f_i \neq f_\delta$ suppose there exists a matching such that $f_i > s_{\psi(i)}$. For f_i to be matched with $s_{\psi(i)}$, f_i must be pushed onto the stack in

------

2.   In Eqs. (4.4) and (4.5) ':=' is an ALGOL-like assignment operator.

Step 4 of the minimal matching procedure before $s_{\psi(i)}$ is recognized in Step 5. This can happen either by starting the pointer of the circular list in the interval from $s_\psi(i)$ to f_i or by starting the pointer outside the interval and skipping over $s_{\psi(i)}$ the first time in Step 3 because the pushdown stack is empty. In either case we will come to f_i before $s_{\psi(i)}$ is recognized and f_i will be pushed onto the stack. Since $s_{\psi(i)} \leq f_i$ we must come to f_δ after f_i and before $s_{\psi(i)}$. At this instant f_δ will be pushed onto the stack above f_i. When we come to $s_{\psi(i)}$ in the list at least f_δ and f_i will be in the stack since f_δ is by definition the element left in the stack at the end of the matching algorithm and f_i cannot have been removed by some previous matching since we assume it will be paired with $s_{\psi(i)}$. However, f_δ is above f_i in the stack, and consequently f_i is not the top element of the stack when $s_{\psi(i)}$ is recognized and cannot be matched with $s_{\psi(i)}$. Hence we have a contradiction and therefore $s_{\psi(i)}$ cannot be less than f_i.

5.   The Minimal Time Permutation with no Crossovers

If the permutation ψ has one cycle then we can construct a schedule from the permutation directly. If it has more than one cycle, then it does not correspond to a schedule because only the records on the same cycle as the pseudo record will be accessed before the schedule terminates. Hence we must obtain a single cycle permutation, call it ϕ^0, for which the latency time is minimal over all one cycle permutations.

The material in this section and the next is developed to enable us to connect as many disjoint cycles in ψ as possible without increasing the cost of the permutation. This strategy parallels one used by Gilmore and Gomory [1964]. In this section, the permutation ψ will be modified to get the permutation ψ' such that $T(\psi') = T(\psi)$ and if $f_i \leq f_j$ then $s_{\psi'(i)} \leq s_{\psi'(j)}$. This last condition can be stated equivalently by requiring that the ordered bipartite graph of the matching related to ψ' have no crossed arcs. The following theorem shows that ψ' can be constructed from ψ by uncrossing, in any order, all crossed arcs in the bipartite graph of ψ. See Fig. 5.1.

Theorem 4. Let ψ' be the permutation constructed from ψ by uncrossing all the arcs of the ordered bipartite graph that are in the complete matching defining ψ. Then

$$T(\psi') = \min\{T(\phi)\} \tag{5.1}$$

where the minimum is taken over all possible permutations ϕ of the N+1 records.

    Proof. Consider any pair of crossed arcs in the matching corresponding to the permutation ψ. From Lemma 1 we know that

$$s_{\psi(i)} \geq f_i \tag{5.2}$$
$$\text{and} \quad s_{\psi(j)} \geq f_j \ . \tag{5.3}$$

The fact the arcs are crossed implies that if we assume

$$f_i < f_j \tag{5.4}$$
$$\text{then} \quad s_{\psi(i)} > s_{\psi(j)} \ . \tag{5.5}$$

This situation is illustrated in Fig. 5.2. Eqs. (5.2) and (5.5) define the following total ordering on the four elements

$$f_i < f_j \leq s_{\psi(j)} < s_{\psi(i)} \tag{5.6}$$

which in turn defines a type 1 (zero cost) interchange. Hence any pair of arcs crossed in ψ can be uncrossed without affecting the cost of the permutation.

138

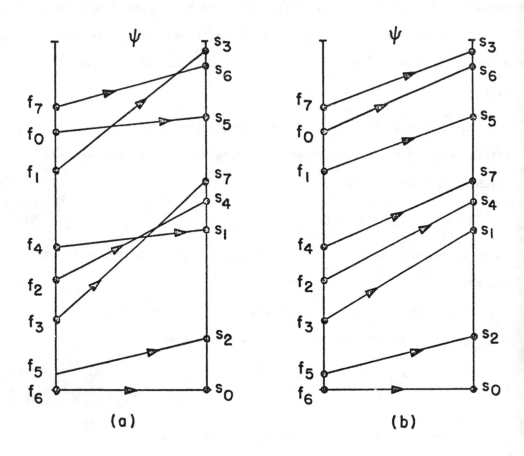

Figure 5.1. An example to illustrate relation between ψ and ψ'.

Corollary 4.1.

$$f_i \le s_{\psi'(i)}, \qquad 0 \le i \le N. \tag{5.7}$$

Proof. From Lemma 1 we know $f_i \le s_{\psi(i)}$ for all i; $0 \le i \le N$. $\psi'(i)$
is different from $\psi(i)$ only if a situation as shown in Fig. 5.2 exists.
In these cases $s_{\psi'(i)} = s_{\psi(j)}$ and $s_{\psi'(j)} = s_{\psi(i)}$. Hence, from Eq. (5.6)
in Theorem 4 we can deduce

$$f_i \le s_{\psi(j)} = s_{\psi'(i)} \tag{5.8}$$

$$\text{and} \quad f_j \le s_{\psi(i)} = s_{\psi'(j)} . \tag{5.9}$$

6. A Minimal Cost, Minimal Component Permutation

Ultimately, we need a permutation that is one continuous cycle and
is of minimal cost. Moving in this direction, the permutation ψ^O is
constructed such that $T(\psi^O) = T(\psi)$ and ψ^O has the minimal number of
disjoint components (cycles).

First we need to establish a fundamental property of permutations.

Lemma 2. (Gilmore and Gomory [1964]). If ϕ is a permutation consisting
of cycles $C_1, \ldots, C_p$ and $X_{i,j}$ is an interchange with i a member of C_r and
j a member of C_s, $r \ne s$, then $\phi * X_{i,j}$ contains the same cycles as ϕ except
that C_r and C_s have been replaced by a single cycle containing all their
nodes.

Proof. This is geometrically evident from Fig. 6.1(a). We note
that if i and j belong to the same cycle, Fig. 6.1(b), the effect is
reversed and the cycle is split.

The general procedure for constructing ψ^O from ψ' is to consider
all possible sequences of zero cost interchanges and choose the sequence
that will transform ψ' into ψ^O, the minimal cost permutation with the

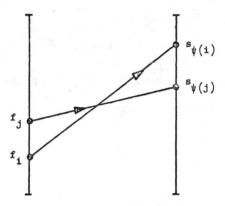

Figure 5.2. A pair of crossed arcs.

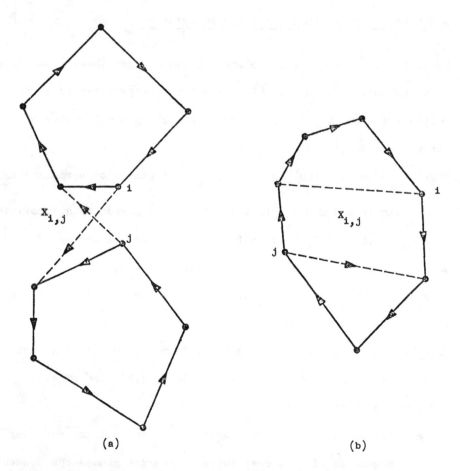

(a)   (b)

Figure 6.1. Using an interchange to merge and split cycles of a
permutation.

minimum number of cycles. The following two lemmas, however, will considerably reduce the work required to transform ψ' to ψ^0.

<u>Lemma 3</u>. Executing any zero cost interchange $X_{i,j}$ on ψ' has the following properties:

1. If

$$f_i \leq f_j \leq f_p \leq f_q \qquad (6.1)$$

then the cost of $X_{p,q}$ is not decreased by executing $X_{i,j}$.

2. If

$$f_r \leq f_s \leq f_i \leq f_j \qquad (6.2)$$

then the cost of $X_{r,s}$ is not changed by executing $X_{i,j}$.

<u>Proof</u>. From Corollary 4.1 it is clear that

$$f_\alpha \leq s_{\psi'}(\alpha) \quad \text{for } \alpha = i,j,p,q,r,s. \qquad (6.3)$$

Hence to prove statement (1) we note that after $X_{i,j}$ is executed, f_j is matched with $s_{\psi'}(i)$. From Eq. (6.1) and the fact ψ' has no crossed arcs it follows that

$$s_{\psi'}(i) \leq s_{\psi'}(j) . \qquad (6.4)$$

Referring to Fig. 2.7 we see the only effect $X_{i,j}$ can have on $X_{p,q}$ is to change it from a type 1 (zero cost) to a type 2 (positive cost) inter-change if $j = p$ and

$$s_{\psi'}(i) < f_p \leq s_{\psi'}(j) . \qquad (6.5)$$

If $j \neq p$ the proof is trivial since $X_{i,j}$ and $X_{p,q}$ do not interact.

Similarly, if $i \neq s$ the proof of statement (2) is trivial since $X_{i,j}$ and $X_{r,s}$ do not interact in any way. If $i = s$ then note that after performing $X_{i,j}$, f_i is matched with $s_{\psi'}(j)$ and from Eqs. (6.2) and (6.4) it follows

$$f_i \leq s_{\psi'(j)} \tag{6.6}$$

which is sufficient to insure the type of $X_{r,s}$ (i.e. $X_{r,i}$) will not be affected.

In an ordered bipartite graph let two arcs be called _adjacent_ if and only if their respective f vertices have no other f vertex between them. For example, arcs (f_2, s_4) and (f_4, s_1) are adjacent in Fig. 5.1(a) but (f_7, s_6) and (f_1, s_3) are not.

<u>Lemma 4.</u> Only adjacent, zero cost (type 1) interchanges need be examined when constructing ψ^0 from ψ'.

<u>Proof.</u> Suppose $X_{i,j}$ is a non-adjacent zero cost interchange in ψ' and i and j are not in the same cycle in ψ'. For all ψ such that

$$f_i \leq f_p \leq f_j \tag{6.7}$$

it is clear from the definition of ψ'

$$s_{\psi'(i)} \leq s_{\psi'(p)} \leq s_{\psi'(j)} \,. \tag{6.8}$$

since ψ' does not have any crossed arcs. Hence it follows

$$f_i \leq f_p \leq s_{\psi'(i)} \leq s_{\psi'(p)} \tag{6.9}$$

which forces $X_{i,p}$ to be a zero cost interchange. Similarly

$$f_p \leq f_j \leq s_{\psi'(p)} \leq s_{\psi'(j)} \tag{6.10}$$

guarantees $X_{p,j}$ will be zero cost.

Therefore if i and p are in the same cycle in ψ', executing $X_{p,j}$ will join the cycles containing i and j. Else if p and j are in the same cycle, executing $X_{i,p}$ will join the cycles containing i and j. Otherwise p is in neither the cycle containing i nor the cycle containing j and executing $X_{p,j}$ and then $X_{i,p}$ will connect all three disjoint cycles at no cost. Hence there is no need to consider the interchange $X_{i,j}$.

Lemmas 3 and 4 make the construction of ψ^0 from ψ' straightforward. Simply consider each adjacent pair of arcs in descending order of the values of the f nodes. If the interchange between the arcs is of zero cost and if the arcs are in different cycles, perform the interchange.

Let $||M||$ denote the number of cycles in the permutation M.

Theorem 5.

$$T(\psi^0) = T(\psi) \qquad\qquad (6.11)$$

$$||\psi^0|| = \min\{||\phi||\} \qquad\qquad (6.12)$$

In the last equation, the minimum is taken over all possible minimal cost permutations, $T(\phi) = T(\psi)$, of the N+1 records.

Proof. ψ^0 is a minimal cost permutation since it was constructed from ψ' by zero cost interchanges and in Theorem 3 we have shown ψ' is a minimal cost permutation.

From Lemma 4 we know it is sufficient to examine only the adjacent arcs defining zero cost interchanges in ψ'. Statement (2) of Lemma 3 assures us that if we execute the necessary zero cost interchanges in decreasing order of the value of their f nodes, applying any zero cost interchange will not affect the cost of following interchanges, i.e. a crucial zero cost interchange will not be transformed to a positive cost interchange (type 2) situation before it is executed. Statement (1) of Lemma 3 guarantees us that after scanning the adjacent arcs once, we do not need to backtrack and rescan any adjacent arcs since the cost of their associated interchange can only increase if we execute the necessary zero cost interchanges in decreasing order.

7. A Minimal Cost, Single Cycle Permutation

The next theorem establishes a lower bound on the cost (time) of a single cycle permutation over the N+1 records and provides some insight as to how to construct a minimal cost, single cycle permutation.

Theorem 6. A lower bound on the total cost (total latency time) of a single cycle permutation is

$$T(\psi^O) + \max\{\Delta T(X_{\delta,q}, \psi^O)\} \tag{7.1}$$

where the maximum operation is taken over all interchanges of the form $X_{\delta,q}$ where q is such that for all f_j, $0 \le j \le N$, if $f_j < f_q$, the vertices j and q are not in the same cycle of ψ^O.

Proof. Let q' be such that $\Delta T(X_{\delta,q'}, \psi^O) = \max\{\Delta T(X_{\delta,q}, \psi^O)\}$. The range of the maximum operation is as defined in the theorem statement. Clearly the cycles containing nodes δ and q' must be connected in order to form a single cycle permutation. Theorem 5 has shown there are no zero cost or negative cost interchanges available to connect the cycles containing δ and q'.

By definition of q', if q'' and q' are in the same cycle of ψ^O, then $q'' \ge q'$ and hence

$$\Delta T(X_{\delta,q''}, \psi^O) \ge \Delta T(X_{\delta,q'}, \psi^O) . \tag{7.2}$$

This situation is shown in Figs. 7.1 and 7.2. Therefore the cheapest interchange available to us is the type 2a interchange $X_{\delta,q'}$ that connects the cycles containing δ and q'.

Another possibility that must be considered here is that there may exist a j such that j < q', and we first connect the cycles containing the nodes δ and j, followed by the connection of cycles containing q' and j. By performing the interchange $X_{\delta,j}$, $X_{j,q'}$ is changed from a type 2 to

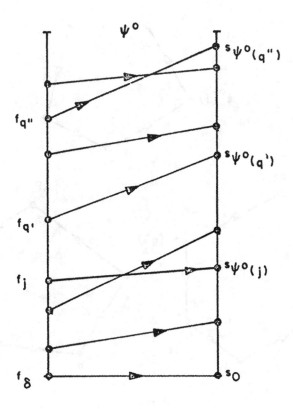

Figure 7.1. The matching representing the permutation ψ^0.

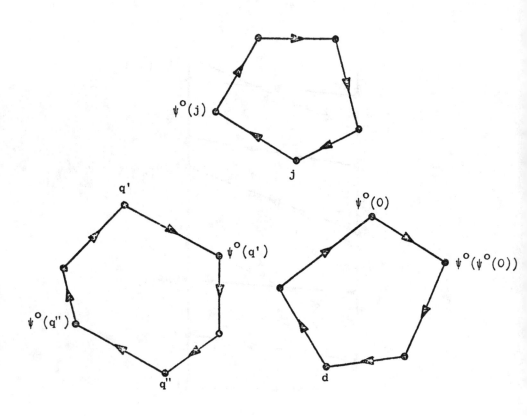

Figure 7.2. The cycles of the permutations ψ^{o}.

a type 2a interchange. This implies that the cheapest way to connect the cycles containing q' and δ is to use the interchange $X_{j,q'}$ with cost

$$\Delta T(X_{j,q'}, \psi^0) = f_{q'} - f_j .$$ (7.3)

However,

$$\Delta T(X_{\delta,j}, \psi^0) + \Delta T(X_{j,q'}, \psi^0 * X_{\delta,j})$$
$$= (f_j - f_\delta) + (f_{q'} - f_j)$$
$$= f_{q'} - f_d$$
$$= \Delta T(X_{\delta,q'}, \psi^0)$$ (7.4)

Therefore, it will cost $\Delta T(X_{\delta,q'}, \psi^0)$ to insure we connect the disjoint components of ψ^0 containing nodes δ and q', regardless of the relative positions of any other disjoint components.

Theorem 6 suggests a simple procedure for the construction of a candidate for the minimal cost, single cycle permutation. Consider each node in the order of increasing value of its associated f value. If the node under consideration and node 0, or equivalently node δ, are not of the same cycle, execute the positive cost, type 2a interchange associated with the current f node and the f node matched to s_0. After all N nodes have been examined let the resulting permutations be called ϕ^0.

All that remains to show is that ϕ^0 is in fact the minimal cost, single cycle permutation we have been looking for.

Theorem 7. The permutation ϕ^0 is a minimal cost (total latency time), single cycle permutation and

$$T(\phi^0) = T(\psi^0) + \max\{\Delta T(X_{\delta,q}, \psi^0)\}$$ (7.5)

where the maximum operation is taken over all interchanges of the form $X_{\delta,q}$ where q is such that for all f_j, $0 \leq j \leq N$, if $f_j < f_q$, the vertices j and q are not in the same cycle of ψ^0.

Proof. From Lemma 2 we know each interchange that is executed in transforming ψ^O to ϕ^O connects previously disjoint cycles. No inter-changes are executed on nodes in the same cycle. Since all cycles contain at least one node, the fact we scan all the nodes is sufficient to insure we have not forgotten any cycles. From the procedure to construct ϕ^O from ψ^O we see

$$\phi^O = \psi^O * X_{\delta, i_1} * \ldots * X_{i_{m-1}, i_m} \tag{7.6}$$

where the nodes $f_{i_1}, \ldots, f_{i_m}$ are found not to be in the same cycle as f_δ as the list of f_i's is scanned as described above. Now it follows directly,

$$
\begin{aligned}
T(\phi^O) &= T(\psi^O * X_{\delta, i_1} * \ldots * X_{i_{m-1}, i_m}) \\
&= T(\psi^O * X_{\delta, i_1} * \ldots * X_{i_{m-2}, i_{m-1}}) \\
&\quad + (f_{i_m} - f_{i_{m-1}})
\end{aligned} \tag{7.7}
$$

$$
\begin{aligned}
T(\phi^O) &= T(\psi^O * X_{\delta, i_1} * \ldots * X_{i_{m-3}, i_{m-2}}) \\
&\quad + (f_{i_{m-1}} - f_{i_{m-2}}) + (f_{i_m} - f_{i_{m-1}}) \\
&= T(\psi^O * X_{\delta, i_1} * \ldots * X_{i_{m-3}, i_{m-2}}) \\
&\quad + (f_{i_m} - f_{i_{m-2}})
\end{aligned} \tag{7.8}
$$

$$\cdot$$
$$\cdot$$
$$\cdot$$

$$T(\phi^O) = T(\psi^O) + (f_{i_m} - f_\delta) \tag{7.9}$$
$$T(\phi^O) = T(\psi^O) + \Delta T(X_{\delta, i_m}, \psi^O) \tag{7.10}$$

which proves Eq. (7.5). Since $T(\phi^O)$ is equal to the lower bound established for a single cycle permutation in Theorem 6, ϕ^O must be a minimal cost, single cycle permutation.

The complete sequence of record accesses is now easily constructed from ϕ^0. $R_{\phi^0(i)}$ is accessed immediately after R_i. Recall that the pseudo record has the index 0 and consequently $R_{\phi^0(0)}$ will be the first record accessed, $R_{\phi^0(\phi^0(0))}$ the second, etc.

8. The Complete Algorithm

In this section the optimal drum scheduling algorithm is explicitly stated. All the steps that are listed here have been implicitly discussed previously in the paper but it should be helpful to see the algorithm brought together and concisely stated.

1. Based on the unique value associated with each node, sort f_0, f_i, and s_i, $1 \leq i \leq N$, into one circular list. If $f_i = s_j$ for any i and j then f_i must precede s_j.

2. Set the list pointer to an arbitrary element in the list.

3. Scan in the direction of nodes with increasing value for the next (first) f_i in the list.

4. Place this f_i on a pushdown stack. (There is no need to explicitly remove this f_i from the circular list.)

5. Move the pointer to the next element and if it is an f_i go to Step 4, else continue on to Step 6. In the latter case, the element must be an s_i.

6. Pop the top f_i from the stack and move the pointer to the next element in the circular list. (Do not attempt to match this f node to an s node as was done in the minimal matching procedure of Sec. 3.)

7. If the circular list has been completely scanned go to Step 8, else if the stack is empty go to Step 3, else go to Step 5.

8. Let the bottom f_i on the pushdown stack be identified as f_δ. Change the circular list to an ordinary list where the bottom element is f_δ.

9. Match f_δ to s_0, and starting from the top of the list match the kth s_i to the kth f_i. (The permutation ψ' has now been constructed.)

10. Determine the membership of the cycles of ψ'.

11. Moving from the top to the bottom of the list, if adjacent arcs define a zero cost interchange and if they are in disjoint cycles perform the interchange. (This step transforms ψ' to ψ^0.)

12. Moving from the bottom to the top of the list, perform the positive cost, type 2a, interchange on the current arc if it is not in the same cycle as the arc containing f_δ. (The permutation defined at the end of this step is the minimal cost, single cycle permutation ϕ^0.)

There are several points about this algorithm that deserve some discussion. First of all, note that the minimal cost permutation ψ is never explicitly constructed. The above algorithm uses a simplified version of the minimal matching procedure of Sec. 3 and is able to proceed directly to the permutations ψ' in Step 9. The reason permutation ψ was introduced was to facilitate proving the properties of ψ'.

In the introduction it was claimed that this is an N*logN algorithm and this can now be seen to be true. In Step 1 we are required to sort 2N+1 elements and hence the first step becomes one of our most expensive computations, requiring work on the order of N*logN [Morris, 1969]. Steps 2-8 constitute a single scan of the list and the computation required for each element in the list is independent of the size of the list. Step 9 is a second simple scan of the elements in the list used to construct ψ'. Determining the connectivity of a graph in Step 10 is in general an N^2 process [Holt and Reingold, 1970] but in our case we only have cycles without any branches and the computation reduces to one proportional to N (see Appendix C). Steps 11 and 12 are a third and fourth pass over the list of N+1 records but at each step in both passes we must determine in what cycle the current f_i is a member. This is logN process (see Appendix C) and consequently steps 11 and 12 require computation on the order of N*logN.

9. An Example

In this section a simple example will be presented in which each major step of the drum scheduling algorithm performs some non-trivial computation. The set of records we will schedule is shown in Fig. 9.1. There are four records that need to be processed and the current position of the drum head, f_0, is between the beginning of record 3, denoted by s_3, and the end of record 2, f_2.

Step 1 of the scheduling algorithm constructs the sorted circular list as illustrated in line (a) of Fig. 9.2. Note that the pushdown stack is initially empty and the pointer into the circular list has arbitrarily been set to s_4 (Step 2). Now Step 3 through 7 are repetitively executed as the pointer scans across the circular list. Fig. 9.2 shows the contents of the pushdown stack after the element currently pointed to in the circular list has been processed. Line (i) of Fig. 9.2 shows f_1 is on the bottom of the stack after the list has been completely scanned; hence f_1 is designated f_6 in Step 8. Now the value of all the nodes are redefined relative to f_6, as implied in Step 8

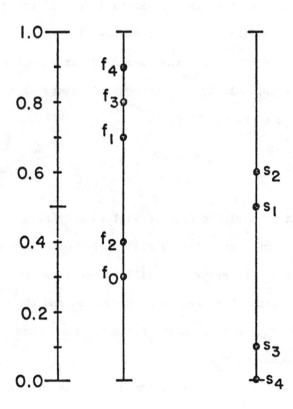

Figure 9.1. Ordered bipartite graph representation of example.

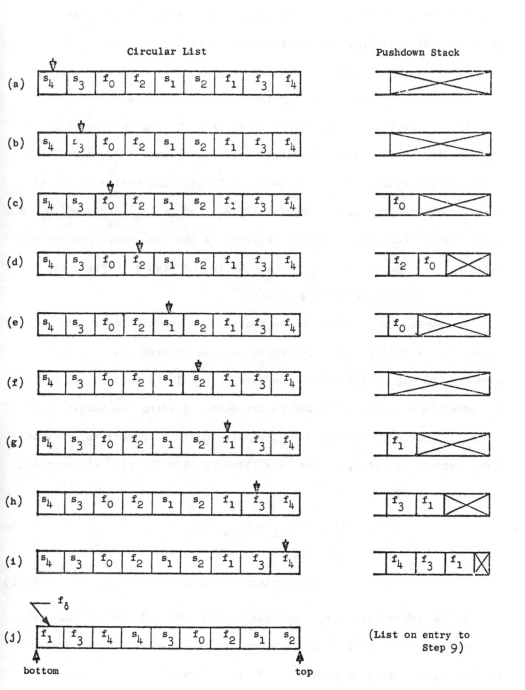

Figure 9.2. Scanning the circular list.

when we made f_δ the bottom of the list. Our example now has the appearance of Fig. 9.3. The no-crossover matching of Fig. 9.3 is constructed by Step 9 and defines the minimal cost permutation ψ'.

Figure 9.4(a) shows the disjoint cycles of ψ' as determined in Step 10. In Step 11 the algorithm moves from the top to the bottom of the matching in Fig. 9.3 and notices arcs (f_0, s_1) and (f_2, s_2) define a zero cost interchange and since they are in disjoint cycles of ψ', the interchange is performed. The arcs (f_4, s_3) and (f_3, s_4) also define a zero cost interchange. However, they are in the same cycle and hence no interchange is performed. At the conclusion of Step 11 we have the permutation ψ^0 as shown in Fig. 9.4(b).

Now moving from the bottom to the top of the matching we find f_1 and f_3 are in disjoint cycles. The positive cost interchange $X_{1,3}$ is executed and Fig. 9.4(c) shows the results. All the records are now connected in a single cycle and we are done. Tracing the single cycle of ϕ^0 in Fig. 9.4(c), starting at f_0, we see that the optimal way to access these records is 2,1,4,3. The total latency time incurred in accessing these records is

$$
\begin{aligned}
T(\phi^0) &= t_{0,2} + t_{2,1} + t_{1,4} + t_{4,3} \\
&= 0.3 + 0.1 + 0.3 + 0.2 \\
&= 0.9 \text{ revolutions of the drum}
\end{aligned} \tag{9.1}
$$

It has often been suggested that a good heuristic to minimize drum latency time is to process the next record the read-write head sees after completing its previous record transfer. If we use this scheduling algorithm, which we are calling SLTF, it is easy to see from Fig. 9.1(a) that we will access the four records in the sequence

$$
1,4,3,2 . \tag{9.2}
$$

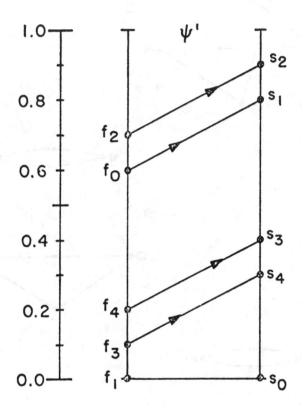

Figure 9.3. Matching on ordered bipartite graph after Step 9.
A minimal cost matching with no crossed arcs.

156

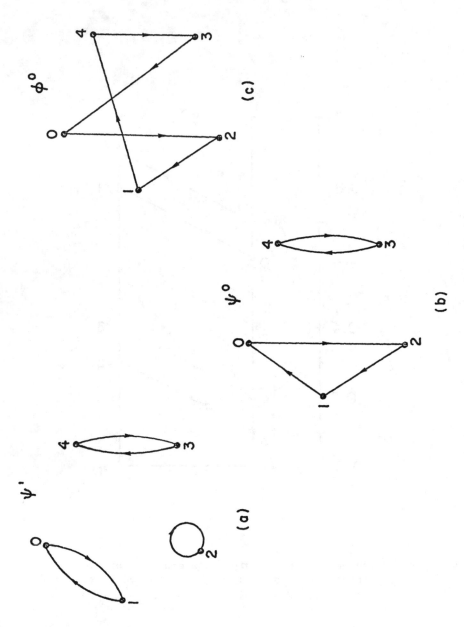

Figure 9.4. The permutations constructed by the drum scheduling algorithm.

The latency time associated with accessing the records by this sequence is

$$T(\phi_{SLTF}) = t_{0,1} + t_{1,4} + t_{4,3} + t_{3,2}$$
$$= 0.2 + 0.3 + 0.2 + 0.8$$
$$= 1.5 \text{ drum revolutions.} \qquad (9.3)$$

This is significantly longer than the total latency time of an optimal schedule for this example.

10. Concluding Remarks

An important practical aspect of the scheduling algorithm discussed in this paper is its computational complexity. As we pointed out in Sec. 8, this algorithm enjoys a computational complexity on the order of N*logN, where N is the number of records that must be scheduled. There exists strong evidence to indicate that no other optimal drum scheduling algorithm can be devised with a smaller growth rate than this. In any scheduling algorithm which handles the problem of accessing records from a drum as discussed in this paper, it is evident there must be at least one step in which the N records are sorted on some attribute. Sorting algorithms have been extensively studied and we have conclusive arguments to indicate no sorting algorithm can enjoy a growth rate less than N*logN [Morris, 1969].

Another factor affecting the efficiency of this scheduling algorithm is the coefficient associated with the N*logN term. Unfortunately, no strong statement can be made on this point since the algorithm has not been implemented on any machine. However, this algorithm has been written in Algol (Stanford's Algol W) and the procedure to initially sort the initial and final points of the records into a circular list requires

more time than the rest of the steps in the algorithm combined. This is
true in spite of the fact that special care was taken to use a very
efficient sorting algorithm [Van Emden, 1970]. The shortest-latency-
time-first algorithm, which has been implemented in practice and found
to be of practical value in various applications, must also sort the
initial and final points of the records into a circular list. While the
above observation does not resolve the question of the algorithm's
efficiency, it does hold out substantial promise that it can be of
practical value in some applications. Moreover, there are several levels
in the computer system at which the scheduling algorithm can be
implemented: software, microcode, or hardware, and the particular level
of implementation can be varied to guarantee the gain achieved in using
the algorithm is not outweighted by the time required to perform it.

Another aspect of this scheduling algorithm that must be considered
in many practical implementations is the dynamic behavior of f_0, the
position of the read-write heads. Clearly the drum will continue to
rotate while we are executing the drum scheduling algorithm. Hence when
we go to use the schedule just constructed, f_0 will have increased in
value and in some cases we may be faced with the unfortunate situation
that f_0 has just passed $s_\phi^0(0)$. This whole problem can be prevented by
adding some $\in$ to f_0 at the beginning of the drum scheduling algorithm,
where $\in$ may be a function of N, such that f_0 at the completion of the
algorithm is less than the initial value of $f_0 + \in$.

The complexity of this algorithm is not required if the drum is
organized as a paging drum, i.e. all the records are the same length and
the records do not partially overlap, since it is straightforward to
show the SLTF algorithm is also an optimal algorithm in this case. The
scheduling of paging drums, however, is often not as simple as it may

first appear. For instance, consider the case where more than one drum is connected to a single I/O channel. If the drums are not synchronized, which they rarely are, we are back to the case where the records will overlap in an arbitrary manner and SLTF is not longer optimal. Another example is an IBM 360/67 computer attempting to use an IBM 2301 drum. Unfortunately 4 1/2 pages fit on a track [IBM, 1971] and if we require that the IBM 2301 be organized as a true paging drum we are forced to put only 4 pages to a track and waste the remaining capacity of the drum.

The scheduling algorithm of this paper is applicable in situations where a batch of records are simultaneously recognized as requiring service. It is intriguing, however, to consider the more general situation in which record requests are allowed to arrive at arbitrary times. This more general case has been studied for FIFO and SLTF scheduling algorithms [Abate and Dubner, 1969; Chapter 2]; unfortunately, it is not obvious how to extend the concepts of this discussion to allow random arrival times. This algorithm can, nevertheless, provide a basis for an admittedly sub-optimal, but hopefully good, scheduling procedure that can handle the random arrival of new requests to process a record. We simply optimally order the queue of current requests with the algorithm of this article and be prepared to reorder the queue whenever a new request arrives. This heuristic has an intuitive appeal since it guarantees it will access the requests in the queue in an optimal order providing no new requests arrive. Again, it would be very interesting to implement this algorithm on a machine and compare its performance with other scheduling strategies such as first-come-first-served (FIFO) or shortest-latency-time-first (SLTF).

Chapter 5

THE EXPECTED DIFFERENCE BETWEEN THE SLTF AND MTPT

DRUM SCHEDULING DISCIPLINES

This chapter is a sequel to an earlier chapter, Chapter 4, that develops a minimal-total-processing-time (MTPT) drum scheduling algorithm. A quantative comparison between MTPT schedules and shortest-latency-time-first (SLTF) schedules, commonly acknowledged as good schedules for drum-like storage units, is presented here. The analysis develops an analogy to random walks and proves several asymptotic properties of collections of records on drums. These properties are specialized to the MTPT and SLTF algorithms and it is shown that for sufficiently large sets of records, the expected processing time of a SLTF schedule is longer than a MTPT schedule by the expected record length. The results of a simulation study are also presented to show the difference in MTPT and SLTF schedules for small sets of records and for situations not covered in the analytic discussion.

1.   Introduction

In Chapter 4 we introduced a drum scheduling algorithm that can efficiently find schedules for sets of I/O requests that minimize the total rotational delay (latency) of the set of I/O requests. The original article, however, is entirely devoted to developing the scheduling algorithm, proving its correctness, and presenting a few examples of the algorithm in operation; this article provides a quantative measure of how much better the new drum scheduling algorithm can be expected to be over conventional scheduling algorithms.

First, briefly reconsider the scheduling problem posed in the original paper. Suppose a fixed-head drum, as illustrated in Fig. 1.1, receives requests to process N I/O records. These requests may be to either read or write a record onto the drum; no distinction is made between reading or writing in this, or the original, discussion. In Fig. 1.1, notice we allow the records to start anywhere around the circumference of the drum and furthermore the record lengths are arbitrary. We assume the drum can only begin reading a record at s_i, the record's starting address, and once started, the drum cannot be pre-empted and will finish processing the record at f_i, the finishing address. The interval of time the drum is delayed waiting for the beginning of the next record is called rotational latency or simply latency. Furthermore, we exclude the possibility of more I/O requests arriving at the drum while the original N requests are being serviced. This is an unrealistic assumption in some cases and more will be said about this in Sec. 6, but for the present we will forbid random arrivals. A scheduling algorithm is developed in the original paper that finds a schedule that processes all N records in the minimal amount of time, and hence we will denote such

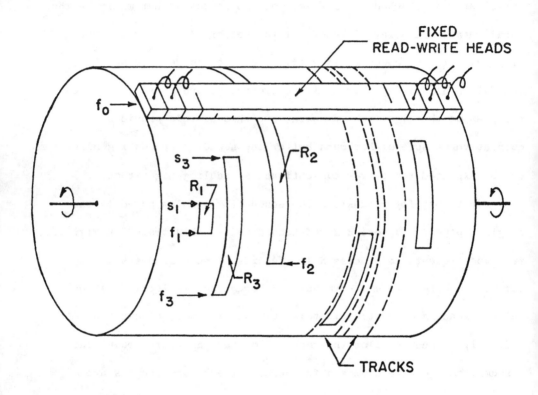

Figure 1.1. A drum storage unit.

a schedule as a <u>minimal-total-processing-time</u> (MTPT) schedule.[*] An
important property of this scheduling algorithm is that it is able to
construct a MTPT schedule in N*logN simple steps.

The algorithm that is commonly acknowledged as a good drum
scheduling algorithm is <u>shortest-latency-time-first</u> (SLTF); for this
reason the MTPT algorithm will be compared to the SLTF algorithm in this
article. A SLTF schedule is simply a schedule that processes the next
record to come under the read-write heads, given that the read-write
heads are not busy servicing another request. In general, an SLTF
schedule is not a MTPT schedule and this article investigates how much
longer than a MTPT schedule a SLTF schedule needs to process a set of N
records. Specifically, this article presents an asymptotic expression
for the expected difference between the SLTF and MTPT schedules and then
concludes with some empirical results to show how the expected difference
of the two algorithms behaves before it approaches its asymptotic value.
These results, along with the least upper bound of one drum revolution
for the difference between SLTF and MTPT schedules developed earlier
[Stone and Fuller, 1971], places us in a good position to quantitatively
evaluate the relative advantages offered by either the MTPT or SLTF
schedules when minimizing the total processing time of a set of I/O
requests is a reasonable objective.

---

[*] The algorithm was called an <u>optimal</u> drum scheduling algorithm in the
original article, but this article refers to the algorithm as the
minimal-total-processing-time (MTPT) drum scheduling algorithm. This
name is more mnemonic and recognizes that other drum scheduling
algorithms may be optimal for other optimality criteria.

This article develops the comparisons between the MTPT and SLTF scheduling algorithms in several steps. This section, Sec. 2, and Sec. 3 introduce the basic concepts and, using an analogy to random walks, prove two properties common to any set of I/O requests waiting for service at a drum. Sections 4 and 5 apply these general results to the MTPT and SLTF scheduling algorithms respectively and Sec. 6 presents an empirical comparison, based on a simulation study, to show the relation of the two drum scheduling algorithms when N is too small to use the asymptotic result and for assumptions concerning the records not covered in the analytic discussion.

2. Basic Notions and Assumptions

The analysis of this article will draw heavily from the notation, and theorems, of the previous paper [Chapter 4]. A complete restatement of the theorems would be impractical, but a statement of the MTPT algorithm is provided in Appendix B and the relevant notation and formalisms developed in more detail in the original paper are outlined quickly below, in conjunction with extensions needed for the present analysis.

A schedule of N I/O requests can be represented by a single-cycle permutation if we let a pseudo-record, with index 0, be defined such that it ends at the current position of the read-write heads, and starts wherever the last record in the schedule ends. Let ψ_{MTPT} and ψ_{SLTF} be the permutations corresponding to the MTPT and SLTF schedules respectively, and let $C(\psi_{MTPT})$ and $C(\psi_{SLTF})$ be the total rotational delay, or latency, associated with the MTPT and SLTF schedules. In Fig. 2.1, for instance,

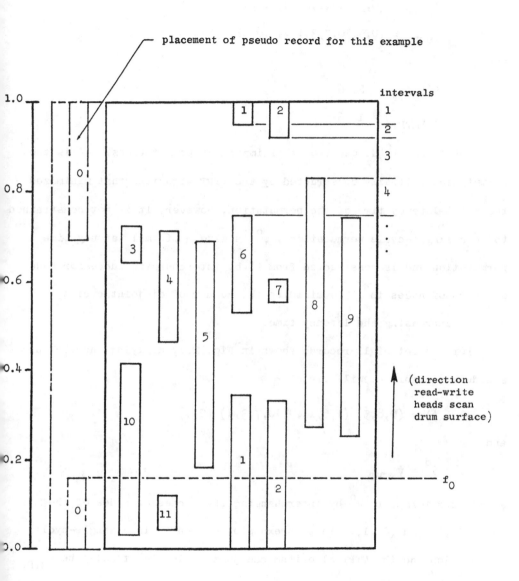

Figure 2.1. An exemplary set of I/O records requesting service.

$$\psi_{SLTF} = (0,5,2,4,1,6,10,7,3,11,9,8)$$
$$\psi_{MTPT} = (0,9,10,7,3,1,4,2,6,11,8,5)$$

and

$$C(\psi_{SLTF}) = 2.08$$
$$C(\psi_{MTPT}) = 1.96$$

Let ψ' and ψ^{o} denote two other important permutations. ψ' is the permutation initially constructed by the MTPT algorithm that minimizes the total latency time of the permutation, however, it is not constrained to be a single-cycle permutation. ψ^{o} is also a minimal latency time permutation and is constructed from ψ' by interchanging successor nodes of pairs of nodes in ψ' to minimize the number of disjoint cycles, without increasing the latency time.

For the set of 11 records shown in Fig. 2.1, applying the MTPT drum scheduling algorithm will yield

$$\psi' = (0,8,5) \ (1,6,11,9,10,7,3,1) \ (2,4)$$

and

$$\psi^{o} = \psi_{MTPT} \ .$$

ψ' is transformed to ψ^{o} by interchanging the successor nodes of the pairs $(1,2)$ and $(0,11)$. In this example, we see ψ^{o} is a single-cycle permutation and the MTPT algorithm can just declare ψ^{o} to also be ψ_{MTPT} without performing any positive cost interchanges. As we will soon see, this is not an uncommon occurrence when we are scheduling a large collection of records.

Let an __interval__ be defined as a region, or sector, of the drum bounded by neighboring endpoints of the N records. The endpoints of these N records can be used to define M intervals, and clearly, M can be no greater than 2N. For example, in Fig. 2.1 the major rectangle

depicts the surface of the drum and the records that require processing

are shown on the drum's surface. The first few intervals defined by

these records are shown in the figure. Let I_k denote the number of

records that are in interval k. A <u>critical interval,</u> for a collection

of I/O requests, is an interval, I_j, such that

$$I_j \geq I_k, \qquad\qquad k = 1,2,\ldots,M \ .$$

Also let

$$I_{crit} = \text{maximum}\{I_k\}, \qquad k = 1,2,\ldots,M \ .$$

Using the position of the read-write heads as a reference point, let the

region bounded by the first and last critical interval be called the

<u>critical region.</u> The critical intervals and critical region of the set

of records shown in Fig. 2.1 are labeled in Fig. 2.2.

In order to proceed with the analysis we need to make some

assumption about the distribution of the starting, s_i, and finishing, f_i,

points around the circumference of the drum. The simplest, reasonable

assumption to make is that all the endpoints are randomly distributed

about the circumference of the drum, i.e. if we let the circumference of

the drum be our unit of length, all the endpoints are independent and

uniformly distributed about the unit circle.

From symmetry it is obvious that the expected distance between

adjacent record endpoints on the drum is 1/M, and the distribution of

the distance between any two adjacent endpoints, call it W, is just the

1st order statistic with mean 1/M and density function

$$\Pr\{W > x\} = M(1 - x)^{M-1} \qquad , \ 0 < x \leq 1;$$

$$= 0 \qquad\qquad , \ \text{otherwise} \ .$$

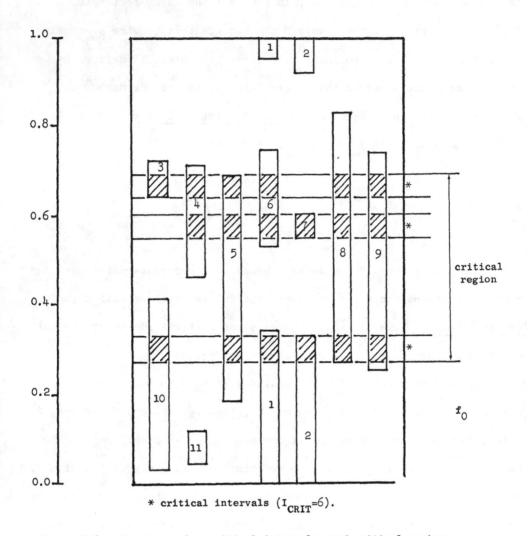

* critical intervals ($I_{CRIT}=6$).

Figure 2.2. The intervals, critical intervals, and critical regions
of the set of I/O records of Fig. 2.1.

Let W_{cr} be the width of the critical region; if the critical region

consists of n intervals, the expected size of the critical region is

the nth-order statistic [cf. Feller, 1971] with mean n/M and density

function

$$Pr\{W_{cr} = x\} = M\binom{M-1}{n-1}x^{n-1}(1 - x)^{M-n} , \quad 0 < x \le 1;$$
$$= 0 \qquad\qquad , \quad \text{otherwise} .$$

3. Critical Intervals and Random Walks

From our assumption that all the endpoints of the records are

independent and uniformly distributed about the circumference of the

drum we can model successive interval sizes as random, unit jumps, and

thereby draw upon the extensive literature associated with random walks

[cf. Barton and Mallows, 1965].

A random walk can be defined as a finite sequence of +1's and -1's,

and at each epoch, or step, in the random walk a Bernoulli trial is

performed to decide if the step should be +1 or -1. In other words,

successive steps in the random walk are independent binary random

variables that take on the values +1 and -1 with equal probability.

Hence there are 2^n equally likely random walks, where n is the number of

steps in the walk.

Now suppose we add the restriction to a random walk of length n

that it have exactly m positive steps, and consequently (n-m) negative

steps. The number of possible paths is now reduced to the number of

ways to distribute m positive steps among the n steps; this is just the

binomial coefficient

$$\binom{n}{m} = \frac{n!}{m!\,(n-m)!}$$

Figure 3.1 is an alternate representation of the set of records shown in Figs. 2.1 and 2.2. The curve of Fig. 3.1 corresponds to the sizes of the intervals around the circumference of the drum.

We can model successive record endpoints as independent events that are equally likely to be a starting or finishing address. If we let a starting address be +1 and a finishing address -1, Fig. 3.2 can be thought of as a random walk of length 2N with the restriction that there are exactly as many +1's as -1's. If we move our point of reference in Fig. 3.1 to the top of an arbitrary critical interval, and if we neglect the difference in interval widths, Fig. 3.1 can be redrawn as Fig. 3.2. Since we chose a critical interval as our new point of reference, the path of interval sizes can never go above the x-axis, and the path of interval sizes starts at coordinate (0,0) and ends at (2N,0).

A random walk, like the one shown in Fig. 3.2, is equivalent to the classic ballot problem originally formulated by Bertrand [1887] and Withworth [1886]; contemporary references that clearly develop the ballot problem, and its many ramifications, are provided by Feller [1968] and Barton and Mallows [1965]. First, consider the following important lemma.

Lemma 3.1 (Reflection Principle). The number of paths from a point A to a point B that touch or cross the x-axis equals the number of all paths from A' to B, where A' is the reflection of A about the x-axis (see Fig. 3.3).

Proof: For a short proof see Feller [1968]; Fig. 3.3, however, makes the proof self-evident. Basically, all that needs to be shown is that there exists a one-to-one correspondence between every path from A' to B with a path from A to B touching, or crossing, the x-axis. Since A' and B are on opposite sides of the x-axis, a path from A' to B must

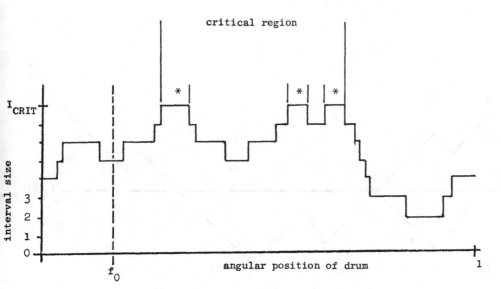

Figure 3.1. The size of intervals as a function of drum position.

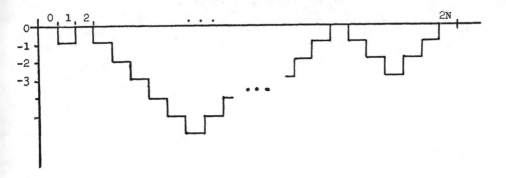

Figure 3.2. An abstract representation of interval size as a
function of the interval index.

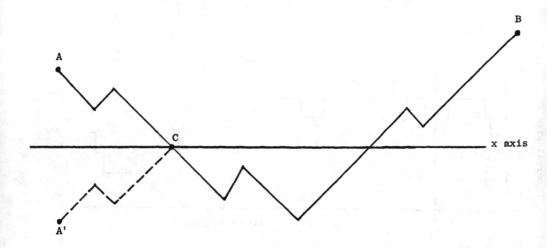

Figure 3.3. Illustration of the A-A' correspondence
in the Reflection Principle.

cross the axis at some point, say C, and Fig. 3.3 shows the unique

corresponding path from A to B, through C.

With the use of the Reflection Principle, we can quickly prove a

special case of a fundamental result of the ballot problem.

Theorem 3.1. Let N be a positive integer. There are exactly

$$P_{2N} = \frac{1}{N+1} \binom{2N}{N} \tag{3.1}$$

paths from the origin, $(0,0)$, to the point $(2N,0)$ that may touch, but

never cross the x-axis, and are below the x-axis.

Proof: There exist as many paths from $(0,0)$ to $(2N,0)$ that do not

cross the x-axis as there are paths from $(0,1)$ to $(2N,1)$ that never

touch the x-axis. From the Reflection Principle, the number of paths

from $(0,1)$ to $(2N,1)$ that touch the x-axis is equal to the number of all

paths from $(0,-1)$ to $(2N,1)$. Hence

$$P_{2N} = \binom{2N}{N} - \binom{2N}{N-1}$$

A simple manipulation of the above difference of binomial coefficients

will show they are equivalent to the right side of Eq. (3.1).

The ballot theorem just discussed can now be used to help us find

the probability of an arbitrary interval being a critical interval. By

construction, interval 0 is a critical interval, and hence interval 1

cannot be a critical interval, and similarly no interval with an odd

index can be a critical interval. The following theorem gives the

probability that an even interval will be a critical interval.

Theorem 3.2. Let N and K be positive integers where $K \leq N$. The

probability that interval 2K is a critical interval is

$$\Pr\{I_{2K} = I_{crit}\} = \frac{N+1}{(K+1)(N-K+1)} \frac{\binom{N}{K}^2}{\binom{2N}{2K}} \tag{3.2}$$

Proof: From Theorem 3.1 we know the number of allowable paths from (0,0) to (2K,0) is

$$P_{2K} = \frac{1}{K+1} \binom{2K}{K} \tag{3.3}$$

Similarly, the number of allowable paths from (2K,0) to (2N,0) is

$$P_{2(N-K)} = \frac{1}{N-K+1} \binom{2(N-K)}{N-K} \tag{3.4}$$

Therefore, the number of allowable paths from (0,0) to (2N,0), passing through (2K,0) is the product of Eqs. (3.3) and (3.4). Dividing the product of Eqs. (3.3) and (3.4) by the total number of admissible paths from (0,0) to (2N,0) yields Eq. (3.2).

If we now use Sterling's approximation, i.e. $n! \sim \sqrt{2\pi} \cdot n^{n+\frac{1}{2}} \cdot e^{-n}$, we see that as N and K get larger, Eq. (3.2) approaches

$$\Pr\{I_{2K} = I_{crit}\} \sim \frac{1}{\sqrt{\pi}} \left[\frac{N}{K(N-K)}\right]^{3/2} \tag{3.5}$$

The following statement can now be made concerning the behavior of the critical region.

Theorem 3.3. For any positive real number ϵ,

$$\lim_{N\to\infty} \Pr\{W_{cr} > \epsilon\} \to 0, \tag{3.6}$$

where W_{cr} is the width of the critical interval.

Proof: For an n such that $n/N < \epsilon/2$, the probability that W_{cr} is greater than ϵ is equivalent to the probability that there exists a critical interval between intervals n and 2N-n in Fig. 3.2. Hence from Theorem 3.2 it follows

$$\Pr\{W_{cr} > \epsilon\} < \sum_{k=n}^{2N-n} \Pr\{I_{2K} = I_{crit}\} \ .$$

For N, and n, sufficiently large we can use Eq. (3.5) and approximate the above inequality with

$$\Pr\{W_{cr} > \epsilon\} < \frac{1}{\sqrt{\pi}} \sum_{k=n}^{2N-n} \left[\frac{N}{K(N-K)}\right]^{3/2} \tag{3.7}$$

As suggested in Fig. 3.4, for large N we can replace the finite sum in Eq. (3.6) by a definite integral. Hence,

$$\Pr\{W_{cr} > \epsilon\} < \frac{1}{\sqrt{\pi}} \int_{n}^{2N-n} \left[\frac{N}{K(N-K)}\right]^{3/2} dK$$

$$= \frac{2}{\sqrt{\pi}} \int_{\epsilon N/2}^{N/2} \left[\frac{N}{K(N-K)}\right]^{3/2} dK$$

$$< \frac{2}{\sqrt{\pi}} \int_{\epsilon N/2}^{\infty} \left[\frac{N}{K(N-\frac{N}{2})}\right]^{3/2} dK$$

$$= \frac{16}{\sqrt{\epsilon \pi N}}$$

In the limit as N approaches infinity the above expression, bounding the width of the critical region, goes to zero.

4. Two Properties of the MTPT Algorithm

Our work with random walks and critical intervals can now be used to prove two properties of the minimal-total-processing-time (MTPT) drum scheduling algorithm.

Theorem 4.1. The distinguished finishing address, f_δ, terminates the critical region.

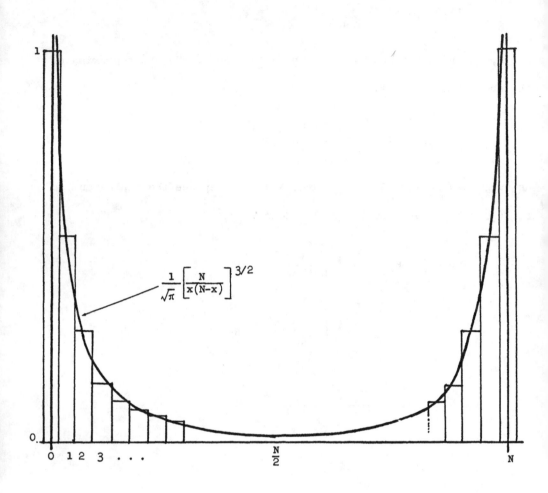

Figure 3.4. Graph of the even interval sizes and
their continuous approximation.

Proof: Figure 4.1 is Fig. 3.2 redrawn with the exception that the position of the read-write heads of the drum, called f_0, is included as a negative step in the graph. Now the path of interval sizes consists of N+1 negative steps and N positive steps and it terminates at $(2N+1,-1)$ rather than $(2N,0)$. The MTPT algorithm finds f_δ by scanning the sorted list of f and s nodes, pushing f nodes onto a push-down stack, and pairing off the top f node of the stack with the s node as it is seen by the scanner. Since Step 2^* of the MTPT algorithm can start the scan of record endpoints anywhere, suppose we start the scan at the f node terminating the critical region; then the distance of the interval path below the x-axis is the stack depth and Fig. 4.1 shows how the f and s nodes are paired off in Step 6. Note that the terminating f node of the critical region moves the path from $(i,0)$ to $(i+1,-1)$ and there is no s node anywhere in the path that moves the interval path back above -1. Hence, the f node terminating the critical region must be the f node remaining in the pushdown stack after the list of f and s nodes has been scanned, and consequently it will be designated f_δ in Step 8.

The assumption that the endpoints of the N records to be scheduled are independent and uniformly distributed about the circumference of the drum guarantees the minimal cost permutation constructed by the MTPT algorithm is a random permutation. It is well known that for a random permutation of N elements, the expected number of cycles is the harmonic number H_N, where

$$H_N = \sum_{k=1}^{N} \frac{1}{k} ,$$

---

* Step 2, and other steps mentioned in this proof refer to the steps of the MTPT scheduling algorithm as enumerated in Appendix B.

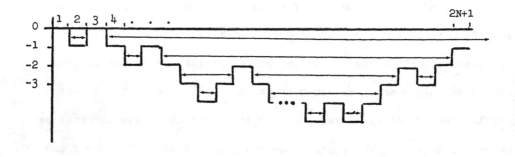

Figure 4.1. Interval sizes as a function of the interval index,

with the inclusion of the pseudo record endpoint f_0.

which is approximately ln N for large N [cf. Knuth, 1969].

Let $||\psi||$ denote the number of cycles in the permutation ψ.

Theorem 4.2.

$$\lim_{N\to\infty} \{||\psi^o||\} = 1$$

Proof: ψ^o is constructed from the random permutation ψ' by looking at the adjacent nodes of a bipartite graph representation of the record endpoints and performing an interchange whenever their arcs form a zero-cost interchange and the nodes are not in the same cycle. ψ' is formed by matching the ith f node with the ith s node, starting from f_δ. Adjacent nodes form a non-zero-cost interchange only if $s_{\psi'(i)}$ comes before f_{i+1}. This situation is equivalent to the path of interval sizes in Fig. 3.2 returning to the x-axis at 2i. From Theorem 3.2 we know

$$Pr\{I_{2i} = I_{crit}\} = \frac{N+1}{(i+1)(N-i+1)} \frac{\binom{N}{i}^2}{\binom{2N}{2i}}$$

and hence as N grows large, the probability that an arbitrary adjacent interchange is a zero-cost interchange approaches one. Hence, with the average number of cycles of ψ^o equal to H_N and the number of adjacent zero-cost interchanges approaching N as N grows large, we see that there is an abundant supply of zero-cost interchanges to connect the disjoint cycles of ψ^o for large N.

5. An Asymptotic Expression for the Expected Difference Between the SLTF and MTPT Algorithms

Before the asymptotic expression between the SLTF and MTPT algorithms can be stated we need the result of the following lemma concerning the behavior of the SLTF drum scheduling algorithm.

Lemma 5.1. The last record of the SLTF drum scheduling algorithm either starts the critical region, or is within the critical region.

Proof: Suppose the last record to be processed in the SLTF drum scheduling algorithm starts outside the critical region. Then the last record starts a non-critical interval and during one of the I_{crit} times the read-write head passes the starting address of the last record it must not have been busy. This is in contradiction to the definition of the SLTF scheduling discipline.

Lemma 5.2.[*] Every SLTF and MTPT schedule passes through the critica region I_{crit} times during the processing of a set of I/O records.

Proof: The critical region contains one or more critical intervals where I_{crit} records share the same interval of the drum's circumference. Clearly no schedule can completely process the set of I/O records without passing through the critical interval at least I_{crit} times. Hence, all that needs to be shown is that neither schedule passes through the critical region more than I_{crit} times.

Consider the last record processed by the SLTF algorithm. Lemma 5.1 requires that it begin in the critical region. Now suppose the SLTF schedule passes through the critical region more than I_{crit} times; then on some revolution the drum must be latent while passing through the critical region. Again we have a contradiction; the SLTF scheduling algorithm does not allow us to pass by the starting address of the last record, or any record, without beginning to process it. In the original article [Chapter 4] the MTPT schedule is shown to process a set of records in less time than any other schedule and hence it cannot pass the critical region more than I_{crit} times either.

---

[*] This Lemma is a stronger case of a theorem first proved by Stone and Fuller [1971].

We can now state the central theorem of this article. Let $E[X]$ denote the mean, or expected value, of the random variable X.

Theorem 5.1. Let N be a positive integer, and if the endpoints of a set of N I/O records are independent random variables uniformly distributed about the drum's circumference

$$\lim_{N\to\infty} E\left[C(\psi_{SLTF}) - C(\psi_{MTPT})\right] = E\left[\text{record length, modulo 1}\right] \quad (5.1)$$

Proof: From theorem 4.1 we know a MTPT schedule terminates at the end of the critical region, for N sufficiently large; Lemma 5.1 guarantees that the last record processed in an SLTF schedule begins within the critical region. Moreover, Theorem 3.3 showed that the width of the critical region goes to zero as $N \to \infty$. Lemma 5.2 assures us that both the SLTF and MTPT schedules pass through the critical region I_{crit} times, so the SLTF schedule must be longer than the MTPT by the expected distance of the finishing address of the last record from the critical region, i.e. the length of the last record modulo the circumference of the drum.

The assumption that all the endpoints of the N I/O requests are independent and uniformly distributed about the drum's circumference implies that the starting and finishing address of a particular record are independent. While this leaves us some freedom to choose a model of drum record length, it leaves us no freedom to model the length of the I/O records, modulo 1; they must be random variables uniformly distributed between 0 and 1. Hence, $E[\text{record length, modulo 1}] = 1/2$ and we could replace the right side of Eq. (5.1) by 1/2, a much simpler expression. In the next section, however, we will discuss generalizations to Theorem 5.1 that suggest the expected value of the record length, modulo the drum circumference, is a more meaningful expression than simply 1/2.

6.   Empirical Observations and Concluding Remarks

Although this article derives an asymptotic expression for the
difference in the MTPT and SLTF drum scheduling algorithms, it leaves
two related and important questions largely unanswered: (i) how does
the difference in MTPT and SLTF schedules look for practical, not
necessarily large, values of N, and (ii) what happens when the two endpoint
of a record are not independent random variables? Analytic solutions
have not yet been found for these questions, but Fig. 6.1 does provide
an empirical answer. The curves of Fig. 6.1 are the result of a Monte
Carlo simulation [Appendix A] and each square in the figure is the
sample mean of the difference in total processing time between MTPT and
SLTF schedules for $10^5/N$ sets of N I/O requests. Figure 6.1 shows that
when the endpoints are independently distributed around the circumference
of the drum, the expected difference in the two schedules is over half
of its asymptotic value for $N > 6$. The other curves in Fig. 6.1 show
the difference in the two schedules for other assumptions that may be of
practical interest. The curves labeled "exp., $\frac{1}{2}$" and "exp., $\frac{1}{4}$" assume
the starting addresses are uniformly distributed about the circumference
of the drum and the record lengths are drawn from an exponential
distribution with means of 1/2 and 1/4 respectively; these assumptions
accurately model the I/O requests for at least one measured system [see
Fig. 2.1 in Chapter 2]. The top curve also assumes the starting
addresses are randomly distributed around the drum, but assumes the
lengths of all records are exactly 1/2 of a drum revolution.

Figure 6.1 suggests that Theorem 5.1 is more general than just for
the case where the endpoints of all the records are independent random
variables uniformly distributed around the drum. Both the set of records

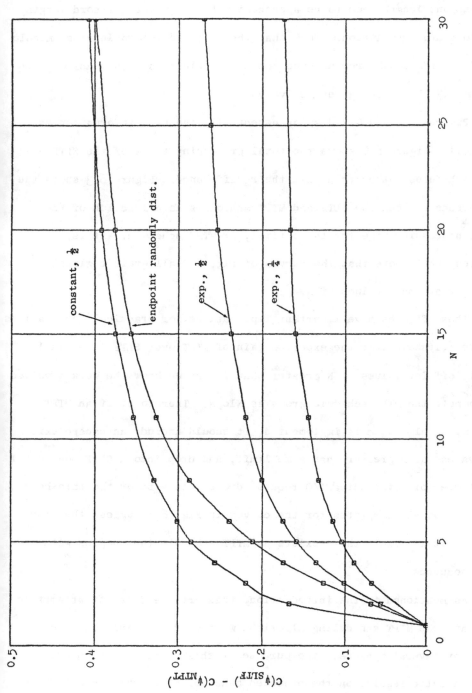

Figure 6.1. Mean difference between the total processing times of SLTF and MTPT schedules.

whose lengths are exponentially distributed as well as the set of records of constant length seem to be approaching their expected record length, modulo a drum revolution. Note that the expected record lengths, modulo 1, of records drawn from an exponential distribution with means 0.5 and 0.25 are .3435 and .2313 respectively.

Figures 6.2 and 6.3 display essentially the same information as Fig. 6.1. Figure 6.2 shows the total processing times of the SLTF and MTPT schedules rather than just their difference. Figure 6.3 shows the difference between the SLTF and MTPT schedules as a fraction of the total processing time for the optimal, or MTPT schedule. It is interesting to note that the curves of Fig. 6.3 all exhibit global maximums at small values of N.

These figures have important implications for practical applications Figure 6.1 shows that the expected gain of MTPT over SLTF essentially levels off for values of N greater than 10 and we know the work involved to compute the MTPT schedule grows as NlogN. Therefore, if an MTPT scheduling algorithm is implemented, it should include an escape exit for values of N greater than some limit, and drop into a SLTF mode until the number of outstanding I/O request drops safely below the threshold. The horizontal asymptotes for the curves in Fig. 6.1 suggest that for large N it is likely there exists an MTPT schedule that begins with an SLTF sequence.

As mentioned in the introduction, this article does not attempt to evaluate the MTPT scheduling algorithm with random arrivals. This is done for several reasons: the purpose of this article is to present some analytic results on the expected behavior of the MTPT and SLTF schedules and these results do not easily generalize to situations with

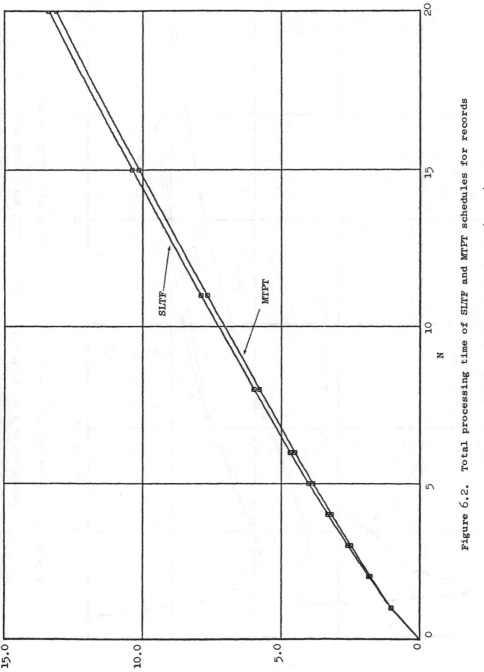

Figure 6.2. Total processing time of SLTF and MTPT schedules for records

with exponentially distributed lengths ($\mu = 2$).

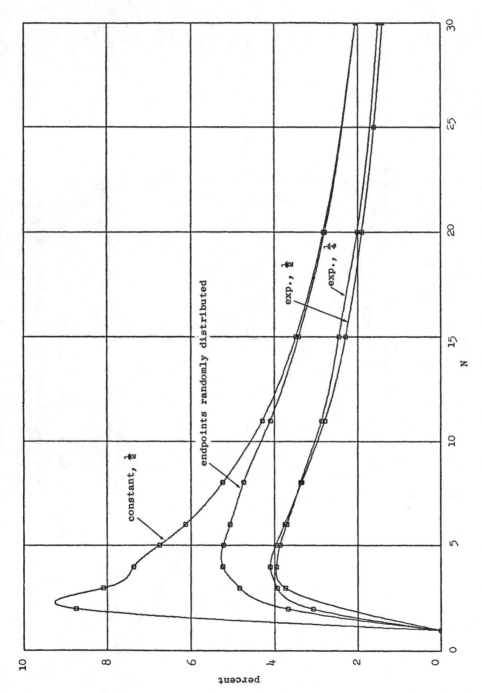

Figure 6.3. Mean difference between the total processing times of SLTF and MTPT schedules as a percentage of the optimal, MTPT, processing time.

random arrivals and moreover applications exist where there are bulk arrivals of requests to the drum or where the requests must be serviced in groups and for these applications an analysis that assumes N requests in a queue just prior to servicing is more appropriate than an analysis that assumes individual, random arrivals of I/O requests.

An example of a situation where I/O requests arrive at random but are best serviced in clusters is a computer system in which the strategy for initiating I/O service is to schedule all the outstanding I/O requests for a device whenever the device completes a previous service interval or is idle. This policy is appropriate in systems where there is insufficient communication between the central and I/O processors to allow incremental scheduling or in systems where the overhead to reschedule after every I/O completion is too costly. File organizations that allow a logical record to be fragmented into several physical records can result in drums experiencing arrivals of blocks of I/O requests rather than seeing only individual I/O request arrivals.

Moving-head disks are devices that may be able to use a MTPT schedule to greatest advantage. In general, the waiting time of an I/O request at a moving-head disk consists largely of alternating intervals of head movement time and service time on cylinders other than the cylinder of the request. A MTPT schedule would minimize the total processing times spent in head positions other than the one on which the I/O request is waiting. A MTPT schedule should show the greatest gains over an SLTF schedule if the number of I/O requests per cylinder is in the region of greatest difference between the MTPT and SLTF schedules, i.e. $2 < N < 10$.

Chapter 6

RANDOM ARRIVALS AND MTPT DISK SCHEDULING DISCIPLINES

This article investigates the application of minimal-total-
processing-time (MTPT) scheduling disciplines to rotating storage units
when random arrival of requests is allowed. Fixed-head drum and moving-
head disk storage units are considered and particular emphasis is placed
on the relative merits of the MTPT scheduling discipline with respect to
the shortest-latency-time-first (SLTF) scheduling discipline. The data
presented are the results of simulation studies. Situations are
discovered in which the MTPT discipline is superior to the SLTF
discipline, and situations are also discovered in which the opposite is
true.

An implementation of the MTPT scheduling algorithm is presented and
the computational requirements of the algorithm are discussed. It is
shown that the sorting procedure is the most time consuming phase of the
algorithm.

1.   Introduction

This article looks at the practical implications of the drum scheduling discipline introduced in Chapter 4. The scope of this paper will include the classes of rotating storage devices shown in Fig. 1.1. Let the device in Fig. 1.1(a) be called a fixed-head file drum, or just fixed-head drum; the essential characteristics of a fixed-head drum is that there is a read-write head for every track of the drum's surface and consequently there is no need to move the heads among several tracks. Furthermore, the drum in Fig. 1.1(a) allows information to be stored in blocks, or records, of arbitrary length and arbitrary starting addresses on the surface of the drum. Physical implementations of a fixed-head file drum may differ substantially from Fig. 1.1(a); for instance, a disk, rather than a drum may be used as the recording surface, or the device may not rotate physically at all, but be a shift register that circulates its information electronically.

The other type of rotating storage unit that will be studied here is the moving-head file disk, or simply moving-head disk, the only difference between a moving-head disk and a fixed-head drum is that a particular read-write head of a moving-head disk is shared among several tracks, and the time associated with repositioning the read-write head over a new track cannot be ignored. A set of tracks accessible at a given position of the read-write arm is called a cylinder. Figure 1.1(b) shows the moving-head disk implemented as a moving-head drum, but this is just to simplify the drawing and reemphasize that 'fixed-head drum' and 'moving-head disk' are generic terms and are not meant to indicate a specific physical implementation.

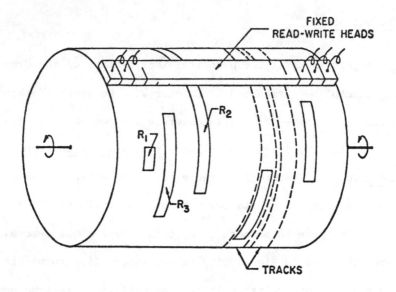

(a) A fixed-head drum storage unit.

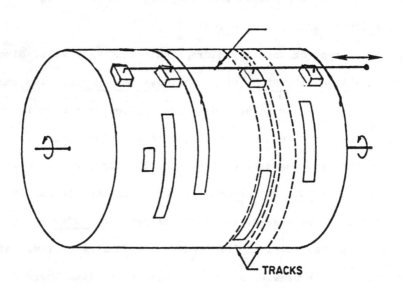

(b) A moving-head drum (disk) storage unit.

Figure 1.1.   Storage units having rotational delays.

The analysis and scheduling of rotating storage units in computer systems has received considerable attention in the past several years [cf. Denning, 1967; Coffman, 1969; Abate et al., 1968; Abate and Dubner, 1969; Teorey and Pinkerton, 1972; Seaman et al., 1966; Frank, 1969]. In these papers, first-in-first-out (FIFO) and shortest-latency-time-first (SLTF) are the only two scheduling disciplines discussed for fixed-head drums or intra-cylinder scheduling in moving-head disks; in [Chapter 4], however, a new scheduling discipline is introduced for devices with rotational delays, or latency. This new discipline finds schedules for sets of I/O requests that minimize the total processing time for the sets of I/O requests. Moreover, if we let N be the number of I/O requests to be serviced, the original article presents a minimal-total-processing-time (MTPT)* scheduling algorithm that has a computational complexity on the order of NlogN, the same complexity as an SLTF scheduling algorithm.

Several other articles have been written since the MTPT scheduling discipline was originally presented, and they develop upper bounds and asymptotic expressions for differences between the SLTF and MTPT scheduling disciplines [Stone and Fuller, 1971; Chapter 5]. Like the original paper, however, these articles address the combinatorial, or static, problem of scheduling a set of I/O requests; new requests are

---

* The algorithm was called an optimal drum scheduling algorithm in the original article, but this article refers to the algorithm as the minimal-total-processing-time (MTPT) drum scheduling algorithm. This name is more mnemonic and recognizes that other drum scheduling algorithms may be optimal for other optimality criteria.

not allowed to arrive during the processing of the original set of I/O requests. Although the MTPT scheduling discipline can always process a set of I/O requests in less time than the SLTF scheduling discipline, or any other discipline, we cannot extrapolate that the MTPT discipline will be best in the more complex situation when I/O requests are allowed to arrive at random intervals. On the other hand, even though the SLTF discipline is never as much as a drum revolution slower than the MTPT discipline when processing a set of I/O requests [Stone and Fuller, 1971], we are not guaranteed the SLTF discipline will take less than a drum revolution longer to process a collection of I/O requests when random arrivals are permitted.

Unfortunately, the analysis of the MTPT scheduling discipline presented in the previous articles does not generalize to MTPT scheduling disciplines with random arrivals. Moreover, attempts to apply techniques of queueing theory to MTPT schedules has met with little success. For these reasons, this article presents the empirical results of a simulator written to investigate the behavior of computer systems with storage units having rotational delays [Appendix A].

Another important question not answered by the earlier papers is what are the computational requirements of the MTPT scheduling algorithm? Although the MTPT scheduling algorithm is known to enjoy a computational complexity on the order of NlogN, where N is the number of I/O requests to be scheduled, nothing has been said about the actual amount of computation time required to compute MTPT schedules. MTPT scheduling disciplines will be of little practical interest if it takes NlogN seconds to compute MTPT schedules, when current rotating storage devices have periods of revolution on the order of 10 to 100 milliseconds. No obvious, unambiguous measure of computation time exists, but this article will present the computation time required for a specific implementation of the MTPT scheduling algorithm, given in Appendix B, on a specific machine, an IBM 360/91.

The next section, Sec. 2, discusses the implementation of the MTPT scheduling algorithm that will be used in this article and presents the computation time required by this algorithm, and Sec. 3 introduces two modifications to the original MTPT algorithm. Section 4 shows the results of using the SLTF and MTPT scheduling disciplines on fixed-head drums where a range of assumptions are made concerning the size and distribution of I/O records. Section 5 continues to present the results of the simulation study but considers moving-head disks. We will see situations with fixed-head drums and moving-head disks, where the MTPT disciplines offer an advantage over the SLTF discipline; and the converse will also be seen to be true in other situations. The ultimate decision as to whether or not to implement a MTPT discipline for use in a computer system will depend on the distribution of record sizes seen by the storage units as well as the arrival rate of the I/O requests; the discussion in the following sections will hopefully provide the insight necessary to make this decision.

2. An Implementation of the Original MTPT Drum Scheduling Algorithm

In this section we will try to add some quantitative substance to the significant, but qualitative, remark that the MTPT drum scheduling algorithm has an asymptotic growth rate of NlogN.

An informal, English, statement of the original MTPT scheduling algorithm is included in Appendix B, along with a well-documented copy

of an implementation of the MTPT scheduling algorithm, called MTPTO.
This implementation of the MTPT algorithm has been done in conjunction
with a larger programming project, and as a result two important
constraints were accepted. First, MTPTO is written to maximize clarity
and to facilitate debugging; the primary objective was not to write the
scheduling procedure to minimize storage space or execution time.
Secondly, the algorithm is written in FORTRAN because this is the
language of the simulator with which it cooperates [Appendix A]. A
glance at MTPTO, and its supporting subroutines: FINDCY, MERGE, and
SORT, shows that a language with a richer control structure, such as
ALGOL or PL/I, would have substantially simplified the structure of the
procedures.

The results of this section were found with the use of a program
measurement facility, called PROGLOOK, developed by R. Johnson and
T. Johnston [1971]. PROGLOOK periodically* interrupts the central
processor and saves the location of the instruction counter. The
histograms of this section are the results of sampling the program
counter as MTPTO is repetitively executed, and then the number of times
the program counter is caught within a 32 byte interval is plotted as a
function of the interval's starting address.

Figure 2.1 is the result of PROGLOOK monitoring MTPTO as it
schedules N requests where N = 2, 3, 4, 6, 8, 10, 13, and 16. The
abscissa of all the histograms is main storage locations, in ascending
order and 32 bytes per line, and the ordinate is the relative fraction

---

* For all the results described here, PROGLOOK interrupted MTPTO every
  500 microseconds.

Legend for Computation Time Histograms of Figure 2.1

1. Initialize data structures.

2. Find f_δ.

3. Redefine record endpoints relative to f_δ.

4. Construct the minimal cost, no-crossover permutation.

5. Find the membership of the cycle of ψ'.

6. Transform the permutation ψ' to the permutation ψ^o.

7. Transform the permutation ψ^o to the single-cycle permutation ϕ^o.

8. Construct MTPT schedule from ϕ^o.

9. Subroutine FINDCY: find cycle in which specified node is a member.

10. Subroutine MERGE: merge two cycles.

11. Subroutine SORT: an implementation of Shellsort.

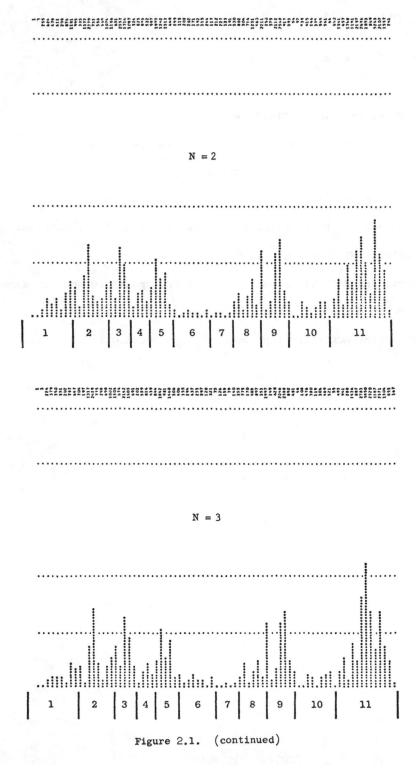

N = 2

N = 3

Figure 2.1. (continued)

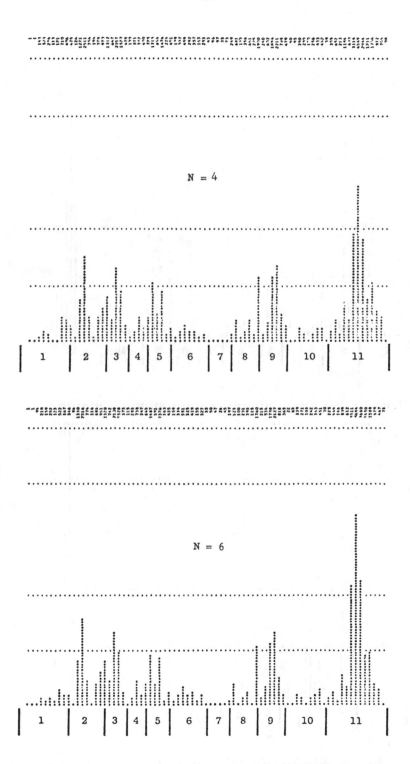

Figure 2.1. Computation time histograms for the MTPTO algorithm.

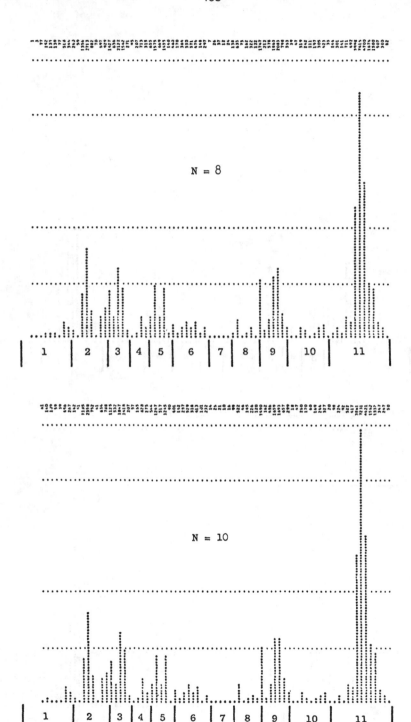

Figure 2.1. (continued)

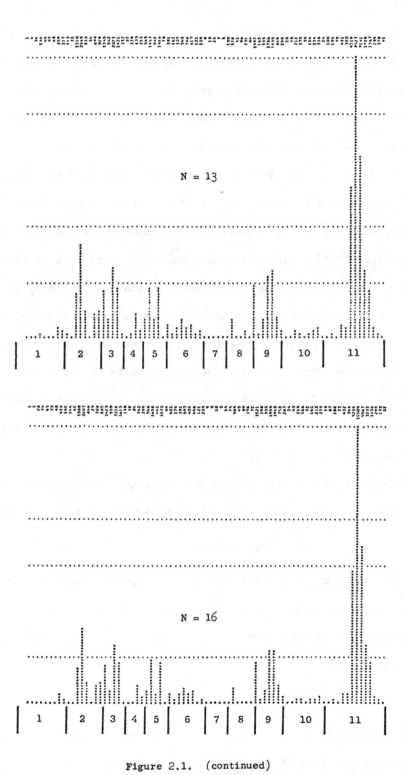

Figure 2.1. (continued)

of time MTPTO spends in an interval in order to schedule a set of N requests. The scales of the histograms in Fig. 2.1 are selected so that an interval whose computation time grows in direct (linear) proportion to N will remain a constant height in all the histograms. Figure 2.1 illustrates that only the sort procedure is growing at a rate perceptively faster than linear; for N in the range of 2 to 16 the rest of MTPTO experiences a linear, or less than linear, growth rate.

The particular sorting algorithm used in MTPTO is Shellsort [Shell, 1959; Hibbard, 1963] because, for most machines, Shellsort is the fastest of the commonly known sorting algorithms for small N [Hibbard, 1963]. If MTPTO is regularly applied to sets of records larger than 10, quicksort, or one of its derivatives [Hoare, 1961; van Emden, 1970 A,B] may provide faster sorting. Whenever the algorithm is used for N more than three or four, Fig. 2.1 indicates that initially sorting the starting and ending addresses of the I/O requests is the most time consuming of the eleven major steps in MTPTO.

The upper curve of Fig. 2.2 is the expected execution time of MTPTO as a function of queue size. Note that it is well approximated by

$$100N + 50 \quad \text{microseconds}$$

for $N < 8$. For $N \geq 8$ the sorting algorithm begins to exhibit its greater than linear growth rate. The lower curve in Fig. 2.2 is the expected execution time for MTPTO minus the time it spends sorting; it can be approximated by

$$50N + 50 \quad \text{microseconds.}$$

The curves of Fig. 2.2 suggest an implementation of MTPTO might maintain a sorted list of the initial and final addresses of the I/O

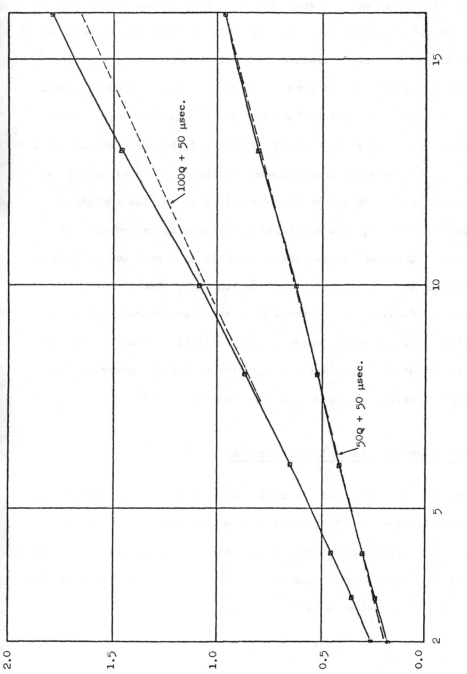

Figure 2.2. Computation time of MTPTO and MTPTO without sort phase, as a function of queue size.

requests at all times: techniques exist to add, or delete, I/O requests from the list in $O(\log N)$ steps [Adel'son-Vel-skiy and Landis, 1962]. Then a schedule could be found more quickly after it is requested since there would be no need to execute the costly sorting step.

Figure 2.2 can only be used as a rough guide to execution times since it is very sensitive to implementation. In particular, these statistics were collected on an IBM 360/91 and they must be appropriately scaled for processors that are slower, or faster. The algorithm is implemented in FORTRAN and has been compiled by the IBM FORTRAN H compiler[*] [IBM, 1971]. An examination of the machine instructions produced by this compiler indicates a factor of 2 or 4 could be gained by a careful implementation in machine language. Furthermore, the starting and final values of the I/O requests are represented as double precision, floating point numbers, and practical implementations of MTPTO would very likely limit the starting and ending addresses to a small set of integers, 128 or 256 for example.

3. Two other MTPT scheduling algorithms

The original MTPT drum scheduling algorithm whose implementation was just discussed in the previous section, is not the only MTPT scheduling algorithm that may be of practical significance; for example, consider Fig. 3.1. Application of the MTPTO scheduling algorithm shows the schedule it constructs is

$$4, 3, 5, 1, 2. \tag{3.1}$$

---

[*] During compilation, the maximum code optimization was requested, i.e.

// EXEC FORTHCLG,PARM.FORT='OPT=2'

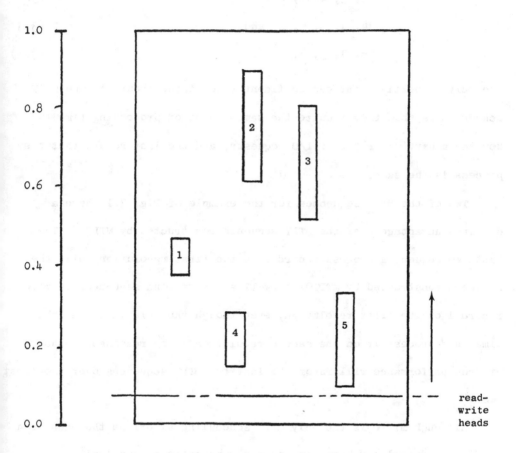

Figure 3.1. An example with four MTPT sequences.

This is a MTPT schedule, but then so are the sequences

$$5, 3, 4, 1, 2; \tag{3.2}$$

$$4, 1, 3, 5, 2; \text{ and} \tag{3.3}$$

$$5, 1, 3, 4, 2. \tag{3.4}$$

The only properties that can confidently be stated about all the MTPT schedules is that they require the same amount of processing time to service a particular set of I/O requests, and the last record that they process is the same.

Two of the MTPT sequences for the example of Fig. 3.1 share a distinct advantage over the MTPT sequence constructed by MTPT0. The last two sequences process record 1 on the first revolution while the sequence constructed by MTPT0, as well as the second sequence, overlook record 1 on the first revolution, even though they are latent at the time, and process it on the second revolution. Any reasonable measure of drum performance will favor the last two MTPT sequences over the first two.

Although MTPT0 is the only MTPT scheduling algorithm that has been studied in detail and known to enjoy a computational complexity of NlogN, the above example indicates that other MTPT algorithms may be of interest. For this reason, two other MTPT scheduling algorithms have been implemented and are listed following the MTPT0 algorithm in Appendix B.

The MTPT1 procedure corrects the deficit in the MTPT0 procedure just illustrated; MTPT1 uses MTPT0 to find a MTPT sequence and then traces through the schedule looking for records, like record 1 in our example, that can be processed at an earlier revolution without disturbing the processing of any of the other records. No claim is made here that MTPT1 is an NlogN process, it is used here to indicate how much better improved MTPT algorithms can be expected to be over MTPT0.

The third MTPT algorithm studied here, MTPT2, is what might be called the shortest-latency-time-first MTPT scheduling algorithm. Like MTPT1 it used MTPT0 to find a MTPT sequence for the I/O requests currently in need of service. Then, it sees if the first record in the MTPT sequence is closest to the read-write heads, if it is not it deletes the record with the shortest potential latency from the set of requests, applies the MTPT0 algorithm to the remaining I/O requests and checks if this new sequence is a MTPT sequence by comparing its processing time to the processing time of the MTPT0 sequence for the N requests. If not, it continues searching for the nearest record that starts a MTPT sequence. As in the case for the MTPT1 algorithm, the MTPT2 algorithm is not an NlogN process, the purpose of discussing it here is to see how the MTPT2 scheduling discipline compares with the other MTPT disciplines, as well as the SLTF discipline. In the example of Fig. 3.1, sequence (3.4) is the MTPT2 sequence and (3.3) is the MTPT1 sequence.

4. Random Arrivals and Fixed-Head Drums

We will now compare the performance of the MTPT0, MTPT1, MTPT2, and SLTF scheduling disciplines when they are used on a fixed-head drum (Fig. 1.1(a)) and I/O requests are allowed to arrive at random points in time. Before proceeding with the results, however, some discussion is needed to clarify the models of drum and record behavior that are used in the simulations.

As successive I/O requests arrive for service, some assumptions
must be made about the location of the starting and ending addresses of
the new I/O request. In at least one real computer system, it is
reasonable to model the starting addresses of successive I/O requests as
independent random variables uniformly distributed around the circumference of the drum, and to model the length of the records as exponentially distributed random variables with a mean of about one third of the
drum's circumference [Chapter 2].

The other assumption made here is that the arrival of I/O requests
form a Poisson process. In other words, the inter-arrival time of
successive I/O requests are independent random variables with the density
function

$$f(t) = \lambda e^{-\lambda t} , \qquad \lambda > 0 \text{ and } t > 0.$$

A more realistic assumption might be to assume that the drum is part of
a computer system with a finite degree of multiprogramming on the order
of 4 to 10. So little is known about the relative merits of SLTF and
MTPT disciplines, however, it is prudent to keep the model as simple as
possible until we have a basic understanding of these scheduling
disciplines.

Several other minor assumptions must be made, and at each point an
attempt was made to keep the model as simple as possible. The time
required to compute the scheduling sequence is assumed to be insignifican
the endpoints are allowed to be real numbers in the interval [0,1), the
period of revolution of the drum will be assumed constant and equal to τ,
no distinction is made between reading and writing on the drum, and no
attempt is made to model the time involved in electronically switching
the read-write heads.

A number of different measures of drum performance are reasonable. In this section, however, three measures will be used: expected waiting time, the standard deviation of the waiting time, and expected duration of drum busy periods. I/O waiting time will be defined here in the common queueing theory sense; that is, the time from the arrival of an I/O request until that I/O request has completed service. Let a drum be defined by busy when it is not idle, in other words the drum is busy when it is latent as well as when it is actually transmitting data.

These three measures of performance will be shown as a fraction of ρ, where ρ is the ratio of the expected record transfer time to the expected interarrival time. Use of the normalized variable ρ assists in the comparison of simulations with records of different mean lengths and always provides an asymptote at $\rho = 1$. In the figures in this section, ρ is shown from 0 to .75. The statistics of drum performance for $\rho > .75$ blow up very fast, and moreover the expense required to run simulations of meaningful precision for large ρ outweighed the possible insight that might be gained. Observed ρ's for operational computer systems are commonly in the range of .1 to .5 [cf. Bottomly, 1970].

The precision of the summary statistics of the following simulations is described in detail in [Appendix A]. All the points on the graphs in this article represent the result of simulation experiments that are run until 100,000 I/O requests have been serviced; this number of simulated events proved sufficient for the purposes of this article. The sample mean of the I/O waiting times, for example, are random variables with a standard deviation less than .002 for $\rho = .1$ and slightly more than .1 for $\rho = .75$.

The corresponding statistics for the expected duration of busy intervals are

$$\sigma_{\overline{x}} = .005 \qquad \text{for } \rho = .1,$$

$$\sigma_{\overline{x}} = .1 \qquad \text{for } \rho = .55 .$$

The variability of the simulation points is often hard to see, but plots of the residuals at the bottom of the graphs often show the experimental error.

All the graphs in this section are really two sets of curves. First, they show the measure of performance as a function of ρ for the four scheduling disciplines studied: MTPT0, MTPT1, MTPT2, and SLTF; and then on the same graph the difference between SLTF and each of the three MTPT disciplines is shown. The residual curves more clearly demonstrate the relative performance of the scheduling disciplines than can be seen from directly studying the original curves. Some of the curves, particularly the residual curves, do not go all the way to the right hand side of the graph; this is simply because it was felt that the marginal gain in insight that might be obtained from the additional points did not justify the additional cost.

Figure 4.1 shows the mean I/O waiting times for a fixed-head drum servicing record with lengths drawn from an exponential distribution with a mean of 1/2, i.e. $\mu = 2$ and density function

$$f(t) = \mu e^{-\mu t} , \qquad t > 0.$$

Figure 4.1 displays an unexpected result, the SLTF and MTPT2 curves lie directly on top of each other to within the accuracy of the simulation. MTPT0 and MTPT1 perform progressively poorer than MTPT2 and SLTF as the arrival rate of I/O requests is increased. MTPT0, MTPT1, and MTPT2 show increasingly smaller mean waiting times; this is

consistent with the observation that MTPT0 is an 'arbitrary' MTPT
schedule while MTPT2, and to a lesser extent MTPT1, look at several MTPT
schedules in the process of deciding how to sequence the set of I/O
requests. We will see in all the figures that follow in this section,
and the next, that MTPT0, MTPT1, and MTPT2 consistently perform in the
same order of performance shown in Fig. 4.1. The observation that
MTPT0 and MTPT1 are poorer scheduling disciplines than the SLTF
disciplines for heavily loaded drums is not too surprising. It is very
rare for large ρ that all the current requests will be processed before
any new request arrives. When an additional request does arrive, a new
MTPT sequence must be calculated and the non-robust nature of the MTPT0
algorithm suggests there will be little resemblance in the two sequences.

Figure 4.2 shows the standard deviation of the I/O waiting time for
a fixed-head drum and records with lengths exponentially distributed
with $\mu = 2$, i.e. the same situation as Fig. 4.1. As in Fig. 4.1, the
SLTF and MTPT2 sequences behave very similarly except that the MTPT2
curve is below the SLTF by a small, but distinct, amount, indicating
that the MTPT2 discipline, while providing the same mean waiting time
exhibits a smaller variance, or standard deviation, than does the SLTF
discipline.

Figures 4.3 and 4.4 show the mean waiting time for drums with
records having exponentially distributed records lengths with means of
1/3 and 1/6 respectively. These figures reinforce our general
impressions from Fig. 4.1. The relatively poor performance of the MTPT0
and MTPT1 disciplines becomes more pronounced as the mean record size
decreases; this follows from the observation that the number of MTPT
sequences, for a given ρ, increases as μ increases. We can see this by

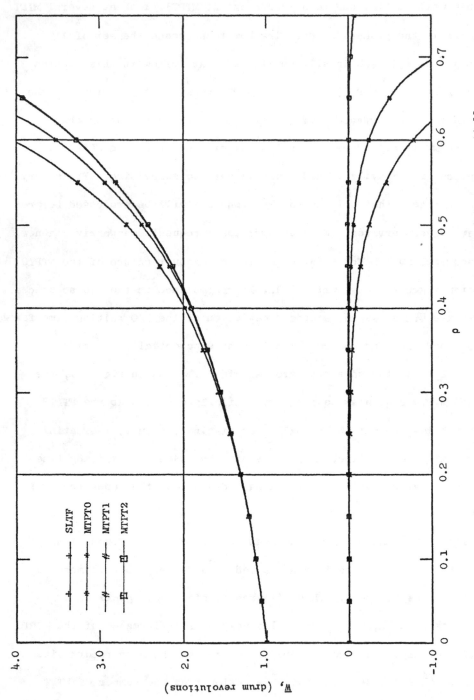

Figure 4.1. The expected waiting time when the records are exponentially distributed records with μ = 2.

211

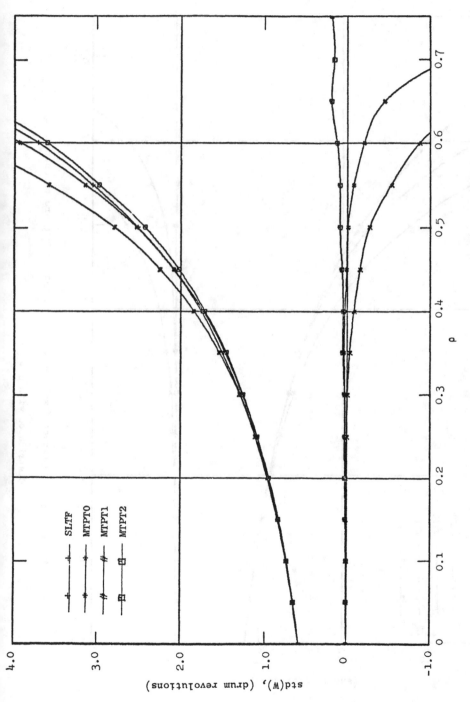

Figure 4.2. Standard deviation of the waiting time for exponentially
distributed records with μ = 2.

212

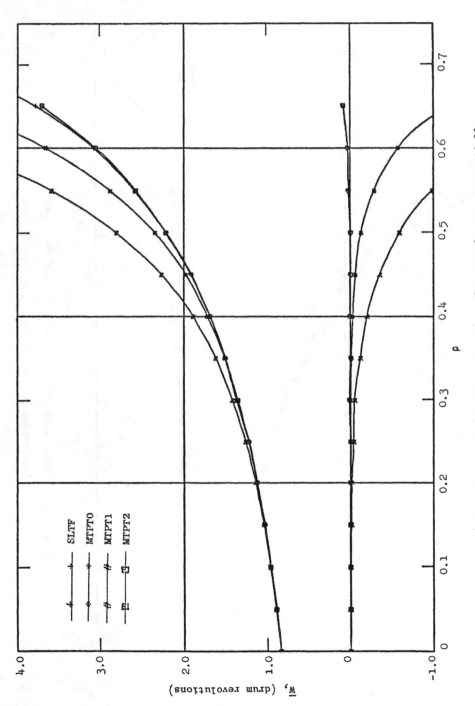

Figure 4.3. The expected waiting time when the records are exponentially distributed with $\mu = 3$.

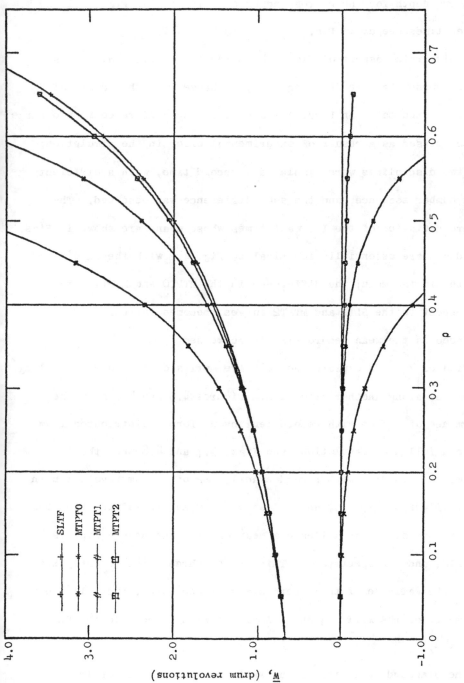

Figure 4.4. The expected waiting time when the records are exponentially distributed with $\mu = 6$.

applying Little's formula, $\overline{L} = \lambda\overline{W}$, or equivalently, $\overline{L} = \rho\overline{W}\mu$. Hence, the mean queue depth for the corresponding ρ coordinate in Figs. 4.1 and 4.4 is three times deeper in Fig. 4.4 than in Fig. 4.1.

A disturbing aspect of Fig. 4.4 is that the MTPT2 sequence is slightly worse than the SLTF sequence, a change from the identical performance indicated in Figs. 4.1 and 4.3. The difference is too large to be dismissed as a result of experimental error in the simulation; these two disciplines were simulated a second time, with a different random number sequence, and the same difference was observed. The standard deviation of the I/O wait times whose means are shown in Figs. 4.3 and 4.4 are essentially identical to Fig. 4.2 with the same trend exhibited in the mean; the difference in the MTPT0 and MTPT1 curves, with respect to the SLTF and MTPT2 curves, becomes increasingly pronounced as the mean record size is decreased.

Figures 4.5-4.8 explore the relative merits of the four scheduling disciplines along another direction. Figures 4.5 and 4.6 show the performance of a drum with record lengths uniformly distributed from zero to a full drum revolution, and Figs. 4.7 and 4.8 show the performance of a drum with records exactly 1/2 of a drum revolution in length. Figures 4.1, 4.5, and 4.7 show the mean I/O waiting time for drums with records that all have a mean of 1/2, but have variances of 1/4, 1/12, and 0 respectively. This set of three curves clearly shows that as the variance of the record sizes is decreased, the relative performance of the MTPT sequences improves with respect to the SLTF discipline.

The standard deviation of the waiting times for uniformly distributed record lengths, Fig. 4.6, and constant record lengths,

215

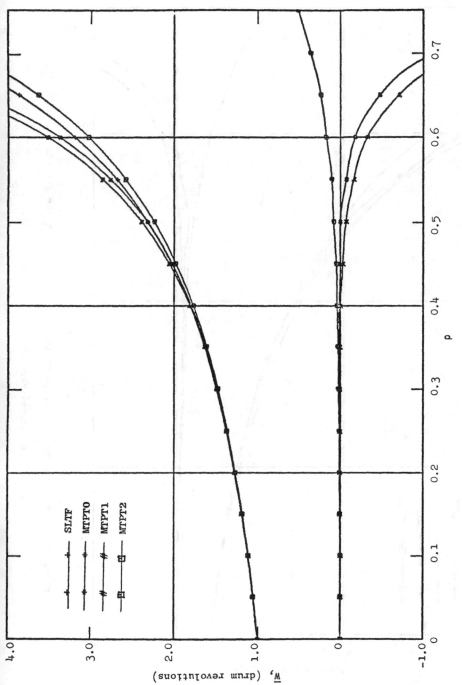

Figure 4.5. The expected waiting time when the records are uniformly distributed from zero to a full drum revolution.

216

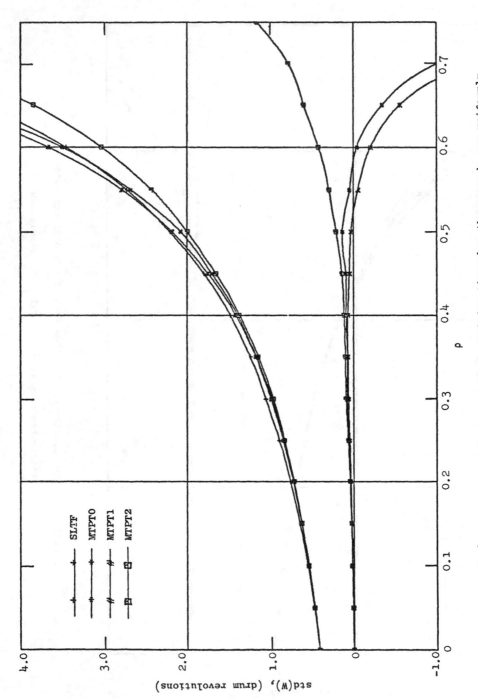

Figure 4.6. The standard deviation of the waiting time when the records are uniformly

distributed between zero and a full drum revolution.

217

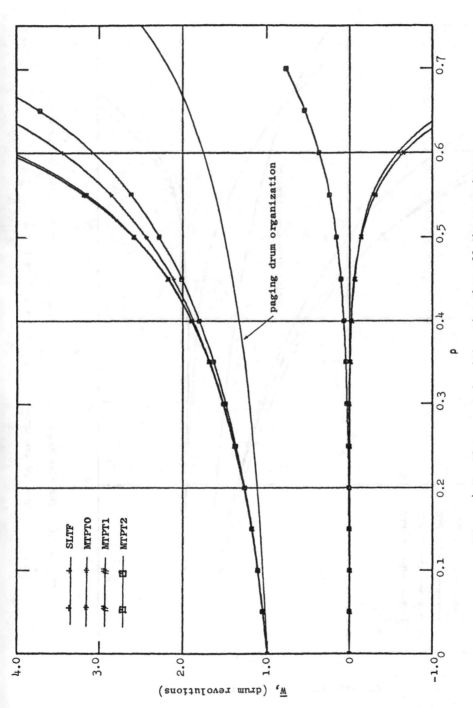

Figure 4.7. The expected waiting time when all the records are 1/2 the drum's circumference in length.

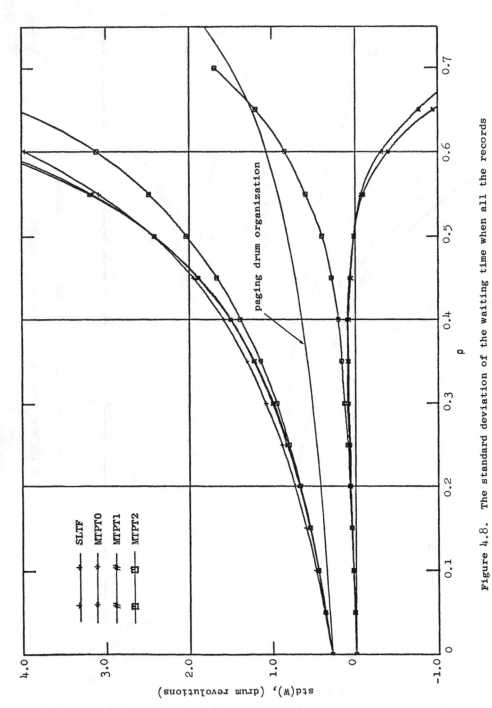

Figure 4.8. The standard deviation of the waiting time when all the records are 1/2 the drum's circumference in length.

Fig. 4.7, show an even more impressive improvement in the MTPT schedules
as the variance of the record lengths are decreased. Clearly the
advantage of MTPT disciplines is enhanced as the variation in the
lengths of records is decreased.

Figures 4.8 and 4.9 include another smooth curve as well as the
four curves already discussed. These curves show the mean and standard
deviation of a drum organized as a paging drum, with 2 pages per track.
There is no need to simulate a paging drum since Skinner [1967] and
Coffman [1969] derived the exact formula for the mean waiting time and
Chapter 3 derived the standard deviation. The paging drum shows a
pronounced improvement over any of the four scheduling disciplines
discussed in this article, and if a drum is only going to service fixed-
size records, Figs. 4.7 and 4.8 indicate the pronounced advantages in
organizing the drum as a paging drum.

Figures 4.9 and 4.10 illustrate another measure of drum performance,
the mean drum busy interval. Since a MTPT scheduling discipline
minimizes the total processing time of the outstanding I/O requests, it
might be suspected the MTPT disciplines will minimize the drum's busy
periods even when random arrivals are allowed. Figure 4.9 shows the
mean drum busy interval for a drum with exponentially distributed
records, $\mu = 2$. The result is surprisingly close to what we might have
guessed from previous combinatorial observations [Chapter 5]. We see
that the expected difference between the MTPT discipline and the SLTF
when no random arrivals are allowed, approached the mean value of the
records' length, modulo the drum circumference, as N gets large. In
other words, for exponentially distributed records, with $\mu = 2$ and the
drum circumference defined to be unity, the mean record length, modulo 1,

220

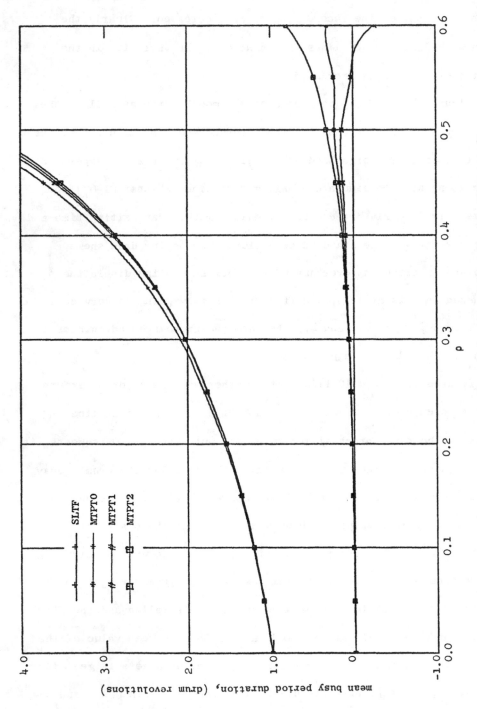

Figure 4.9. The mean duration of the busy intervals when the records are exponentially distributed with μ = 2.

221

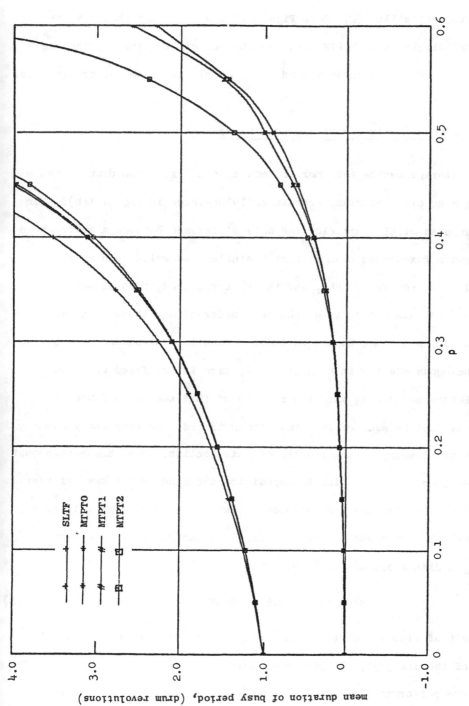

Figure 4.10. The mean duration of the busy intervals when the records are all 1/2 the drum's circumference in length.

For fixed-size records, the mean record length, modulo a drum revolution is still 1/2. Both Figs. 4.9 and 4.10 show that the best of the MTPT disciplines, MTPT2, and the SLTF discipline are approaching a difference of the expected record size, modulo the drum's circumference.

5. Random Arrivals and Moving-Head Disks

A storage device even more common than a fixed-head drum is the moving-head disk, or drum, schematically depicted in Fig. 1.1(b). For the purposes of this article, the only difference between a moving-head disk and a fixed-head drum is that a single read-write head must be shared among several tracks, and the time required to physically move the head between tracks is on the same order of magnitude of a drum revolution, and hence cannot be ignored even in a simple model, as was the analogous electronic head-switching time in the fixed-head drum.

Before proceeding with the results of this section a few more comments must be made on the simulations in order to completely specify conditions leading to the results of this section. Some assumption must be made concerning the time to reposition the head over a new cylinder. Let ΔC be the distance, in cylinders, that the head must travel, then the following expression roughly models the characteristics of the IBM 3330 disk storage unit [IBM, 1971]:

$$\text{seek time} = 0.6 + .0065 \, \Delta C \, . \tag{5.1}$$

Our unit of time in Eq. (5.1) is a disk (drum) revolution, and in the case of the IBM 3330, the period of revolution is 1/60 of a second. The relative performance of the four scheduling disciplines of this article is insensitive to the exact form of Eq. (5.1) and replacing Eq. (5.1) by

$$\text{seek time} = 1 + .07 \ \Delta C,$$

which approximates the IBM 2314 [IBM, 1965] does not change any of the
conclusions of this section.

A decision has to be made concerning the inter-cylinder scheduling
discipline. Although an optimal disk scheduling discipline might
integrate the intra-queue and inter-queue scheduling disciplines, in
this article they will be kept separate. The inter-queue scheduling
discipline chosen for this study is called SCAN, [Denning, 1967] (also
termed LOOK by Teorey and Pinkerton [1972]). SCAN works in the following
way: when a cylinder that the read-write heads are positioned over is
empty, and when there exists another cylinder that has a non-empty queue,
the read-write heads are set in motion toward the new cylinder. Should
more than one cylinder have a non-empty queue of I/O requests the read-
write heads go to the closest one in their preferred direction; the
preferred direction is simply the direction of the last head movement.
This inter-cylinder discipline is called SCAN because the read-write
heads appear to be scanning, or sweeping, the disk surface in alternate
directions.

SCAN gives slightly longer mean waiting times than the SSTF
(shortest-seek-time-first) inter-cylinder scheduling discipline.
However, from Eq. (5.1) we see the bulk of the head movement time is not
a function of distance, and SCAN has the attractive property that it
does not degenerate, as SSTF does, into a 'greedy' mode that effectively
ignores part of the disk when the load of requests becomes very heavy
[Denning, 1967].

An I/O request arriving at a moving-head disk has a third attribute,
in addition to its starting address and length, the cylinder from which

it is requesting service. In the spirit of keeping this model as simple as possible, we will assume that the cylinder address for successive I/O records are independent and uniformly distributed across the total number of cylinders. While no claim is made that this models reality, like the Poisson assumption it simplifies the model considerably and allows us to concentrate on the fundamental properties of the scheduling disciplines. Furthermore, the results of this section are shown as a function of the number of cylinders on the disk, where we let the number of cylinders range from 1 (a fixed-head disk) to 50. Conventional disk storage units have from 200 to 400 cylinders per disk but for any given set of active jobs, only a fraction of the cylinders will have active files. Therefore, the results of this section for disks with 5 and 10 cylinder is likely to be a good indication of the performance of a much larger disk that has active files on 5 to 10 cylinders.

Finally, in all the situations studied here, the records are assumed to be exponentially distributed with a mean of 1/2. This assumption is both simple and realistic and the observations of the previous section for other distributions of record lengths indicates the sensitivity of this assumption.

Figure 5.1 is the mean I/O waiting time for the SLTF, MTPT0, MTPT1 and MTPT2 scheduling disciplines for the disk model just described; the numbers of cylinders per disk include 1, 2, 5, 10, 25 and 50. Note the abscissa is now labeled in arrivals per disk revolution (λ) rather than ρ, and the curves for one cylinder are just the curves of Fig. 4.1, and are included here for comparative purposes. Figure 5.1 shows quite a different result than seen for fixed-head drums of the last section. As the number of cylinders increases, the MTPT disciplines show more and

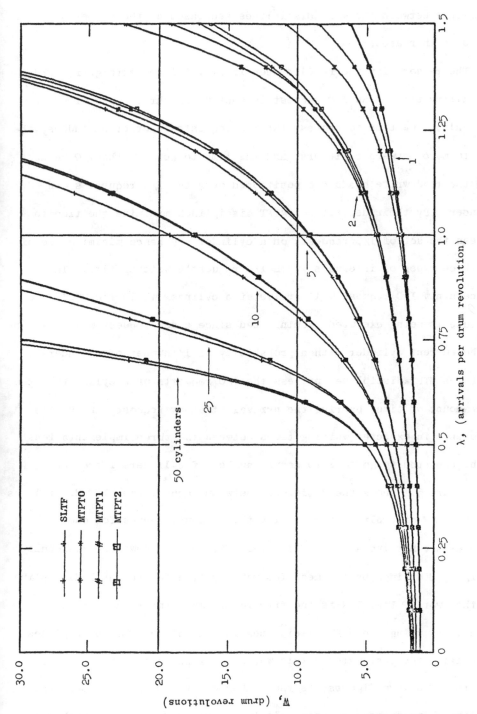

Figure 5.1. The expected waiting time of moving-head disks.

more of an advantage over the SLTF scheduling discipline and also the difference between the MTPT disciplines decreases as the number of cylinders increases.

The reasons for the results seen in Fig. 5.1 are straightforward. The waiting time on an I/O request is made up of three types of intervals: the time to process the I/O requests on other cylinders, the time to move between cylinders, and the time to service the I/O request once the read-write heads are positioned over the I/O request's own cylinder. By their definition, MTPT disciplines minimize the time to process the set of I/O requests on a cylinder and hence minimize one of the three types of intervals in an I/O request's waiting time. The chance a new I/O request will arrive at a cylinder while the MTPT schedule is being executed is minimized since a new request will only go to the current cylinder with a probability of 1/(number of cylinders). All three MTPT disciplines process the I/O requests on a cylinder in the same amount of time, barring the arrival of a new request, and so the difference in expected waiting times between the three implementations can be expected to go to zero as the number of cylinders increases.

Figure 5.2 shows the difference between each of the MTPT disciplines and the SLTF discipline; for clarity the residual curves for one cylinder are not included in Fig. 5.2. Figure 5.3 shows the residuals of Fig. 5.2 divided by the mean I/O waiting time for the SLTF discipline. In other words, Fig. 5.3 is the fractional improvement that can be expected by using the MTPT disciplines instead of the SLTF disciplines. Normalizing the residuals in this way shows a phenomenon not obvious from the first two figures; as the number of cylinders increases, the fractional improvement becomes relatively independent of the number of

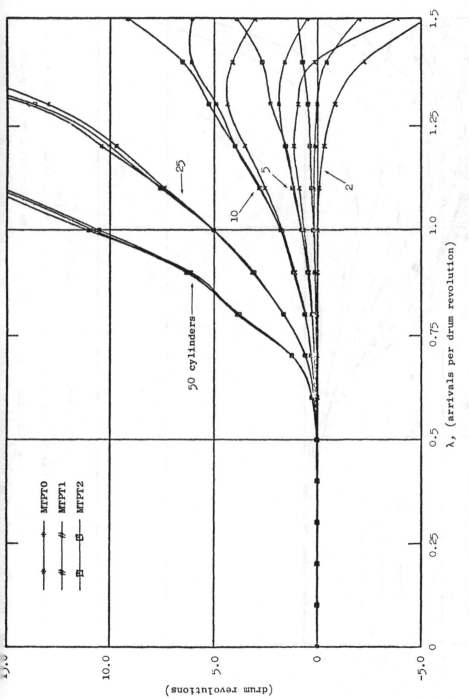

Figure 5.2. The difference between the expected waiting time of a moving-head disk when using the SLTF discipline and a MTPT discipline.

228

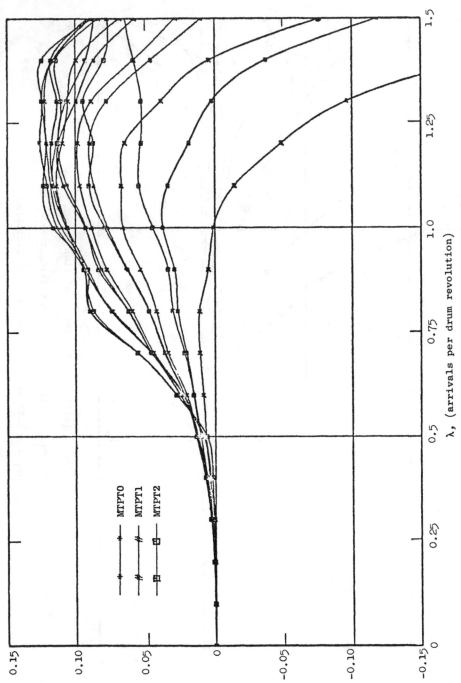

Figure 5.3. The difference between the expected waiting time of moving-head disks when using the SLTF discipline and a MTPT discipline, divided by the $\overline{W}$ for the SLTF discipline.

cylinders and is slightly more than 10 per cent for heavily loaded
situations.

Figure 5.4 shows the standard deviation of the cases shown in Fig.
5.1. The remarks made concerning the mean I/O waiting time apply
unchanged to the standard deviation of the I/O waiting times. The only
additional observation that can be made is that the coefficient of
variation, i.e. the standard deviation divided by the mean, is
decreasing as the number of cylinders increases, and this is independent
of the scheduling discipline used. This would be expected since the I/O
waiting time is made up of intervals of processing time at other
cylinders that are independent, random variables, and from the property
that the mean and variance of a sum of independent random variables is
the sum of the individual means and variances, respectively, we know the
coefficient of variation of the waiting time should decrease as the
square root of the number of cylinders.

6. Conclusions

The graphs of Secs. 4 and 5 are the real conclusions of the
simulation study reported on in this article.

The purpose of this article is to empirically examine what
application MTPT disciplines will have in situations with random
arrivals. Section 3 shows that in situations where: (i) the
coefficient of variation of record sizes is less than one, (ii) it is
important to minimize the variance in waiting times, or (iii) it is
important to minimize the mean duration of busy intervals; MTPT
disciplines offer modest gains. It is important, however, to implement

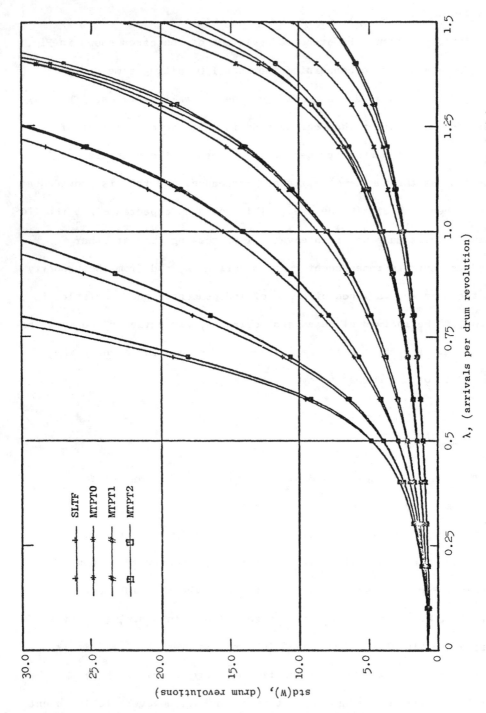

Figure 5.4. The standard deviation of the waiting time for moving-head disks.

as good a MTPT discipline as possible, and unfortunately only the MTPT0 algorithm has been shown to enjoy an efficient computation time, on the order of 100N + 50 microseconds for the naive implementation presented here. More work will be required in order to find efficient algorithms for the MTPT1 and MTPT2 scheduling disciplines.

Although the relative performance of the SLTF and MTPT scheduling disciplines have been considered here, little insight has been gained into what the optimal drum scheduling algorithm is when random arrivals are allowed, or even how close the disciplines studied in this article are to an optimal scheduling discipline. An intriguing topic of further research in this area will be to investigate optimal scheduling disciplines for random arrivals, and even if algorithms to implement the discipline are too complex to allow practical application, they will still provide an excellent measure of the sub-optimality of more practical scheduling disciplines.

The results of applying the MTPT discipline to a moving-head disk is encouraging. For heavy loads improvements of over 10 per cent are consistently achieved and just as importantly, it is relatively unimportant which of the MTPT disciplines is used. In other words, MTPT0, which has an efficient implementation, offers very nearly as much of an improvement over SLTF as does MTPT1 and MTPT2 when 5 or more cylinders are actively in use.

In the course of this study, the performance of MTPT2 was traced several times. It was observed that as the queue of outstanding requests grew, the probability that the MTPT2 discipline could use the shortest-latency record also grew. This observation leads to the reasonable, but as yet unproved, property of MTPT schedules that as the queue of I/O requests grows, with probability approaching unity there exists a MTPT sequence that begins with a SLTF sub-sequence. If this conjecture is true, then an obvious implementation feature of MTPT disciplines appears; when the depth of the I/O queue exceeds some threshold, suspend the MTPT algorithm in favor of a SLTF algorithm until the queue size drops below the threshold.

Chapter 7

CONCLUSIONS AND TOPICS FOR FURTHER RESEARCH

This final chapter reviews the significant results of this
dissertation and attempts to put them in some perspective with respect
to their importance and potential for practical application. A
discussion is also included of those research topics, related to the
work present here, that seem solvable, important, or both.

1.   Summary of Results

Table 6.1 and Fig. 6.1 of Chapter 2 provide an excellent perspective from which to approach the potential gains in performance available with rotating storage units through the use of different scheduling disciplines and drum organizations. They show that the expected waiting time of an I/O request, $\overline{W}$, for the FIFO file drum, FIFO paging drum, and the SLTF paging drum exhibit hyperbolic growth with respect to the rate of arrival of I/O requests. Specifically:

$$\overline{W} = a + b \frac{\xi}{1-\xi}$$

where a and b are constant coefficients and ξ is a linear function of the arrival rate. $\overline{W}$ for the SLTF file drum grows slightly faster than hyperbolically, and working with the result of simulation experiments in Sec. 5 of chapter 2 we found

$$\overline{W} = (\tfrac{1}{2} + \overline{R}) + \frac{\rho}{1-\rho} + .37\left[\frac{\rho}{1-\rho}\right]^{3/2} .$$

An important observation concerning the measurements of the IBM 360/91 at the Stanford Linear Accelerator Center is that it is shown that a reasonable model of I/O request to a file drum is to let the starting addresses be random variables uniformly distributed about the circumference of the drum and let the lengths of the records be exponentially distributed random variables with a mean record size on the order of one third of the circumference of the drum.

Chapter 3 provides some useful, practical information of immediate use to designers and users of computer systems with paged, e.g. virtual memory systems. It shows that $\overline{W}$ for an I/O channel supporting k paging drums can be divided into two terms: one independent of the load of I/O requests to the drum and another that monotonically increases with increasing load. Furthermore, the load varying term of $\overline{W}$ is nearly proportional to $(2 - 1/k)$. Therefore the only reasons to put more than one drum on a single I/O channel is to get additional capacity or reliability. Even in the case where more than one paging drum must be attached to a single I/O channel, the computer system will gain in performance if it can confine most accesses to a single drum. For example, if several drums are attached to a single I/O channel, it is better to put the heavily used files on a single drum rather than spread them evenly across several drums. Of course, if more than one I/O channel is available to connect the drums to the main store, every attempt should be made to evenly balance the load of I/O requests between the I/O channels, before assigning all the heavily used files allocated to a particular I/O channel to a single drum.

Chapter 4 of this dissertation presents a new drum scheduling discipline that minimizes the total amount of rotational latency (and processing time) for a set of I/O requests. Although the analysis of Chapter 4 does not allow the random arrival of requests, the scheduling discipline has a number of applications that can be justified just from the combinatorial properties presented in Chapters 4 and 5. Many computer architectures [IBM, 1964] do not provide sufficient communication primitives between the central and I/O processors to allow the ideal scheduling assumptions used in this dissertation. In addition, the overhead in starting I/O operations is sometimes so large that it is impractical to initiate I/O operations individually. If a queue of several I/O requests is present at a drum or disk, many IBM S/360 computers, for instance, will 'chain' a set of I/O requests to the same device together, and then not service the queue for that I/O device again until all the I/O requests in the 'chain' have been completed. Clearly in these situations, scheduling disciplines are needed that minimize the total processing time of the set of I/O requests.

One of the major attractions of the scheduling algorithm of Chapter 4 is that it has a computational complexity of NlogN. This is a very small growth rate for the algorithm since finding a schedule to minimize the total processing time is equivalent to a special case of the traveling salesmen problem; a problem whose general solution, and many subcases, do not have efficient solutions. Not only is it a very small growth rate, the measurements of Chapter 6 indicate at a naive implementation of the scheduling algorithm has an actual computation time requirement of approximately (100 + 50N) microseconds. A more sophisticated implementation of the algorithm, and coding it directly in machine language, should provide a reduction in computation time on the order of 2 to 4.

Chapters 5 and 6 deal with the performance of the MTPT scheduling discipline. It is shown that the SLTF scheduling discipline is never as much as a drum revolution longer than the MTPT discipline to process a set of I/O requests and the expected difference in the two disciplines is equal to the average record length, in the limit as N gets large.

Figures 4.1 and 5.1 in Chapter 6 are probably the two most important figures in this thesis with respect to the practical implications of the MTPT scheduling discipline. Figure 4.1 shows the expected waiting time of a fixed-head drum with I/O record lengths exponentially distributed with a mean of 1/2 the circumference of the drum. Only MTPT2, the shortest latency-time-first version of the MTPT scheduling algorithm was as good as the SLTF scheduling algorithm. The other figures in Sec. 4 of Chapter 6 show that when: the coefficient of variation of record sizes is less than one, it is important to minimize the variance of the waiting time, or it is important to minimize the mean duration of busy intervals, MTPT disciplines offer some gains over the SLTF discipline. If the MTPT discipline is to be used on drums with random arrivals the results here show it is necessary to use a more sophisticated MTPT scheduling algorithm than MTPT0, the one shown in Chapter 4 to have a computational complexity of NlogN.

Figure 5.1 shows that the real application of the MTPT scheduling algorithm may lie in the intra-cylinder scheduling of moving-head disks. The difference between the improvement of the MTPT schedules over the SLTF schedules gets arbitrarily large as the rate of arrival of I/O requests increases. Thus the MTPT schedules exhibit the attractive property that they offer the most improvement when the disk is congested, i.e. when it needs an efficient scheduling discipline the most.

2. Topics for Further Research

As the introduction stated, this dissertation is not a complete analysis of devices having rotational delays; many questions remain unanswered with respect to the modeling and behavior of rotating storage units. The reasons to continue to pursue research in this area are the same as the ones that initiated this dissertation: auxiliary storage devices have a major impact of the global performance of computer systems, and in order to develop effective models of computer systems, realistic yet tractable models of rotating storage units must be developed. There is also the additional incentive, as shown in Chapter 3,

that insight into the behavior of the auxiliary storage unit, e.g. the
SLTF paging drum, may provide criteria by which to design better
auxiliary storage units in the future.

The following is a list of topics that appear solvable, but are as
yet unsolved; would have important practical implications if solved or
in several cases are both important and potentially solvable.

* In either the stochastic (Chapter 2) or the combinatorial
  (Chapter 4) analysis of drums, allow I/O requests to have varying
  priorities. In particular, differentiate between read and write
  operations.

* Allow read requests to have a starting address and length specified,
  but let write requests have only the length specified and be free
  to begin operation at any convenient starting address.

* Analyze the shortest-processing-time-first (SPTF) drum scheduling
  algorithm for a file drum in a manner analogous to the analysis of
  the SLTF discipline in Chapter 2. Consider the cases of preempt/
  repeat and nonpreemptive SPTF disciplines.

* Find an exact analysis for $\underset{\sim}{W}(s)$ or even just $\overline{W}$, for an I/O channel
  with multiple paging drums. See Skinner [1967] for some
  suggestions of possible approaches and references to other articles
  that may be helpful.

* Compare the sectored file drum of Chapter 2 to the file drum for
  the SLTF scheduling discipline. Consider the case where each of
  the sectors of an individual field may be read separately, i.e.
  remove the assumption that processing a record is an indivisible
  process. This models drums that associate error checking and
  correcting codes to physical records of one sector in length [CDC,

196X]. It appears likely that such a drum organization may offer
superior performance to a pure file drum, while still processing
I/O requests of arbitrary length.

* Find efficient implementations of the MTPT1 and MTPT2 scheduling
  algorithms of Chapter 6. It is conjectured that as N gets large,
  there exists an MTPT sequence that begins with an SLTF sub-sequence.

* Although the SLTF scheduling discipline and the MTPT discipline of
  Chapter 4 can be implemented with algorithms having a computational
  complexity of NlogN, the SLTF discipline has an obvious incremental
  algorithm with a complexity of logN. Find an efficient incremental
  implementation of the MTPT drum scheduling algorithm.

* Find the optimal drum scheduling algorithm when the arrival of I/O
  requests form a Poisson process. Find the optimal drum scheduling
  discipline for the simple cyclic queueing models of computer
  systems discussed in Sec. 6 of Chapter 2.

* Generalize Theorem 5.1 of Chapter 5 to include the case where the
  endpoints of a record may be dependent random variables.

Appendix A

A SIMULATOR OF COMPUTER SYSTEMS WITH STORAGE UNITS

HAVING ROTATIONAL DELAYS

This note describes a simulator for computer systems with secondary storage units having rotational delays, i.e. drums and disks. This simulator is able to model a wide range of drums and disks and is primarily intended to be used to study alternative scheduling disciplines for rotating storage devices. A discussion is included on the precision of the summary statistics of the simulator, and a short user's guide is provided to aid others in the use of the simulator.

1. Introduction

This note describes a Monte Carlo simulator written to study the performance of computer systems with storage units having rotational delays. Figure 1.1 illustrates the computer systems that the simulator is capable of modeling; it is notable both for its simplicity and its relative emphasis on the rotating storage unit rather than the central processor.

The simulator's simplicity is a result of writing it as an adjunct and aid to analytic studies in Chapters 2, 3, 5, and 6. Unlike many simulation experiments, this simulator is not designed to validate details or incremental changes to computer systems; rather it is designed to explore the fundamental problems associated with scheduling devices having rotational delays. Every reasonable attempt has been made to keep the number of independent parameters of the simulator to a minimum with the expectation that the user will be able to relate the parameters of the model to the results obtained. Simulation experiments that include a multitude of parameters may be the only way to get realistic answers to problems that otherwise escape analysis, but the very fact that they include so many details in many cases precludes the opportunity to gain much qualitative information or cause and effect relationships.

Experience has shown that a simulator, like the one described here, is a valuable tool for the following applications. First, it can verify assumptions made in some analytic models. For instance, the exact analysis of a shortest-latency-time-first (SLTF) file drum is an extremely difficult problem, and this simulation has been used to study the relative merits of different approximate models of SLTF file drums

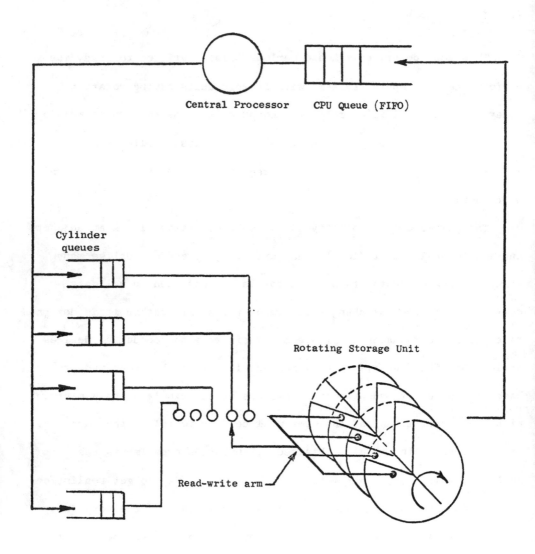

Figure 1.1. Model of computer system with rotating storage unit.

[Abate and Dubner, 1969; Chapter 2]. The simulator is also useful in the initial stages of analytic work as an aid in developing an intuitive understanding that can lead to conjectures of fundamental principles and starting points for analytic work.

This note is written to serve two, hopefully compatible, functions: provide documentation for a simulator that was used in several studies reported in Chapters 2, 3, 5, and 6, and provide sufficient information on the capabilities and structure of the simulator to allow others to take advantage of it in their own studies of storage units having rotational delays. Toward these ends, this section has given a very general description of the computer system simulator, and Sec. 2 will more precisely define the models that can be simulated as well as describe the structure of the simulator itself. An analysis of the stochastic convergence, i.e. the precision of the summary statistics, of the simulator is presented in Sec. 3. Finally, Sec. 4 is a brief user's guide.

2. General Description

This section will first consider the scope of computer systems the simulator is capable of modeling and then some comments will be made concerning the organization and flow of control in the simulator itself.

Referring back to Fig. 1.1, we see there is one central processor; at the central processor first-in-first-out (FIFO), non-preemptive scheduling is assumed. There is only one data channel between the storage unit and main memory; this is depicted in Fig. 1.1 as a single read-write head structure that can only be connected to a single I/O queue at one time.

The unit of time for the simulator is the period of rotation of the storage unit. The read-write heads of the storage units are movable and the surface of the storage unit that is accessible at a particular head position is called a cylinder. The number of cylinders in the storage unit is variable, and setting the number of cylinders to one gives the storage unit the characteristics of a fixed-head drum (or disk). Separate queues for I/O requests are maintained for each cylinder and the scheduling algorithms between cylinder queues, as well as within cylinder queues, is meant to be flexible. FIFO, shortest-latency-time-first (SLTF), and MTPT [Chapter 4] scheduling algorithms are implemented and available for intra-cylinder scheduling and SCAN [Denning, 1967] is available for inter-cylinder scheduling. The simulator is designed to allow, and encourage, the implementation of other inter-queue, intra-queue, or unified scheduling strategies.

The time required to move the read-write heads is

$$a + b\delta$$

where δ is the distance, in cylinders, to be traveled and a and b are easily altered parameters that initially have the values:

$$a = 1,$$
$$b = .07 .$$

These values approximate the time involved in an IBM 2314 disk [IBM, 1965B].

The structure of the simulator itself is best described by the flow chart in Fig. 2.1. It follows the conventional form on an event-driven simulation. The listing, in FORTRAN, of the main loop of the simulator is provided at the end of this note to provide more detailed information

245

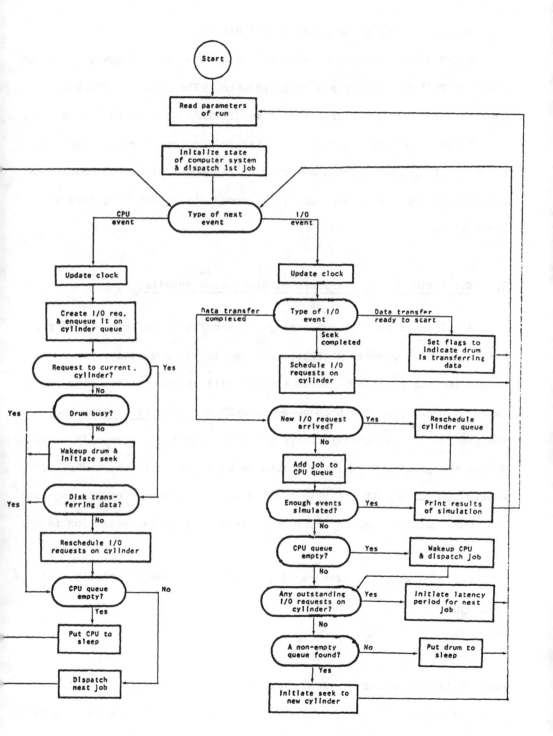

Figure 2.1. Flow chart of computer system simulation.

that will be useful to users of the simulator.

FORTRAN was selected over other, general purpose languages such as ALGOL or PL/I for purely pragmatic reasons. The group of FORTRAN compilers readily available, WATFIV and FORTRAN H, provide faster compilation and better object code than do the compilers available for the other languages. The simplicity of the model described above does not require the use of such special purpose simulation languages as GPSS and Simula.

3. Estimation of the Variance of Simulation Results

A difficult problem concerning any simulation is determining the variance of the summary statistics. Clearly, in any well-designed simulation the precision of the results will improve as the simulation is run longer, and this phenomenon is called stochastic convergence. The problem with stochastic convergence is that it is slow. In order to double the precision of a simulation we must quadruple the number of events simulated. This section will discuss the number of I/O requests that must be simulated in order to achieve a specified precision in the summary statistics.

The simulation's estimate of the mean of a random variable, call it $\overline{X}$, is just

$$\overline{X} = \frac{1}{n} \sum_{i=1}^{n} X_i$$

where n is the number of times an event is simulated and X_i is the value of the ith occurrence of the event. A few examples of events of interest in this simulation are: I/O waiting time, central processor busy intervals, I/O busy intervals, and I/O latency times. Furthermore, let

σ^2 be the variance of X and $\sigma_{\overline{X}}^2$ be the variance of the sample mean $\overline{X}$.

Suppose the X_i's are independent, identically distributed (iid) random variables; successive CPU busy intervals, or I/O busy intervals are good examples of iid random variables. The Central Limit Theorem guarantees that the sample mean is normally distributed for large n and from the linearity properties of the expectation operation [cf. Parzen, 1960, p. 206] it directly follows that

$$\sigma_{\overline{X}}^2 = \frac{\sigma^2}{n} \qquad (3.1)$$

Hence the standard deviation of $\overline{X}$, which we will use as a convenient measure of precision, is just

$$\sigma_{\overline{X}} = \frac{\sigma}{\sqrt{n}}$$

This expresses a fundamental property of Monte Carlo simulation; the precision of the simulation's summary statistics are proportional to $1/\sqrt{n}$. While this simple analysis is sufficient for the estimation of busy intervals and processor utilization, it is not adequate to estimate the precision of the sample mean of events that are correlated; I/O waiting time is an important instance of a random event that is likely to be correlated with neighboring events (I/O waiting times). A simple analysis, however, can still be of value even in this more complex case. The variance of the sum of a set of identically distributed random variables is

$$\sigma_{\overline{X}}^2 = \frac{\sigma^2}{n} + \frac{2\sigma^2}{n} \sum_{k=1}^{n} (1 - \frac{k}{n})\rho(k) \qquad (3.2)$$

where $\rho(k)$ is the autocorrelation coefficient of events with lag k. The simulator described in this note is capable of executing 10^4 to 10^6 events in a reasonable amount of time, and the autocorrelation coefficient for I/O waiting times were observed to be insignificant for k > 100. Therefore, for I/O waiting times, Eq. (3.2) can be approximated by

$$\sigma_{\overline{X}}^2 = \frac{\sigma^2}{n} \left[1 + 2 \sum_{k=1}^{100} \rho(k) \right]$$

Table 3.1 lists σ^2, the sum of the autocorrelation coefficients, $\sigma_{\overline{X}}^2$, and $\sigma_{\overline{X}}$ for the I/O waiting times of a fixed-head drum with SLTF scheduling and a range of arrival rates. Note the strong dependence of $\sigma_{\overline{X}}$ on the load imposed on the drum. A practical number of I/O operations to simulate for an individual run is 10^5, and the last column in Table 3.1 enumerates $\sigma_{\overline{X}}$ for $n = 10^5$. While this table is for I/O waiting times for drums with SLTF scheduling, the technique can be directly applied to other sample means in the simulation.

Another practical technique for estimating the precision of the sample mean of correlated events is discussed by M. Fishman [1967]. He suggests a spectral analysis of the time series of successive events to determine the equivalent number of independent events, and then uses Eq. (3.1) to estimate the precision of the sample mean.

4. A Short User's Guide

Input parameters. The parameters of a particular simulation are read with a NAMELIST format. For specific details of NAMELIST see [IBM, 1971A]. The input variables are listed below with the default values in parentheses.

RHO	ratio of mean I/O transfer time to mean CPU service time. (0.5)
MU	reciprocal of mean I/O transfer time. (1.0)
IOLIM	Number of I/O requests that will be simulated. (10000)

mean inter-arrival time / mean data transfer time	σ^2	$\sum_{k=1}^{100} \rho(k)$	$\sigma_{\bar{x}}^2$	$\sigma_{\bar{x}}$ for $n = 10^5$
.10	0.354	0.105	$\dfrac{0.564}{n}$	0.002
.25	0.891	0.785	$\dfrac{2.46}{n}$	0.005
.50	5.119	16.14	$\dfrac{37.4}{n}$	0.019
.75	64.28	554.3	$\dfrac{1170}{n}$	0.108

Table 3.1. Variance, and related statistics, of the I/O wait time for a fixed-head drum with SLTF scheduling.[*]

---

[*] The sums of autocorrelation coefficients of I/O waiting times are sample means calculated as

$$\sum_{k=1}^{100} \rho(k) = \frac{1}{(n-101)} \sum_{i=101}^{n} \sum_{j=1}^{100} (x_i - \bar{x})(x_{i-j} - \bar{x})$$

where $n = 30,000$.

SHAFTS   When the storage unit is configured as a set of paging drums, the number of drums attached to the I/O channel. (1)

NUMCYL   The number of cylinders in the storage unit. (1)

NUMJOB   The degree of multiprogramming. (1000 -- for simulating Poisson arrivals)

CPUSED   Random number seed for CPU service times. (1)

RECSED   Random number seed for parameters of I/O requests. (1)

Output. Figure 4.1 is an example of the summary statistics that are printed following each simulation. The statistics shown in the figure are generally self-descriptive. The latency statistics, however, require some clarification. The somewhat arbitrary decision was made to define the latency period associated with an I/O request as the entire time the drum is latent prior to the actual servicing of the request. For example, a scheduling algorithm such as SLTF may initially be latent waiting for I/O request i to come under the read-write heads, but upon the arrival of one or more new I/O requests, it may switch to waiting for record j. In this instance, the whole latent period will be associated with the processing of I/O request j. The other form of output is the following set of parameters and summary statistics. Depending on the definition of FORTRAN data set 7, these parameters and statistics can go to any output device, but the default device is the card punch. As with the input parameters, the NAMELIST format is used. The output parameters and statistics are:

RHO   ratio of mean I/O service time to mean CPU service time

MU   reciprocal of mean I/O transfer time

CPUM   mean CPU busy interval

```
                    RESULTS OF SIMULATION.  (SLTF SCHEDULE)


PARAMETERS OF MODEL:
  NUMBER OF CYLINDERS ON DISK =   1;
  NUMBER OF SPINDLES ON I/O CHANNEL =   1;
  DEGREE OF MULTIPROGRAMMING =   5;
  CPU SERVICE TIMES ARE DRAWN FROM EXPONENTIAL DIST. WITH MEAN = 0.833333  ;
  RECORD LENGTHS ARE DRAWN FROM AN EXPONENTIAL DIST. WITH MEAN = 0.333333  ;
  (LAMBDA/MU) = 0.400000
  RANDOM NUMBER SEEDS:  (   2718281,   5772156,   1618033);

NUMBER OF I/O REQUESTS PROCESSED =   50000;
TOTAL ELAPSED TIME = 43540.767  ;  (UNIT OF TIME IS PERIOD OF THE DRUM)

SUMMARY OF CPU PERFORMANCE:
  BUSY INTERVAL:   MEAN = 8.8685047  ;  VARIANCE = 246.12662  ;  STD. DEVIATION = 15.688423  ;
                   MAX. INTERVAL = 161.02283 ;
  UTILIZATION =0.95853120  ;  NUMBER OF INTERVALS =   4706;

SUMMARY OF DRUM PERFORMANCE:
  BUSY INTERVAL:   MEAN = 3.2614382  ;  VARIANCE = 19.727833  ;  STD. DEVIATION = 4.4416025  ;
                   MAX. INTERVAL = 54.247054 ;  NUMBER OF INTERVALS =   10599;
  UTILIZATION =0.79392225  ;  VARIANCE = 1.6803061  ;  STD. DEVIATION = 1.2962662  ;
  WAIT TIME:   MEAN = 1.5378478  ;  E(W) - E(W(NL)) =0.7045438  ;
               MAX. WAIT = 14.213228  ;
  DRUM QUEUE LENGTH:   MEAN = 1.7659861  ;
  LATENCY:   MEAN =0.35686846  ;  VARIANCE =0.718410094D-01;  STD. DEVIATION =0.26803189  ;
             MAX. LATENCY =0.99987701 ;
```

Figure 4.1. Example of summary statistics.

CPUV	variance of CPU busy intervals
CPUU	mean CPU utilization
IOM	mean I/O busy interval
IOV	variance of I/O busy intervals
IOU	mean I/O utilization
IOWM	mean I/O waiting time
IOWV	variance of I/O waiting times

Execution Time Requirements. The execution time of the simulator is heavily dependent on the congestion of requests at the I/O device. For example, running the simulator with RHO = 0.2 and using SLTF scheduling on a drum, the simulator can progress at roughly 5000 I/O completions per second on an IBM 360/91. Increasing RHO to 0.8, however, reduces the simulator to 1000 I/O completions per second. Should it become necessary to improve the performance of this simulator the user is encouraged to use a program monitor such as PROGLOOK [Johnson and Johnston, 1971]. Using PROGLOOK on the current version of the simulator indicates the random number generator is the most heavily used section of the code and a significant improvement in execution speed could be achieved with a more efficient random number generator, i.e. recoding the subroutine in assembly language.

General Comment. This simulator is not meant to be used by those with little knowledge of programming. Much of the flexibility can be obtained only through modifications to the FORTRAN source statements. For this reason the following pages are a listing of the main loop of the simulator. It is a direct implementation of the flow chart of Fig. 2.1. A reasonable modification to the source code, for example, would be to change "CALL SLTF" to "CALL FIFO" to alter the scheduling of the I/O devices from SLTF to FIFO.

```
      INTEGER*4 CURCYL,CYL,TARCYL,NUMCYL,DELTA,SHAFTS/1/
      INTEGER*4 CPUBN,IOBN,IOCPLT
      INTEGER*4 I,J,K,N,IOLIM/1000/,IOTYPE,NUMJOB/1000/
      INTEGER*4 CPURDN,RECRDN,SEKRDN,CPUSED/1/,RECSED/1/,SEKSED/1/
      INTEGER*2 CPUJOB,IOJOB,NXTJOB
      INTEGER*2 LINK(1000),QSIZE(10),Q(1000,10),QMAX/1000/,SDOREC
      LOGICAL*1 CPUBSY,DBUSY,LATENT,SEEKNG,TRANS,RESCHD,LOCK
      REAL*8 CLOCK,CPUMRK,IOMARK,LATMRK,INTRVL,CPUTIM,IOTIM
      REAL*8 START(1000),FINISH(1001),ARIVAL(1000),LENGTH(1000)
      REAL*8 CPUB1,CPUB2,CPUBM,IOB1,IOB2,IOBM,LAT1,LAT2,LATM
      REAL*8 WAIT1,WAIT2,WAITM,DISTAN,HDPOS,PERIOD,INFIN/1.0D64/
      REAL*8 MEAN,VAR,STD,UTIL,RANDFL,BURST,CPUGEN,GENER
      REAL*8 RHO/0.5D0/,MU/1.0D0/,CPUAVR,RECAVR,SEKTIM
      REAL*8 CPUM,CPUV,CPUU,IOM,IOBV,IOU,IOWM,IOWV
C
      COMMON START,FINISH,SDOREC,RESCHD
      COMMON /CPUCOM/CPUAVR,LOCK
      COMMON /STAT1/MEAN,VAR,STD
      COMMON /RECCOM/RECAVR,RECRDN,NUMCYL
C
      NAMELIST /PARMS/RHO,MU,IOLIM,SHAFTS,NUMCYL,NUMJOB,
     1CPUSED,RECSED,SEKSED
      NAMELIST /SIM/RHO,MU,CPUM,CPUV,CPUU,IOM,IOBV,IOU,IOWM,IOWV
C
      PERIOD = 1.0D00
      SDOREC = 1001
      NUMCYL = 1
      RECRDN = 1
   50 READ(5,PARMS,END=2000)
      RECAVR = 1.0D0/MU
      CPUAVR = 1.0D0/(MU*RHO)
      CPURDN = CPUSED
      RECRDN = RECSED
      SEKRDN = SEKSED
C
C
C         INITIALIZE THE COMPUTER SYSTEM STATE
C
C         DATES
      CLOCK = 0.0D0
      CPUMRK = INFIN
      IOMARK = INFIN
      LATMRK = INFIN
C       CPU IMAGE
      CPUJOB = 0
      CPUTIM = INFIN
      CPUBSY = .FALSE.
C       DRUM IMAGE
      IOJOB = 0
      IOTIM = INFIN
      CURCYL = 1
      DELTA = 1
      SEEKNG = .FALSE.
      LATENT = .FALSE.
      DBUSY = .FALSE.
      LOCK = .FALSE.
      TRANS = .FALSE.
      RESCHD = .TRUE.
      DO 100 I=1,NUMCYL
         QSIZE(I) = 0
  100 CONTINUE
```

```
C          JOB IMAGES
      NXTJOB = 1
      DO 110 I=1,NUMJOB
         LINK(I) = I+1
  110 CONTINUE
      LINK(NUMJOB) = 0
C
C          INITIALIZE COUNTERS
C
C          CPU COUNTERS
      CPUBN = 0
      CALL CLEAR(CPUB1,CPUB2,CPUBM)
C          I/O COUNTERS
      IOBN = 0
      IOCPLT = 0
      CALL CLEAR(IOB1,IOB2,IOBM)
      CALL CLEAR(LAT1,LAT2,LATM)
      CALL CLEAR(WAIT1,WAIT2,WAITM)
C
C          DISPATCH FIRST JOB TO GET SIMULATION STARTED.
C
      CPUJOB = NXTJOB
      NXTJOB = LINK(NXTJOB)
      CPUMRK = CLOCK
      CALL RANDK(CPURDN,RANDFL)
      CPUTIM = CPUGEN(RANDFL)
      CPUBSY = .TRUE.
C
C          ENTER MAIN LOOP OF SIMULATION
C
  150 CONTINUE
      IF (IOTIM .LT. CPUTIM) GO TO 500
C
C          NEXT EVENT IS COMPLETION OF SERVICE ON CPU
C
      CLOCK = CPUTIM
C          CREATE I/O RECORD ATTRIBUTES
      CALL RECGEN(CYL,START(CPUJOB),LENGTH(CPUJOB),FINISH(CPUJOB))
      ARIVAL(CPUJOB) = CLOCK
C          ENQ RECORD ON APPROPIATE CYLINDER QUEUE
      QSIZE(CYL) = QSIZE(CYL) + 1
      IF (QSIZE(CYL).GT.QMAX) CALL TROUBL(CYL)
      Q(QSIZE(CYL),CYL) = CPUJOB
      IF(LOCK.OR.SEEKNG) GO TO 215
      IF (CYL .NE. CURCYL) GO TO 211
C          RESCHEDULE I/O REQUESTS ON CURRENT CYLINDER
      IF (TRANS) GO TO 212
      HDPOS = DMOD(CLOCK,PERIOD)
      CALL SLTF(QSIZE(CURCYL),Q(1,CURCYL),HDPOS)
      IF (LATENT) GO TO 210
         IOMARK = CLOCK
         LATMRK = CLOCK
         DBUSY = .TRUE.
         LATENT = .TRUE.
         IOTYPE = 2
C          SCHEDULE NEXT I/O RECORD TO BE PROCESSED
  210    DISTAN = START(Q(1,CURCYL)) - HDPOS + PERIOD
         IOTIM = CLOCK + DMOD(DISTAN,PERIOD)
         GO TO 215
  211    IF(DBUSY) GO TO 215
C          WAKE UP THE DRUM
```

```
                  DBUSY = .TRUE.
                  IOMARK = CLOCK
C             INITIATE SEEK
                  TARCYL = CYL
                  SEEKNG = .TRUE.
                  IOTIM = CLOCK + SEKTIM(CURCYL,TARCYL)
                  IOTYPE = 1
                  GO TO 215
   212      RESCHD = .TRUE.
C
C           GENERATE NEXT CPU COMPLETION DATE IF CPU QUEUE NOT EMPTY
C
   215      IF (NXTJOB .EQ. 0) GO TO 220
                  CPUJOB = NXTJOB
                  NXTJOB = LINK(NXTJOB)
                  CALL RANDK(CPURDN,RANDFL)
                  CPUTIM = CLOCK + CPUGEN(RANDFL)
                  GO TO 150
C
C           CPU QUEUE IS EMPTY.  COLLECT STATISTICS AND PUT CPU TO SLEEP
C
   220            CPUJOB = 0
                  CPUBSY = .FALSE.
                  CPUTIM = INFIN
                  INTRVL = CLOCK - CPUMRK
                  CPUB1 = CPUB1 + INTRVL
                  CPUB2 = CPUB2 + INTRVL**2
                  IF (INTRVL .GT. CPUBM) CPUBM = INTRVL
                  CPUBN = CPUBN + 1
                  GO TO 150
C
C           NEXT EVENT IS RELATED TO ONE OF THE THREE I/O EVENTS
C                1.   COMPLETION OF SEEK.
C                2.   COMPLETION OF LATENT PERIOD.
C                3.   COMPLETION OF DATA TRANSMISSION.
C
   500 CLOCK = IOTIM
       HDPOS = DMOD(CLOCK,PERIOD)
       GO TO (600,700,800), IOTYPE
C
C           COMPLETION OF SEEK OPERATION
C
C                FIX-UP DRUM IMAGE
   600            CURCYL = TARCYL
                  SEEKNG = .FALSE.
                  LATMRK = CLOCK
                  LATENT = .TRUE.
                  IOTYPE = 2
C                SCHEDULE I/O REQUESTS ON CYLINDER
                  CALL SLTF(QSIZE(CURCYL),Q(1,CURCYL),HDPOS)
                  DISTAN = START(Q(1,CURCYL)) - HDPOS + PERIOD
                  IOTIM = CLOCK + DMOD(DISTAN,PERIOD)
                  GO TO 150
C
C           END OF LATENCY PERIOD.  RECORD POSITIONED FOR TRANS.
C
C                FIX-UP DRUM IMAGE
   700            IOJOB = Q(1,CURCYL)
                  TRANS = .TRUE.
                  LATENT = .FALSE.
                  IOTIM = CLOCK + LENGTH(IOJOB)
                  IOTYPE = 3
```

```
C               COLLECT STATISTICS ON LATENCY
            INTRVL = CLOCK - LATMRK
            LAT1 = LAT1 + INTRVL
            LAT2 = LAT2 + INTRVL**2
            IF (INTRVL .GT. LATM) LATM = INTRVL
            GO TO 150
C
C
C        COMPLETION OF DATA TRANSMISSION
C
C               FIX-UP DRUM IMAGE
  800       TRANS = .FALSE.
            QSIZE(CURCYL) = QSIZE(CURCYL) - 1
            N = QSIZE(CURCYL)
            DO 801 I=1,N
               Q(I,CURCYL) = Q(I+1,CURCYL)
  801       CONTINUE
            IF(RESCHD) CALL SLTF(QSIZE(CURCYL),Q(1,CURCYL),HDPOS)
C               ADD JOB TO CPU QUEUE
            LINK(IOJOB) = NXTJOB
            NXTJOB = IOJOB
            IF (CPUBSY) GO TO 810
C               WAKEUP CPU
               CPUJOB = NXTJOB
               NXTJOB = LINK(NXTJOB)
               CPUMRK = CLOCK
               CALL RANDK(CPURDN,RANDFL)
               CPUTIM = CLOCK + CPUGEN(RANDFL)
               CPUBSY = .TRUE.
C            COLLECT I/O WAIT TIME STATISTICS
  810       INTRVL = CLOCK - ARIVAL(IOJOB)
            WAIT1 = WAIT1 + INTRVL
            WAIT2 = WAIT2 + INTRVL**2
            IF (INTRVL .GT. WAITM) WAITM = INTRVL
            IOCPLT = IOCPLT + 1
            IF (IOCPLT .EQ. IOLIM) GO TO 1000
C
            IF (QSIZE(CURCYL) .EQ. 0) GO TO 820
C               ELSE QUEUE IS NOT EMPTY; SCHEDULE NEXT REQUEST.
               LATENT = .TRUE.
               LATMRK = CLOCK
               DISTAN = START(Q(1,CURCYL)) - HDPOS + PERIOD
               IOTIM = CLOCK + DMOD(DISTAN,PERIOD)
               IOTYPE = 2
               GO TO 150
C
C            SEE IF ANY OTHER CYLINDERS HAVE A NON-EMPTY QUEUE
            CALL SEEK(CURCYL,TARCYL)
            IF(TARCYL.EQ.CURCYL) GO TO 850
               SEEKNG = .TRUE.
               IOTIM = CLOCK + SEKTIM(CURCYL,TARCYL)
               IOTYPE = 1
               GO TO 150
C
C            DRUM QUEUE IS EMPTY, PUT DRUM TO SLEEP
  850          DBUSY = .FALSE.
               IOTIM = INFIN
C               COLLECT STATISTICS ON DRUM BUSY INTERVALS
            INTRVL = CLOCK - IOMARK
            IOB1 = IOB1 + INTRVL
            IOB2 = IOB2 + INTRVL**2
            IF (INTRVL .GT. IOBM) IOBM = INTRVL
            IOBN = IOBN + 1
            GO TO 150
```

```
C
C          SIMULATION COMPLETED.
C          CALCULATE SUMMARY STATISTICS AND PRINT THEM OUT.
C
 1000 CONTINUE
C
C     (STATEMENTS TO PRINT STATISTICS OF SIMULATION.)
C
      GO TO 50
 2000 WRITE(6,2001)
 2001 FORMAT(1H1,'ALL DATA HAS BEEN PROCESSED.')
      STOP
      END
```

```
      SUBROUTINE RANDK(IY,YFL)
          INTEGER IY
          DOUBLE PRECISION YFL
C
C         THIS RANDOM NUMBER GENERATOR IS BASED ON
C         THE COMMENTS IN SEC. 3.6 OF KNUTH, THE ART
C         OF COMPUTER PROGRAMMING (1969).
C
          IY = IY*314159269 + 453806245
C         NEXT STATEMENT NECESSARY BECAUSE OF A BUG IN
C         THE FORTRAN H COMPILER
          IY = IY + 0
          IF(IY .GE. 0) GO TO 10
             IY = IY + 2147483647 + 1
   10     YFL = IY
          YFL = YFL*.4656612393077393D-9
          RETURN
      END
```

```
      SUBROUTINE SLTF(QSIZE,QUEUE,HDPOS)
C
C         THIS SUBROUTINE IMPLEMENTS AN SLTF(SHORTEST-
C         LATENCY-TIME-FIRST) SCHEDULING POLICY FOR I/O
C         REQUESTS ON A CYLINDER QUEUE.  OTHER POLICIES
C         THAT HAVE BEEN IMPLEMENTED ARE:
C
C         FIFO(FIRST-IN-FIRST-OUT)
C
C         MTPT(MINIMAL-TOTAL-PROCESSING-TIME.  FOR DETAILS
C            SEE (FULLER, 1971))
C
      END
```

```
      DOUBLE PRECISION FUNCTION CPUGEN(X)
C
C        GENERATES CPU SERVICE TIME.  NEGATIVE EXP.
C        CURRENTLY IMPLEMENTED.
C
      END


      DOUBLE PRECISION FUNCTION BURST(X)
C
C        GENERATES A BURST OF (NUMJOB-1) JOBS WITH 0 LENGTH
C        SERVICE TIME, FOLLOWED BY 1 SERVICE TIME
C        EQUAL TO RHO/MU., AND REPLACES CPUGEN WHEN
C        STUDYING COMBINATORIAL PROPERTIES OF SCHEDULES.
C
      END




      SUBROUTINE RECGEN(CYL,START,LENGTH,FINISH)
C
C        GENERATES PARAMETERS OF I/O REQUESTS.
C
      END


      DOUBLE PRECISION FUNCTION SEKTIM(I,J)
C
C     CALCULATES DISK SEEK(HEAD MOVEMENT) TIME.
C
      END


      SUBROUTINE SCAN(CURCYL,TARCYL)
C
C        THIS SUBROUTINE IS AN IMPLEMENTATION OF THE
C        SCAN INTER-CYLINDER SCHEDULING POLICY(DENNING,
C        1967); ALSO CALLED LOOK BY PINKERTON AND
C        THOERY(1972).
C
      END
```

Appendix B

IMPLEMENTATION OF THE MTPT DRUM SCHEDULING ALGORITHM

This appendix lists the implementation, in FORTRAN IV, of the MTPT drum scheduling algorithm developed in Chapter 4. The results discussed in Chapters 5 and 6 are based upon the subroutines listed here, and the formal parameters of the subroutines are compatible with the conventions of the simulator described in Appendix A. Three versions of the MTPT scheduling algorithm are included here: MTPT0, an implementation of the original MTPT algorithm of Chapter 4; MTPT1, an obvious modification to MTPT0; and MTPT2, a shortest-latency-time-first version of MTPT0. Both MTPT1 and MTPT2 are described in detail in Chapter 6. Also included in this appendix is a restatement, in English, of the original MTPT drum scheduling algorithm.

1. A Statement of the Original MTPT Drum Scheduling Algorithm

Listed here is an informal, English statement of the original minimal-total-processing-time (MTPT) drum scheduling algorithm developed in Chapter 4. The notation used is consistent with Chapters 4 and 5.

The Minimal-Total-Processing-Time Scheduling Algorithm

1. Based on the unique value associated with each node, sort f_0, f_i, and s_i, $1 \leq i \leq N$, into one circular list. If $f_i = s_j$ for any i and j then f_i must precede s_j.

2. Set the list pointer to an arbitrary element in the list.

3. Scan in the direction of nodes with increasing value for the next (first) f_i in the list.

4. Place this f_i on a pushdown stack.

5. Move the pointer to the next element and if it is an f_i go to Step 4, else continue on to Step 6. In the latter case, the element must be an s_i.

6. Pop the top f_i from the stack and move the pointer to the next element in the circular list.

7. If the circular list has been completely scanned go to Step 8, else if the stack is empty go to Step 3, else go to Step 5.

8. Let the bottom f_i on the pushdown stack be identified as f_δ. Change the circular list to an ordinary list where the bottom element is f_δ.

9. Match f_δ to s_0, and starting from the top of the list match the kth s_i to the kth f_i. (This constructs the permutation ψ'.)

10. Determine the membership of the cycles of ψ'.

11. Moving from the top to the bottom of the list, if adjacent arcs define a zero cost interchange and if they are in disjoint cycles perform the interchange. (This step transforms ψ' to ψ^0.)

12. Moving from the bottom to the top of the list, perform the positive cost, type 2a, interchange on the current arc if it is not in the same cycle as the arc containing f_δ. (The permutation defined at the end of this step is ψ_{mtpt}.)

2. Implementation of the Original MTPT Algorithm, MTPTO

```
      SUBROUTINE MTPTO(QSIZE,QUEUE,START,FINISH,HDPOS,SDOREC,RESCHD)
      :NTEGER*2 QSIZE,QUEUE(1),SDOREC
      REAL*8 START(1),FINISH(1),HDPOS
      LOGICAL*1 RESCHD
C
C          This subroutine is an implementation of the drum
C      scheduling algorithm described in 'An Optimal Drum
C      Scheduling Algorithm', (Fuller, 1971).  This procedure
C      finds a schedule for the outstanding I/O requests
C      such that the total processing time is minimized.
C
C          The formal parameters have the following inter-
C      pretation:
C
C          QSIZE  ::= the number of requests to be scheduled.
C
C          QUEUE  ::= a vector of length QSIZE that contains
C                     the integer identifiers of the I/O requests
C                     to be scheduled.  The current implementation
C                     restricts the identifiers to be positive
C                     integers less than 1001.
C
C          START  ::= START(i) is the starting address of I/O
C                     request i.
C
C          FINISH ::= FINISH(i) is the finishing address of
C                     I/O request i.
C
C          HDPOS  ::= the present position of the read-write heads.
C
C          SDOREC ::= the identifier of the pseudo record.
C
C          RESCHD ::= a boolean variable to signal when rescheduling
C                     is required.
C
      INTEGER I,J,N,COMPNS,QPLUS1,QMIN1,QMIN2,TEMP,K,L,M
      INTEGER FINDCY
      INTEGER*2 STACK,FPOINT,SPOINT,DELTA,DELTAS
      INTEGER*2 FNODES(1001),F(1001),SNODES(1001),S(1001)
      REAL*8 PERIOD/1.00/
      REAL*8 LATEND,LATSTR,SJ,FJ,ADJUST
C
      COMMON /OPTIM/ PERM,CYCLE,LEVEL
      INTEGER*2 PERM(1001),CYCLE(1001),LEVEL(1001)
C
      RESCHD = .FALSE.
      IF(QSIZE.LE.1) RETURN
C
C          Initialize data structures and constants
C
      QPLUS1 = QSIZE + 1
      QMIN1 = QSIZE - 1
      QMIN2 = QSIZE - 2
      DO 100 I=1,QSIZE
          FNODES(I) = QUEUE(I)
          SNODES(I) = QUEUE(I)
  100 CONTINUE
```

```
C          Enter current position of read-write heads.
               FNODES(QPLUS1) = SDOREC
               FINISH(SDOREC) = HDPOS
C
C          Sort list of F and S nodes.
C
       CALL SORT(FNODES,FINISH,QPLUS1)
       CALL SORT(SNODES,START,QSIZE)
C
C          Find F(DELTA).
C
       STACK = 0
       FPOINT = 1
       SPOINT = 1
       N = 2*QSIZE + 1
       DO 300 I=1,N
          IF(FINISH(FNODES(FPOINT)).LE.START(SNODES(SPOINT))) GO TO 310
             IF(STACK.GT.0) STACK = STACK - 1
             SPOINT = SPOINT + 1
             IF(SPOINT.LE.QSIZE) GO TO 300
                IF(STACK.GT.0) GO TO 335
                   DELTA = FPOINT
                   DELTAS = 1
                   GO TO 335
  310          IF(STACK.GT.0) GO TO 330
                   DELTA = FPOINT
                   DELTAS = MOD(SPOINT-1,QSIZE) + 1
  330          STACK = STACK + 1
               FPOINT = FPOINT + 1
               IF(FPOINT.GT.QPLUS1) GO TO 335
  300 CONTINUE
C
C          redefine S and F nodes relative to F(DELTA).
C
  335 DO 340 I=1,QSIZE
          F(I) = FNODES(MOD(DELTA+I-2,QPLUS1)+1)
          S(I+1) = SNODES(MOD(DELTAS+I-2,QSIZE)+1)
  340 CONTINUE
      F(QPLUS1) = FNODES(MOD(DELTA+QPLUS1-2,QPLUS1)+1)
      DELTA = 1
      ADJUST = PERIOD - FINISH(F(DELTA))
C
C          Construct the permutation Psi'.
C
      PERM(F(1)) = SDOREC
      DO 400 I=2,QPLUS1
          PERM(F(I)) = S(I)
  400 CONTINUE
C
C          Determine the membership of the cycles of Psi'.
C
      DO 500 I=1,QPLUS1
          CYCLE(F(I)) = F(I)
  500 CONTINUE
      COMPNS = 0
      DO 501 K=1,QPLUS1
          I = F(K)
          IF(CYCLE(I).NE.I) GO TO 501
             COMPNS = COMPNS + 1
             LEVEL(I) = 1
             J = I
```

```
502        J = PERM(J)
           IF(J.EQ.I) GO TO 501
               LEVEL(I) = 2
               CYCLE(J) = I
               GO TO 502
 501 CONTINUE
     IF(COMPNS.EQ.1) GO TO 800
C
C        Transform Psi' to Psi(0).
C
     DO 600 I=1,QMIN1
     J = QPLUS1 -I
     IF(DMOD(ADJUST+START(S(J)),PERIOD).LT.
   1    DMOD(ADJUST+FINISH(F(J+1)),PERIOD) .OR.
   2    (FINDCY(F(J)).EQ.FINDCY(F(J+1)))) GO TO 600
           CALL MERGE(F(J),F(J+1))
           COMPNS = COMPNS - 1
           IF(COMPNS.EQ.1) GO TO 800
 600 CONTINUE
C
C        Transform Psi(0) to Phi(0).
C
     DO 700 I=2,QPLUS1
     IF(FINDCY(F(DELTA)).EQ.FINDCY(F(I))) GO TO 700
         CALL MERGE(F(DELTA),F(I))
         DELTA = I
         COMPNS = COMPNS - 1
         IF(COMPNS.EQ.1) GO TO 800
 700 CONTINUE
C
C        Construct schedule from Phi(0).
C
 800 J = SDOREC
     DO 810 I=1,QSIZE
        J = PERM(J)
        QUEUE(I) = J
 810 CONTINUE
     RETURN
     END




     INTEGER FUNCTION FINDCY(NODE)
        INTEGER*2 NODE
        COMMON /OPTIM/ PERM,CYCLE,LEVEL
        INTEGER*2 PERM(1001),CYCLE(1001),LEVEL(1001)
C
C        This is a function subroutine whose value is an
C        integer identifying the cycle of the permutation in
C        which NODE is a member.  CYCLE is a tree structure
C        defining the cycles of the permutation.
C
        FINDCY = NODE
  10    IF(FINDCY.EQ.CYCLE(FINDCY)) RETURN
           FINDCY = CYCLE(FINDCY)
           GO TO 10
     END
```

```
      SUBROUTINE MERGE(NODE1,NODE2)
         INTEGER*2 NODE1,NODE2
C
C        MERGE connects the tree representation of CYCLE1
C     and CYCLE2.  The integer vectors CYCLE and LEVEL
C     define the membership of the cycles of the permutation.
C        MERGE also executes the interchange of the successors
C     of NODE1 and NODE2.
C
         INTEGER*2 C1,C2,TEMP
         INTEGER FINDCY
         COMMON /OPTIM/ PERM,CYCLE,LEVEL
         INTEGER*2 PERM(1001),CYCLE(1001),LEVEL(1001)
         C1 = FINDCY(NODE1)
         C2 = FINDCY(NODE2)
C
C        Merge the two cycle structures.
C
         IF(LEVEL(C1).GE.LEVEL(C2)) GO TO 100
            CYCLE(C1) = C2
            GO TO 200
  100    IF(LEVEL(C1).EQ.LEVEL(C2)) LEVEL(C1) = LEVEL(C1) + 1
         CYCLE(C2) = C1
C
C        Perform the interchange on the permutation.
C
  200    TEMP = PERM(NODE1)
         PERM(NODE1) = PERM(NODE2)
         PERM(NODE2) = TEMP
      RETURN
      END


      SUBROUTINE SORT(NODES,VALUE,N)
         INTEGER*2 NODES(1),N
         REAL*8 VALUE(1)
C
C           Shellsort.  For further discussion of Shellsort
C        see Shell(1959), Hibbard(1963), and Knuth(1971).
C
         INTEGER*4 I,J,D,Y
         REAL*8 VALUEY
         D = 1
  200    D = D + D
         IF(D - N) 200,208,207
  207       D = D/2
  208       D = D - 1
  201    IF(D.LE.0) RETURN
         I = 1
  202    J = I
         Y = NODES(I+D)
         VALUEY = VALUE(NODES(I+D))
  203    IF(VALUEY.LT.VALUE(NODES(J))) GO TO 204
  205       NODES(J+D) = Y
            I = I + 1
            IF((I+D).LE.N) GO TO 202
               D = (D-1)/2
               GO TO 201
  204       NODES(J+D) = NODES(J)
            J = J-D
            IF(J.GT.0) GO TO 203
               GO TO 205
      END
```

3.   An Obvious Modification to MTPT0, MTPT1

```
      SUBROUTINE MTPT1(QSIZE,QUEUE,START,FINISH,HDPOS,SDOREC,RESCHD)
         INTEGER*2 QSIZE,QUEUE(1),SDOREC
         REAL*8 START(1),FINISH(1),HDPOS
         LOGICAL*1 RESCHD
C
         INTEGER I,J,N,COMPNS,QPLUS1,QMIN1,QMIN2,TEMP,K,L,M
         INTEGER FINDCY
         INTEGER*2 STACK,FPOINT,SPOINT,DELTA,DELTAS
         INTEGER*2 FNODES(1001),F(1001),SNODES(1001),S(1001)
         REAL*8 PERIOD/1.00/
         REAL*8 LATEND,LATSTR,SJ,FJ,ADJUST
C
         CALL MTPT0(QSIZE,QUEUE,START,FINISH,HDPOS,SDOREC,RESCHD)
         QMIN2 = QSIZE - 2
         IF(QMIN2.LE.2) RETURN
         LATSTR = PERIOD - DMOD(HDPOS,PERIOD)
         DO 900 I=1,QMIN2
            J = I + 1
            LATEND = DMOD(LATSTR+START(QUEUE(I)),PERIOD)
            DO 920 J=J,QMIN1
               SJ = DMOD(LATSTR+START(QUEUE(J)),PERIOD)
               IF(SJ.GT.LATEND) GO TO 920
               FJ = DMOD(LATSTR+FINISH(QUEUE(J)),PERIOD)
               IF((FJ.LT.SJ).OR.(FJ.GT.LATEND)) GO TO 920
                  TEMP = QUEUE(J)
                  K = J - I
                  DO 930 L=1,K
                     M = J-L
                     QUEUE(M+1) = QUEUE(M)
930               CONTINUE
                  QUEUE(I) = TEMP
               LATEND= DMOD(LATSTR+START(TEMP),PERIOD)
920         CONTINUE
            LATSTR = PERIOD - DMOD(FINISH(QUEUE(I)),PERIOD)
900      CONTINUE
         RETURN
      END
```

4. The Shortest-Latency-Time-First MTPT Algorithm, MTPT2

```
      SUBROUTINE MTPT2(QS,Q,START,FINISH,HD,SDOREC,RESCHD)
         INTEGER*2 QS,Q(1),SDOREC
         REAL*8 START(1),FINISH(1),HD
         LOGICAL*1 RESCHD
C
         INTEGER I,J,K,REND,RBEGIN
         INTEGER*2 QSM1
C
         IF(QS.LE.1) RETURN
         CALL MTPT0(QS,Q,START,FINISH,HD,SDOREC,RESCHD)
         IF(QS.LE.2) RETURN
         RBEGIN = Q(1)
         REND = Q(QS)
         QSM1 = QS - 1
C
         DO 100 I=1,QS
            CALL SLTF(QS,Q,START,FINISH,HD,SDOREC,RESCHD,I)
            IF(Q(1).EQ.RBEGIN) RETURN
            DO 200 J=2,QS
  200          QT(J-1) = Q(J)
            CALL MTPT0(QSM1,QT,FINISH(Q(1)))
            RESCHD = .TRUE.
            IF(QT(QSM1).EQ.REND) RETURN
  100    CONTINUE
         WRITE(6,101) QS
  101    FORMAT(10X,'ERROR IN MTPT2;   QS = ',I4,';')
         CALL MTPT0(QS,Q,START,FINISH,HD,SDOREC,RESCHD)
         RETURN
      END
```

Appendix C

SOME EFFICIENT ALGORITHMS AND DATA STRUCTURES

FOR HANDLING PERMUTATIONS

1.   Introduction

Consider the following interesting problem often discussed in the study of graphs. Given any two nodes in an arbitrary graph G, does there exist a path between the nodes in G?   In other words, are the nodes in the same component of G or are they in disjoint components? Holt and Reingold [1970] have discussed this problem and show the computation involved is of an order not less than N^2 if G is allowed to be any arbitrary graph and arcs in G are represented as elements of an N $\times$ N matrix. In the discussion that follows we will restrict the graph G to be a description of a permutation of N elements. Consequently, each node in G will have exactly one arc entering it and one arc leaving it. Furthermore, instead of representing the arcs of G by entries in an N $\times$ N matrix, a different data structure will be used involving at most 2N words.

Algorithms will now be discussed which can be used to construct and modify the data structure representing G. A procedure will also be presented with a computational complexity on the order of logN which discovers if two nodes in G are in the same cycle, i.e., there exists a path between them.

2.   A Tree Representation for Permutations

Fig. 2.1 shows the general tree structure that will be used to represent a permutation ψ on N+1 elements. Each element, or node, in ψ is given a unique cell in the lowest level of the tree. If this cell contains the distinguished identifier, Λ in Fig. 2.1, then this element is fixed by ψ, and is therefore in a cycle of length 1. In general,

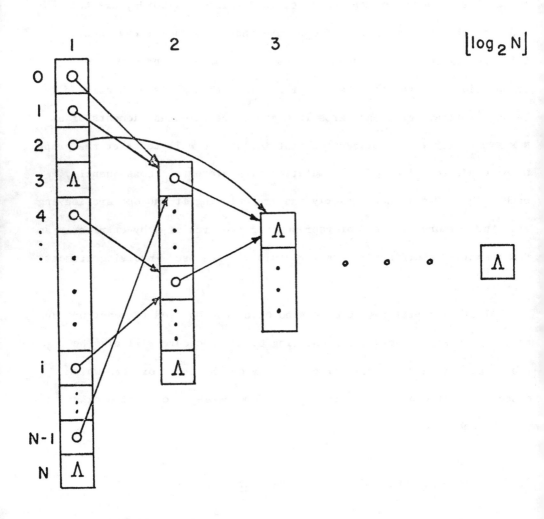

Figure 2.1. The tree representation of the cycles of a permutation.

however, more than one element will be included in some cycles of ψ. In this case, every element of a given cycle will have a pointer from its cell in stage 1 to some unique cell in stage 2. This cell in stage 2 will now contain Λ. Clearly, the first two levels of the tree in Fig. A.1 are sufficient in order to completely describe any permutation.

In the last section of this appendix the ALGOL procedure Findcycles is stated which constructs a tree representation of some permutation ψ. Findcycles is able to build the tree structure of ψ in a single scan of the nodes in ψ. Furthermore, the work required at each node in ψ is independent of the size ψ. Consequently, the computation performed by Findcycles is a linear function of the number of nodes of ψ.

A related problem to that of the construction of a representation of ψ is the problem of efficiently modifying the representation of ψ to reflect a change in ψ's structure. The specific problem considered here is the case where two cycles in ψ are transformed into one cycle. This particular type of modification arises in combinatorial problems where the solution requires a single cycle permutation. The method used to combine two cycles in the tree structure of Fig. 2.1 is very straight-forward. If the two cycles to be merged both have their terminal node in the ith level of the tree, then their terminal nodes are replaced by pointers to the same cell in level i+1 of the tree. This new cell in the i+1 level now becomes the terminal node of the new cycle and is assigned the value Λ. If the terminal node of one cycle is at a lower level than the other terminal node the lower terminal node will be made to point to the higher terminal node and we are done.

The tree structure of Fig. 2.1 has at most $\log_2 N$ levels and the number of cells at level i+1 is not greater than 1/2 the number at level

i. This is obvious from the fact that a node is created at the i+1st level only if two cycles must be merged with terminal nodes both at level i. Otherwise the cycles can be merged by adding a pointer from the lower to the higher terminal node without increasing the depth of the tree. The procedure Merge is listed in the final section of this appendix and is an implementation of the merging process just described. Note that the work required to merge two cycles is independent of N, the size of the permutation.

Finally, to find out which cycle any particular element of the permutation is in, we need only be given its cell address at the first level and then follow at most $\log_2 N$ pointers to discover the terminal node of the cycle in which the element is a member. This process is explicitly stated in the procedure Identifycycle at the end of this appendix.

3. The Collapsed Tree Representation

In order to simplify the three procedures just described, the actual data structure used is a "collapsed" version of the tree of Fig. 2.1. This new structure is shown in Fig. 3.1. All that has really been done is to collapse all $\log_2 N$ levels onto the first level, and add an attribute to each cell in the collapsed tree to identify which level it currently represents.

For example, consider the cycle continuing elements j and N in Fig. 2.1. The terminal cell in level 2 has been moved on top of cell j in level 1. Cell N points to the terminal node as before, and j does not need a pointer since it is now the terminal node. Similarly the three

273

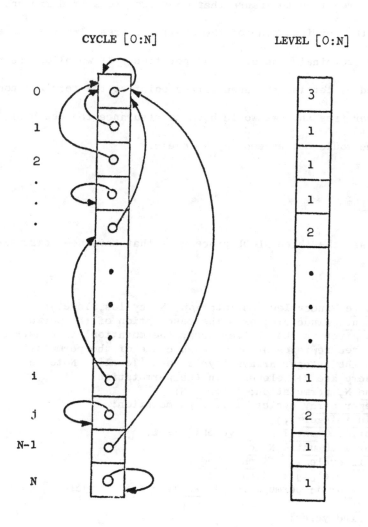

Figure 3.1. The collapsed tree representation.

level tree including elements 0,1,2,i, and i+1 has been collapsed and cell 0 is the terminal node with a level attribute of 3. The level attribute is required to insure that when two trees of different depths are merged the terminal node of the shallower tree always is made to point to the terminal node of the deeper tree. If we allow the trees to be merged by letting the deeper tree point to the terminal node of the shallower tree then we would have no assurance the depth of the maximal tree would not exceed $\log_2 N$ levels.

4.   Algorithms

Below are the three ALGOL procedures that have been discussed in this appendix.

```
procedure Findcycles (permutation, N, cycles, level);
    Comment  Findcycles uses the description of the permutation
        as given in the integer array 'permutation' to construct
        a tree representation of each cycle of the permutation
        in the integer arrays 'cycle' and 'level'.  Note that
        there are N+1 elements in the permutation;
    value N, permutation; integer N;
    integer array cycles, level, permutation;
    begin integer i,j;
        for i:=0 until N do cycle[i] := i;
        for i:=0 until N do
            if cycle[i] = i then begin
                level[i] := 1; j := i;
                for j:=permutation[j] while j ≠ i do cycle[j] := i
            end
    end Findcycles;

integer procedure Identifycycle (cycle, node);
    Comment  Identifycycle is a function procedure whose
        value is an integer identifying the cycle of the permutation
        in which 'node' is a member.  Cycle is a tree structure
        defining the cycles of the permutation;
    value cycle, node; integer node; integer array cycle;
    begin
        for node := cycle[node] while node ≠ cycle[node] do;
        Identifycycle := node
    end Identifycycle;
```

```
procedure Merge (cycle, level, cycle1, cycle2);
   Comment  Merge connects the tree representation of cycle1
     and cycle2 of the permutation defined in the integer
     arrays cycle and level;
   value cycle1, cycle2; integer cycle1, cycle2;
   integer array cycle, level;
   if level[cycle1] < level[cycle2]
     then cycle[cycle1] := cycle2
     else begin
       if level[cycle1] = level[cycle2] then
         level[cycle1] := level[cycle1] + 1;
       cycle[cycle2] := cycle1
     end Merge;
```

Appendix D

AN ALTERNATE DERIVATION OF $Q(z)$: THE MOMENT GENERATING

FUNCTION OF SECTOR QUEUE SIZE

This appendix is an alternate derivation to the one presented in
Chapter 3, Sec. 3, for the moment generating function, $Q(z)$, of sector
queue size. This approach follows the technique employed by Coffman
[1969] in his analysis of the special case of a single drum per I/O
channel.

The point of departure from the analysis of Chapter 3, Sec. 3 is in the way we embed the first Markov chain into the drum model. Originally we defined our Markov epochs as those points in time when the read-write heads see the start of the sector. In Fig. 3.2 we labeled these points ①. Now define the Markov epochs as those points in time when the read-write heads reach the end of the sector. Recalling $\alpha_n(t)$ is the probability of n I/O request arriving in an interval of t seconds duration we can write the defining recurrence relation from our new Markov chain. As before, let g_n denote the equilibrium probability of n I/O requests in the sector queue.

$$g_n = \sum_{0 \leq i \leq n} \alpha_i(\tau)[\underset{\sim}{F}g_{n-i+1} + (1-\underset{\sim}{F})g_{n-i}]$$

$$+ g_o \underset{\sim}{F}[\alpha_o(\frac{r-1}{r}\tau)\alpha_n(\frac{\tau}{r}) + \sum_{1 \leq i \leq n} \alpha_i(\frac{r-1}{r}\tau)\alpha_{n-i+1}(\frac{\tau}{r})]$$

The above recurrence relation can be used to find the moment generating function of the sequence $\{g_n\}$

$$G(z) = \frac{g_o \underset{\sim}{F} \alpha_o(\frac{r-1}{r}\tau)(1-z) \, A(z,\frac{\tau}{r})}{z - [\underset{\sim}{F} + z(1-\underset{\sim}{F})] \, A(z,\tau)} \tag{1.1}$$

It is now possible to find the equilibrium probabilities of queue lengths for any angular displacement, θ, where $0 \leq \theta < 2\pi$. After the read-write heads have passed the end of the sector, I/O requests can only arrive at the sector, none can leave, and so we have

$$q_n(\theta) = \sum_{0 < i \leq n} g_i \, \alpha_{n-i}(\frac{\theta\tau}{2\pi})$$

where $q_n(t)$ is the equilibrium probability of n requests in the sector queue θ radians after the sector has finished service. We can simply remove the conditioning of $p_n(\theta)$ in θ by integrating over the interval $[0,2\pi]$, i.e.

$$q_n = \int_0^{2\pi} q_n(\theta)d\theta \ .$$

The corresponding relation for the generating function of the sequence $\{q_n\}$ is

$$Q(z) = \int_0^{2\pi} G(z) \ A(z,\frac{\theta\tau}{2\pi})d\theta$$

$$= \frac{1 - e^{-\lambda_q\tau(1-z)}}{\lambda_q\tau(1 - z)} \ G(z) \ .$$

Replacing $G(z)$ by Eq. (1.1) in the last line yields an expression for $Q(z)$ identical to Eq. (3.13) of Chapter 3 and hence concludes the alternate derivation of $Q(z)$.

The approach just presented removes the dependence of queue size on the angular position of the drum by integration, while our original approach made use of the fact that the distribution of queue sizes immediately after the departure of a request is the same as the equilibrium distribution of queue sizes. It might also be noted in passing that the basic recurrence relation in our original approach (recall we embedded the Markov epochs at the start of a sector) is considerably simpler than the corresponding recurrence relations for the alternate approach in which the Markov epochs are defined at the end of a sector.

REFERENCES

Abate, J. and Dubner, H. (1969) Optimizing the performance of a drum-like storage. IEEE Trans. on Computers C-18, 11 (Nov., 1969), 992-996.

Abate, J., Dubner, H., and Weinberg, S. B. (1968) Queueing analysis of the IBM 2314 disk storage facility. J. ACM 15, 4 (Oct., 1968), 577-589.

Adel'son-Vel'skiy, G. M. and Landis, E. M. (1962) An algorithm for the organization of information. Doklady, Akademiia Nauk SSSR, TOM 146, 236-266. Also available in translation as: Soviet Mathematics 3, 4 (July, 1962), 1259-1263.

Arden, B. W. and Boettner, D. (1969) Measurement and performance of a multiprogramming system. 2nd Symposium on Operating Principles (1969), 130-146.

Barton, D. E. and Mallows, C. L. (1965) Some aspects of the random sequence. Ann. Math. Statist. 36 (1965), 236-260.

Baskett, F. (1971) Mathematical models of multiprogrammed computer systems. TSN-17 Computation Center, Univ. of Texas, Austin, Texas (Jan., 1971).

Berge, C. (1962) The Theory of Graphs. John Wiley and Sons, New York, N.Y. (1962).

Berge, W. H. and Konheim, A. G. (1971) An accessing model. J. ACM 18, 3 (July, 1971), 400-404.

Bertrand, J. (1887) Solution d'un probleme. C. R. Acad. Sci. Paris 105 (1887), 369.

Boothroyd, J. (1963) Algorithm 201, Shellsort. C. ACM 6, 8 (Aug., 1963), 445.

Bottomly, J. S. (1970) SUPERMON statistics. SFSCC Memo. (August 13, 1970), Stanford Linear Accelerator Center, Stanford, Calif.

Brooks, F. P. (1969) Mass memory in computer systems. IEEE Trans. on Magnetics MAG-5, 3 (Nov., 1969), 635-639.

Burroughs. (1970) Burroughs B6375 disk file optimizer. New Product Announcement, Burroughs Corp., Detroit, Mich. (Feb., 1970).

CDC. (196X) CDC 862/863/865 Drum subsystems. Production specification, Control Data Corp., Minneapolis, Minn.

Chandler, J. P. and Harrison, W. C. (1970) Remark on algorithm 201, Shellsort. C. ACM 13, 6 (June, 1970), 373-374.

Coffman, E. G. (1969) Analysis of a drum input/output queue under scheduling operation in a paged computer system. J. ACM 16, 1 (Jan., 1969), 73-90.

Conway, R W., Maxwell, W. L., and Miller, L. W. (1967) Theory of Scheduling. Addison-Wesley, Reading, Mass. (1967).

Cox, D. R. and Smith, W. L. (1961) Queues. Monographs on Applied Probability and Statistics, Chapman and Hall Ltd., London. (1961).

Denning, P. J. (1967) Effects of scheduling on file memory operations. Proc. AFIPS SJCC 30 (1967), 9-21. Keywords: drum scheduling, queueing models.

Edmonds, J. and Fulkerson, D. R. (1965) Transversals and matroid partition. J. of Research of the National Bureau of Standards 69B, 3 (July-Sept., 1965), 147-153.

Fishman, G. S. (1967) Problems in the statistical analysis of simulation experiments; the comparisons of means and the length of sample records. C. ACM 10, 2 (February, 1967), 94-99.

Feller, W. (1968) An Introduction to Probability Theory and Its Applications, Volume 1. Wiley and Sons, Inc., New York, N.Y. (1968).

Feller, W. (1970) An Introduction to Probability Theory and Its Applications, Volume 2. Wiley and Sons, Inc., New York, N.Y. (1970).

Foster, C. C. (1965) Information storage and retrieval using AVL trees. ACM 20th National Conference (Aug., 1965), 192-265.

Fuller, S. H., Price, T. G., and Wilhelm, N. C. (1971) Measurement and Analysis of a multiprogrammed computer system. IEEE Workshop on Measurement and Performance Evaluation, Argonne, Ill. (Oct. 1971).

Gale, D. (1968) Optimal assignments in an ordered set: an application of matroid theory. J. Combinatorial Theory, 4 (1968), 176-180.

Gaver, D. P. (1967) Probability models for multiprogramming computer systems. J. ACM 14 (July, 1967), 423-438.

Gilbert, E. N. (1956) Enumeration of labelled graphs. Canadian J. of Math. 8 (1956), 405-411.

Gill, A. (1960) The optimal organization of serial memory transfers. IRE Trans. on Elec. Computers EC-12, 3 (March, 1960), 12-15.

Gilmore, P. C. and Gomory, R. E. (1964) Sequencing a one state-variable machine: a solvable case of the traveling salesman problem. Operations Research, 12, 5 (Sept-Oct., 1964), 655-679.

Gordon, W. J. and Newell, G. F. (1967) Closed queueing systems with exponential servers. Operations Research 15 (1967), 254-265.

Greenberg, M. L. (1971) An algorithm for drum storage management in time-sharing systems. ACM Third Symposium on Operating Principles (1971), 141-148.

Hearn, A. C. (1967) Reduce user's manual. A.I. memo 50. Stanford
    Artificial Intelligence Project, Stanford Univ., Stanford, Calif.
    (Feb., 1967).

Hibbard, T. N. (1963) An empirical study of minimal storage sorting.
    C. ACM 6, 5 (May, 1963), 206-213.

Hoare, C.A.R. (1961) Algorithm 64, quicksort. C. ACM 4, 7 (July, 1961),
    321.

Hoare, C.A.R. (1961) Quicksort. Computer J. 5 (1962), 10-15.

Holt, R. C. and Reingold, E. M. On the time required to detect cycles
    and connectivity in directed graphs. Tech. Report No. 70-63, Dept.
    of Computer Science, Cornell Univ., Ithaca, N.Y. (June, 1970).

IBM. (1964) IBM system/360 principles of operation. File No. S360-01,
    Form A22-6821-7.

IBM. (1965A) IBM system/360 component descriptions -- 2820 storage control
    and 2301 drum storage. File No. S360-07, Form A22-6895-2.

IBM. (1965B) IBM system/360 component descriptions -- 2314 direct access
    storage facility and 2844 auxiliary storage control. File No.
    S360-07, Form A26-3599-2.

IBM. (1971A) IBM system/360 and system 370 FORTRAN IV Language. File
    No. S360-25, Order No. GC28-6515-8.

IBM. (1971B) IBM 2835 storage control and IBM 2305 fixed head storage
    module. Form GA26-1589-2.

IBM. (1971C) IBM 3830 storage control and 3330 disk storage. Order No.
    GA26-1592-1.

Jackson, J. F. (1963) Jobshop-like queueing systems. Management
    Science 16, 1 (Oct. 1963), 131-142.

Jewell, W. S. (1967) A simple proof of: L = λW. Operations Research
    15 (1967), 1109-1116.

Johnson, R. and Johnston, T. (1971) PROGLOOK user's guide SCC-007,
    Stanford Computation Center, Stanford University, Stanford, Calif.
    (Oct., 1971).

Khintchine, A. Y. (1969) Mathematical Methods in the Theory of Queueing.
    Griffin's Statistical Monographs and Courses, Hafner Publishing Co.,
    New York, N.Y. (1969).

Knapp, M. A. and McIntyre, D. E. (1971) Bulk storage applications in
    the Illiac IV system. IEEE Trans. on Magnetics MAG-7, 4 (Dec.,
    1971), 838-847.

Knuth, D. E. (1968) The Art of Computer Programming, Volume 1/ Fundamental Algorithms. Addison-Wesley Co., Reading, Mass. (1968).

Knuth, D. E. (1970) The Art of Computer Programming, Volume 2/ Seminumerical Algorithms. Addison-Wesley Co., Reading, Mass. (1970).

Kruskal, J. B. (1956) On the shortest spanning subtree of a graph and the traveling salesman problem. Proc. Amer. Math. Soc. 7, 1 (Feb., 1956), 48-50.

Kuhn, H. W. (1955) The Hungarian method for the assignment problem. Naval Research Logistics Quarterly 2 (1955), 83-97.

Little, J.D.C. A proof for the queueing formula L = λ*W. Operations Research 9, 3 (May, 1961).

Liu, C. L. (1968) Introduction to Combinatorial Mathematics. McGraw-Hill, New York, N.Y. (1968).

Matick, R. E. (1972) Review of Current proposed technologies for mass storage systems. Proc. of the IEEE 60, 3 (March, 1972), 266-289.

McFarland, K. and Hashiguchi, M. (1968) Laser recording unit for high density permanent digital data storage. Proc. AFIPS FJCC 33 (1968), Thompson, Washington, D.C., 1369-1380.

Morris, R. (1969) Some theorems on sorting. SIAM J. of Applied Math. 17, 1 (Jan., 1969), 1-6.

Morse, P. M. (1958) Queues, Inventories and Maintenance. John Wiley and Sons, New York, N.Y. (1958).

Naylor, T. H. (1971) Computer Simulation Experiments with Models of Economic Systems. Wiley and Sons, Inc., New York, N.Y., (1971).

Parzen, E. (1960) Modern Probability Theory and Its Applications. John Wiley and Sons, Inc., New York, N.Y. (1960).

Pinkerton, T. B. (1968) Program behavior and control in virtual storage computer systems. CONCOMP TR-4, University of Michigan, Ann Arbor, Mich. (April 1968).

Pinkerton, T. B. (1969) Performance monitoring in a time-sharing system. C. ACM 12, 11 (Nov., 1969), 608-610.

Randell, B. (1969) A note on storage fragmentation and program segmentation. C. ACM 12, 7 (July, 1969), 365-369, 392.

Saaty, T. L. (1961) Elements of Queueing Theory. McGraw-Hill, New York, N.Y. (1961).

Shedler, G. S. (1970) A cyclic-queue model of a paging machine. RC-2814, IBM T. J. Watson Research Center, Yorktown Heights, N.Y. (March, 1970).

Shell, D. L. (1959) A high-speed sorting procedure. C. ACM 2, 7 (July, 1959), 30-32.

Sherman, S., Baskett, F., and Browne, J. C. (1971). Trace driven mode'ing and analysis of CPU scheduling in a multiprogramming system. ACM Workshop on System Performance Evaluation, Harvard Univ. (April, 1971), 173-199.

Skinner, C. E. (1967) Priority queueing systems with server-walking time. Operations Research 15, 2 (1967), 278-285.

Stone, H. S. and Fuller, S. H. (1971) On the near-optimality of the shortest-access-time-first drum scheduling discipline. Technical Note 12, Digital Systems Lab., Stanford Univ., Stanford, Calif., (Oct., 1971).

Teorey, T. J. and Pinkerton, T. B. (1972) A comparative analysis of disk scheduling policies. C. ACM 15, 3 (March, 1972), 177-184.

Teorey, T. J. (1972) Disk storage performance with rotational position sensing. Unpublished report, University of Wisconsin, Madison, Wis. (April, 1972).

Tutte, W. T. (1971) Introduction to the Theory of Matroids. American Elsevier, New York, N.Y. (1971).

van Emden, M. H. (1970A) Algorithm 402, increasing the efficiency of quicksort. C. ACM 13, 11 (Nov., 1970), 693-694.

van Emden, M. H. (1970B) Increasing the efficiency of quicksort. C. ACM 13, 9 (Sept., 1970), 563-667.

Weingarten, A. (1966) The Eschenback drum scheme. C. ACM 9, 7 (July, 1966), 509-512.

Weingarten, A. (1968) The analytical design of real-time disk systems. Proc. IFIPS Congress (1968), D131-137.

Whitworth, W. A. (1886) Choice and Chance (4th ed.). Deighton Bell, Cambridge (1886).

Worlton, W. J. (1971) Bulk storage requirements in large-scale scientific calculations. IEEE Trans. on Magnetics MAG-7, 4 (Dec., 1971), 830-833.

Lecture Notes in Economics and Mathematical Systems